Lecture Notes in Computer Science 4652

Commenced Publication in 1973
Founding and Former Series Editors:
Gerhard Goos, Juris Hartmanis, and Jan van Leeuwen

Dimitrios Georgakopoulos   Norbert Ritter
Boualem Benatallah   Christian Zirpins
George Feuerlicht   Marten Schoenherr
Hamid R. Motahari-Nezhad (Eds.)

Service-Oriented Computing ICSOC 2006

4th International Conference
Chicago, IL, USA, December 4-7, 2006
Workshops Proceedings

 Springer

Volume Editors

Dimitrios Georgakopoulos
Telcordia, Austin, TX 78701, USA
E-mail: dimitris@research.telcordia.com

Norbert Ritter
University of Kaiserslautern, Germany
E-mail: ritter@informatik.uni-kl.de

Boualem Benatallah
University of New South Wales, Sydney NSW 2052, Australia
E-mail: boualem@cse.unsw.edu.au

Christian Zirpins
University of Hamburg, Germany
E-mail: Zirpins@informatik.uni-hamburg.de

George Feuerlicht
University of Technology, Sydney, NSW 2007, Australia
E-mail: jiri@it.uts.edu.au

Marten Schoenherr
Technical University Berlin, Germany
E-mail: MSchoenherr@sysedv.tu-berlin.de

Hamid R. Motahari-Nezhad
The University of New South Wales (UNSW), Australia,
E-mail: hamidm@cse.unsw.edu.au

Library of Congress Control Number: Applied for

CR Subject Classification (1998): C.2, D.2, D.4, H.4, H.3, K.4.4

LNCS Sublibrary: SL 2 – Programming and Software Engineering

ISSN   0302-9743
ISBN-10   3-540-75491-1 Springer Berlin Heidelberg New York
ISBN-13   978-3-540-75491-6 Springer Berlin Heidelberg New York

Springer is a part of Springer Science+Business Media

springer.com

© Springer-Verlag Berlin Heidelberg 2007
Printed in Germany

Typesetting: Camera-ready by author, data conversion by Scientific Publishing Services, Chennai, India
Printed on acid-free paper   SPIN: 12170272   06/3180   5 4 3 2 1 0

Preface

Service-oriented computing is a cross-disciplinary paradigm for distributed computing that enables the development of networks of collaborating applications distributed within and across organizational boundaries. Service-oriented computing fundamentally changes the way software applications are designed, architected, delivered and consumed. The ICSOC conference series covers the entire spectrum from theoretical results to empirical evaluations and industrial solutions. Due to its broad scope and its dedicated community, ICSOC is currently recognized as one of the leading conferences in the service-oriented computing area.

The 4th International Conference on Service-Oriented Computing (ICSOC 2006) and associated workshops followed on the success of three previous events in Amsterdam, The Netherlands (2005), New York City, USA (2004) and Trento, Italy (2003).

ICSOC 2006 solicited the submission of workshop proposals on any of the conference topics including: Business Service Modeling, Service Assembly, Service Management, SOA Runtime, Quality of Service, and Grid Services. Particularly, workshops on key research challenges with the following properties were encouraged:

- Multidisciplinary: involve synergy between different scientific communities and research disciplines
- Domain specific: focus on complete service-oriented solutions for specific application domains, e.g., healthcare, telecommunications, government and public sector, military, etc.
- Operationally extreme: focus on solutions intended/designed for specific operational environments/requirements, e.g., providing 24x7 services, supporting communities of mobile/partially connected services, etc.
- Collaborative: promote collaboration between academic institutions, industry, and communities of users

Out of six workshop submissions (not including the separately organized PhD symposium), the following two met the specified criteria best and were selected as ICSOC 2006 workshops:

- 2nd International Workshop on Engineering Service-Oriented Applications: Design and Composition (WESOA 2006),
- Modeling the SOA – Business Perspective and Model Mapping (SOAM 2006).

Both ICSOC 2006 workshops were held as one-day workshops on December 4, 2006, i.e., the day before the major conference program of ICSOC 2006 started. This volume contains separate descriptions of both workshops as well as all high-quality paper contributions to these two workshops. In order to reflect the natural concern of scientific workshops as well as to ensure the indispensable high quality of papers to be included into the proceedings it was decided to provide post-workshop proceedings.

Thus, besides the regular reviewing process performed by the two workshop Program Committees in order to invite workshop contributions there was a second quality assurance process performed after the workshops ensuring that all original reviewer comments as well as comments given during the respective workshop were taken into account in order to further improve the papers. This way, as we think, high-quality post-workshop proceedings can be provided in this volume, which we hope all readers will find very interesting and stimulating!

The excellent contributions you will find in this volume reflect the hard work of numerous people involved in preparing, organizing and conducting the workshops and observing high-quality standards. Since a great amount of this work was performed by the Organization Committees of the two workshops, we want to thank all members of the two teams. As representatives we want to mention Christian Zirpins and George Feuerlicht from the WESO 2006 team as well as Marten Schoenherr from the SOAM 2006 team. We also want to acknowledge the contributions of all Program Committee members of the two workshops. A special thanks goes to ICSOC 2006 Local Arrangements Chair Julie Wulf for being continuously supportive and prompt in responding to all kinds of requests. Further we want to thank the ICSOC 2006 General Chairs, Ian Foster and Carlo Ghezzi, for their support. Last but not least we would like to acknowledge the contributions of Hamid R. Motahari-Nezhad in putting together this volume.

May 2007

Dimitrios Georgakopoulos
Norbert Ritter
Boualem Benatallah

Organization

ICSOC 2006 Workshop Chairs

Dimitrios Georgakopoulos, Telcordia, USA
Norbert Ritter, Hamburg University, Germany

WESO 2006 Organizers

George Feuerlicht, Sydney University of Technology, Australia
Christian Zirpins, University College London, UK
Guadalupe Ortiz Bellot, University of Extremadura, Spain
Yen-Jao Chung, IBM T.J. Watson Research Center, USA
Winfried Lamersdorf, University of Hamburg, Germany
Wolfgang Emmerich, University College London, UK

SOAM 2006 Organizers

Marten Schönherr, Technical University Berlin, Germany
Maximilian Ahrens, Deutsche Telekom Laboratories, Germany

ICSOC 2006 Publication Chair

Boualem Benatallah, The University of New South Wales, Australia

2nd International Workshop on Engineering Service-Oriented Applications: Design and Composition

George Feuerlicht[1], Christian Zirpins[2], Guadalupe Ortiz Bellot[3], Yen-Jao Chung[4], Winfried Lamersdorf[5], and Wolfgang Emmerich[2]

[1]Sydney University of Technology, Australia
Jiri@it.uts.edu.au
[2]University College London, UK
C.Zirpins|W.Emmerich@cs.ucl.ac.uk
[3]University of Extremadura, Spain
GOBellot@unex.es
[4]IBM T.J. Watson Research Center, USA
JYChung@us.ibm.com
[5]University of Hamburg, Germany
Lamersdorf@informatik.uni-hamburg.de

1 Workshop Goals and Contents

Growing acceptance of service-oriented computing and an increasing number of large-scale Web service projects raise an urgent need for the research community and industry practitioners to develop comprehensive methodologies that support the entire software development lifecycle (SDLC) of service-oriented applications. To ensure that resulting services are stable, reusable and extendable, such methodologies must be based on sound engineering principles and guide developers through the analysis, design, implementation and deployment phases of the service-oriented SDLC.

A key challenge that needs to be addressed involves the unification of service design and composition methods. Service-oriented design needs to determine what constitutes a service component and decide about the appropriate level of service granularity. It is equally important to correctly define the assembly of complex composite services over multiple levels of abstraction, and to use these aggregated services to construct application systems. The current lack of agreement about basic principles that should guide service design and composition makes it difficult for comprehensive service-oriented SDLC-methodologies to emerge.

Both service design and service composition are active research areas at present. However, the problem areas overlap and can benefit from interchange of ideas and unification of approaches. To reflect on dependencies and synergies between service design and service composition, the WESOA 2006 workshop aimed to discuss unified design and composition methods for reusable service components. Moreover, we sought a multidisciplinary perspective to address the challenges of service design and composition in the context of various domains and to bring together researchers and practitioners for exchange of ideas.

Our call for papers led to 32 submissions. Each paper was comprehensively reviewed by at least 3 reviewers, resulting in acceptance of 11 papers for presentation and publication. This corresponds to an acceptance rate of 34%. The outcome is a rich variety of work revolving around design and composition of services. A number of authors tackled service-oriented SDLC at the level of *business processes* (Schaffner et al.) and *business services* (Werth et al.). QoS-aware design of service composition is another common concern discussed in the context of *requirements specification* (Baligand et al.), *prediction* (Wu et al.), *dynamic verification* (Rouached et al.) and a *reliability study* (Wassermann et al.). Other papers dealt with AI topics including *formal semantics* (Küster et al.) and *effect-based reasoning* (Wang et al.) as well as data engineering approaches (Feuerlicht). Of particular interest are case studies on service-oriented software systems development for *asset management* (Pathak et al.) and *online auctions* (Benyoucef et al.).

2 Workshop Organization

WESOA 2006 was organized by an international group of researchers listed as the authors of this article. The event would not have been possible without the invaluable contribution of the international Program Committee. We would therefore like to thank the Program Committee members that include the following experts:

- Marco Aiello *(University of Trento, Itlay)*
- Djamal Benslimane *(LIRIS, France)*
- Andrew Blair *(Biz Integration, Australia)*
- Paul Brebner *(CSIRO Canberra, Australia)*
- Mark Cameron *(CSIRO ICT Centre, Australia)*
- Jen-Yao Chung *(IBM T.J. Watson Research Center, USA)*
- Vincenzo D'andrea *(University of Trento, Itlay)*
- Schahram Dustdar *(Technical University of Vienna, Austria)*
- Wolfgang Emmerich *(University College London, UK)*
- Opher Etzion *(IBM Haifa Research Center, Israel)*
- George Feuerlicht *(Sydney University of Technology, Australia)*
- Howard Foster *(Imperial College London, UK)*
- Ian Gorton *(UNSW NICTA, Australia)*
- Paul Greenfield *(CSIRO, Australia)*
- Roy Gronmo *(SINTEF ICT, Norway)*
- John Grundy *(University of Auckland, New Zealand)*
- Manfred Hauswirth *(DERI Galway, Ireland)*
- Juan Hernandez *(University of Extremadura, Spain)*
- Cai Hong *(IBM China Research, China)*
- Winfried Lamersdorf *(University of Hamburg, Germany)*
- Yinsheng Li *(Fudan University, China)*
- Mark Little *(Arjuna, USA)*
- Zheng Lu *(University of Wollongong, Australia)*
- Heiko Ludwig *(IBM Research, USA)*
- E. Michael Maximilien *(IBM Almaden Research, USA)*
- Massimo Mecella *(University of Rome La Sapienza, Italy)*
- Harald Meyer *(HPI Potsdam, Germany)*
- Daniel Moldt *(University of Hamburg, Germany)*

- Josef Noll *(Telenor, Norway)*
- Guadalupe Ortiz Bellot *(University of Extremadura, Spain)*
- Mike Papazoglou *(Tilburg University, The Netherlands)*
- Greg Pavlik *(Oracle, USA)*
- Thomas Risse *(Fraunhofer Society, Germany)*
- Colette Rolland *(University of Paris, France)*
- Dumitru Roman *(DERI Innsbruck, Austria)*
- Subbu N. Subramanian *(Tavant Technologies, USA)*
- Willem-Jan van den Heuvel *(Tilburg University, The Netherlands)*
- Bruno Wassermann *(University College London, UK)*
- Jim Webber *(ThoughtWorks, Australia)*
- Andreas Wombacher *(University of Twente, The Netherlands)*
- Aoying Zhou *(Fudan University, China)*
- Christian Zirpins *(University College London, UK)*

Finally, we would like to thank the ICSOC organizers, especially the Workshop Chairs Dimitrios Georgakopoulos and Norbert Ritter, the Publication Chair Boualem Benatallah and the Local Arrangements Chair Julie Wulf, for their guidance and support.

Ist International Workshop on Modeling Service-Oriented Architectures: Business Perspective and Model Mapping

Marten Schönherr[1] and Maximilian Ahrens[2]

[1]Faculty of Computer Science and Electrical Engineering,
Technical University Berlin, Germany
mschoenherr@sysedv.tu-berlin.de
[2] Deutsche Telekom Laboratories, Berlin, Germany
maximilian.ahrens@telekom.de

1 Workshop Topics and Objectives

In the last few years both scientists and practitioners have been discussing the issue of service-oriented architectures (SOA). Recently, vendors of enterprise information systems presented first releases of their service-enabled system architectures. From the business perspective the paradigm of service orientation promises more flexibility by aligning business requirements and information technology functionalities.

Modeling the business processes is the first step in formalizing (functional and non-functional) service requirements. There are many methodologies, notations and tools for business process modeling but few which consider the full stack of service orientation specifics. BPEL as an executable model and the dominant standard in the SOA modeling discipline does not cover all aspects of business process modeling. For modeling business processes using notations apart from BPEL, the process models have to be mapped to executable formal models which are necessary to orchestrate services to fulfill defined business requirements. Therefore, different modeling notations need to be combined to fulfill the requirements of a holistic SOA approach. Further aspects such as service life-cycles, roles and service management issues need to be considered.

Main objectives of the workshop were the identification and definition of necessary modeling issues, the introduction of innovative solutions or enhancements for those modeling aspects that are currently not properly supported, and the examination of all aspects of (model) mappings between different SOA model(ing aspect)s. These topics are relevant for research as well as industry practitioners. Thus, the workshop invited important multi-disciplinary contributions in order to start a substantial discussion and finally generate a lasting contact between academic and industrial researchers.

As a result of a double-blind review and an acceptance rate of 40%, the workshop publishes six papers on different issues mentioned above: Modeling of Service Composition (Jaeger), An Approach for QoS Prediction of BPEL Processes (Wu), a Pattern-Based Approach to Business Process Modeling and Implementation in Web Services (Brahe et al.), An Extension of the UN/CEFACT Modeling Methodology and Core Components for Intra-Organizational Service Orchestration (Offermann et al.), An Integration of Semantic Business Policy into Web Service Composition Meng et al.), and A Model-Driven Approach of Service Domain Analysis(Aier et al.).

2 Workshop Organization

The workshop was organized by the authors of this article. We would like to thank the following Program Committee members:

- Maximilian Ahrens *(Deutsche Telekom Laboratories Berlin, Germany)*
- Stephan Aier *(IWI-HSG, University of St. Gallen, Switzerland)*
- Udo Bub *(Deutsche Telekom Laboratories, Germany)*
- Jens Dietrich *(OSCI, UNCEFACT, Germany)*
- Dirk Draheim *(SCCH, Austria)*
- Mathias Ekstedt *(KTH, Sweden)*
- Michael Elhadad *(Ben Gurion University, Israel)*
- Marten Schoenherr *(Berlin University of Technology, Germany)*
- Johannes Siedersleben *(T-Systems International, Germany)*
- Gerald Weber *(University of Auckland, New Zealand)*

We would like to thank the Workshop Chairs Dimitrios Georgakopoulos and Norbert Ritter, the Publication Chair Boualem Benatallah and the Local Arrangements Chair Julie Wulf.

Table of Contents

Part I: Second International Workshop on Engineering Service-Oriented Applications: Design and Composition

Part II: First International Workshop on Modeling Service-Oriented Architectures: Business Perspective and Model Mapping

Part I

Second International Workshop on Engineering Service-Oriented Applications:
Design and Composition

Managing SOA Through Business Services – A Business-Oriented Approach to Service-Oriented Architectures

Dirk Werth, Katrina Leyking, Florian Dreifus, Jörg Ziemann,
and Andreas Martin

Institute for Information Systems (IWi)
at the German Institute for Artificial Intelligence (DFKI)
Stuhlsatzenhausweg 3, Geb. D3 2
66123 Saarbrücken
Germany
{werth,leyking,dreifus,ziemann,a.martin}@iwi.dfki.de

Abstract. The idea of more flexible, modular system structures thanks to web service interfaces feed expectations towards a novel degree of business agility. However, the challenge of the information system community consists in developing methods and techniques to vest service-orientation with business concepts that deploy a SOA according to organizational requirements. This paper tackles this challenge by introducing Business Service Management as an interdisciplinary discipline for business-driven deployment of SOA. It approaches this ambitious objective by utilizing business processes as semi-formalized representations of an enterprise's characteristics and requirements towards IT.

Keywords: Business Process, Business process management, Business Services, Service-oriented Architectures, Web Services.

1 Introduction

The current omnipresence of service-oriented architectures (SOA) could lead one to believe in the rise of a new software paradigm that will revolutionize IT landscapes especially in business environments. The idea of more flexible, modular system structures through web service interfaces feed expectations towards a novel degree of business agility. The dream of leveraging and integrating system resources on demand based on market requirements has been dreamed by business already multiple times. SOA shares the concept of flexible, business-driven system architectures with previous approaches such as business components or business objects. Thus, the legitimate question comes up what distinguishes SOA from them. Why should service-orientation become the envisioned panacea for bridging the gap between IT and business which all other concepts failed to be? Whether the SOA vision will turn out as short-dated fad or as durable step towards plug-and-play software architectures is not only a matter of technological progress but also of its seamless applicability to real business situations. In fact, SOA will primarily add complexity to managerial tasks instead of disburden them. Introducing SOA brings about novel unprecedented

D. Georgakopoulos et al. (Eds.): ICSOC 2006 Ws, LNCS 4652, pp. 3–13, 2007.

challenges for the manageability of the IT landscape. The common business goal of efficient and transparent processes over the whole value chain becomes much fuzzier and very difficult to accomplish. In order to reconcile the conflictive objectives of flexibility promised by a SOA and manageability targeted by business (process) management, a rigorous approach to reduce complexity from service-orientation is needed. Thus, the challenge of the information system community consists in developing methods and techniques to vest service-orientation with business concepts that deploy a SOA according to organizational requirements [1]. This paper tackles this challenge by introducing Business Service Management as a mediating discipline for business-driven deployment of SOA. It approaches this ambitious objective by utilizing business processes as semi-formalized representations of an enterprise's characteristics and requirements towards IT and web services as representatives for the IT application landscape. Due to ever accelerating developments on the market, business processes are all but stable entities. They are subject to changes in the product portfolio, redefinition of core competencies, most innovative production techniques, etc. On the other hand, companies must not only deal with agility of their markets but also manage their constantly aging IT infrastructure characterized by heterogeneity, distribution, and out-dated technology. We define Business Services as the ultimately durable layer between rapidly changing business requirements represented by business processes and steadily evolving system landscape that ought to meet these requirements. The goal is to have a set of business-oriented building blocks that embody core functionalities, executed via composite web services, to be flexibly reused and combined to processes. The paper will finish by indicating the most urgent research questions to consolidate the new discipline of business service management in the context of business process management.

2 On the Relation Between Business Process and Service Orientation

2.1 Business Process Management

In order to design, analyze and control organizational structures as well as business activities companies nowadays are increasingly following the process orientation paradigm [2]. A business process is a "continuous series of enterprise tasks, undertaken for the purpose of creating output" [3]. In line with these efforts Business Process Management (BPM) is widely-used as a framework for having formal and repeatable proceedings in place. Various approaches to adopt BPM in companies have emerged in recent years. Besides approaches such as the Zachman Framework or PROMET the architecture of Integrated Information Systems (ARIS) is accepted as a standard framework for business process (re-)engineering throughout the community. Beyond notation and modeling dimensions the ARIS House of Business Engineering provides an overall BPM methodology which supports the entire BPM life cycle combining process design, process control, workflow control and process application implementation [4]. Generally speaking, concepts of business process management can be identified as requirements engineering approaches that take the needs of the business domain and relate them to implemented information technology (IT).

Therefore, IT plays an important role in the context of BPM .It allows the automation of business processes, leading to higher productivity and quality gains. Nowadays, there are of-the-shelf products for almost common business process Applications such as Enterprise Resource Planning (ERP) or Customer Relationship Management (CRM), emerged and offered by software vendors in the nineties, perform the task of supporting business processes. They combine and provide modeled and automated processes for companies of various industries following best practices. However, since applications such as the ERP or the CRM are focusing on selected divisions of a company and therefore using independent databases, the exchange of information within a company gets very difficult and between companies sometimes impossible. In this context the term silo emerged for enterprise applications, reflecting the fact that the application might be full up with valuable data, but that data is divided by technological walls. At the time when enterprise application emerged, most markets companies acted on were steady and competition was manageable; hence the problem of data exchange and communication between applications was neglected. Companies' primary intention was to utilize the productivity gains associated with the use of IT. If any action was taken to tackle the problem of transferring data between applications proprietary solutions, using Application Programming Interfaces for example, were applied, resulting in inflexible, costly and unstable stovepipe connections between applications. However, hardening markets and increasing competition coming along with new business models such as process networks or the real time enterprise as well as utilized productivity gains of IT in the context of BPM, confront IT with increasing demand on its interoperability and flexibility. In times of collaborative business [5] and real time enterprises processes have to be modeled and implemented across borders within the company (i.e. across divisions) as well as across the companies' external borders (i.e. to partners, suppliers and customers), in a flexible and manageable way [6]. Despite notable progress in Workflow Systems and Enterprise Application Integration (EAI) products as well as agreed and widely used industry standards for data exchange (e.g. RosettaNet), integrating applications along end-to-end business processes has remained the major challenge regarding an integrated BPM approach. In order to satisfy the demand of business of such an integrated BPM approach a successor of the widespread client server architecture is needed. In this context Service Oriented Architecture is discussed as the most recent and promising approach to satisfy the demand of an application architecture which allows the implementation of end-to-end processes in a flexible and agile way [7].

2.2 Service-Oriented Architectures

The Service-oriented Architecture aims at developing Applications Systems easily adoptable to business requirements. Therefore, in a SOA components are developed based rather on organizational criteria than on technical criteria, e.g. a SOA component should rather resemble business functions than for example a fine grained module that establishes a Database connection. SOA components are commonly implemented in form of Web Services that a service provider offers via a network. According to the SOA idea, the service provider is also supposed to publish the Service in a central service registry and to describe functional characteristics of the Web Service, not only its technical interface which is described by the Web Service

Description Language (WSDL). Since business functions can be expected to have fewer and less detailed parameters than technical modules, it implies a coarse granularity of SOA Web Service. This, and the fact that Web Services are late bound (e.g. it is only decided at runtime which Web Service is to be invoked), results in a loose coupling of the SOA components. Apart from having components that are being distributed, loosely coupled and easy to discover, an important further characteristic of a SOA is process orientation [13, 8]. This is realized on the one hand side by providing process components (e.g. Web Services) that might be (re-) composed in various sequences, on the other hand by providing process description standards that compose the Web Service into a process. Note, that thus the process flow is separated from programming code contained in single modules. The most prominent example for a Web Service Business Process standard is BPEL. Most of the SOA characteristics mentioned are not new but represent classical software engineering requirements, e.g. the concept of modularization and information hiding was proposed as early as 1972 [9]. But due to internet technology and vendor independent standards (e.g. XML, WSDL, SOAP, HTTP) today these concepts have a better chance to be realized. For example, a comparable technology to Web Service flows as realized by BPEL, formerly Workflow-Management-Systems were used to separate business process from business components. Nonetheless, workflow standards were vendor dependent, thus components could only be used in the scope of a proprietary workflow systems. Today, the vendor independent standard WSDL allows for an invocation of Web Service across boundaries of different workflow-engines (now also called orchestration engines) and possibly also of different organizations.

Nonetheless, SOA development is still a relatively young discipline with few practical experiences and various challenges remain. For example, methods are needed to ensure that SOA processes are compliant with conceptual processes as designed by business analysts. Though first approaches exist to transform EPC to BPEL [10], they have to be refined and put on a broader conceptual basis.

3 Business Service Management Bridging the Concepts

3.1 Business Services

In order to leverage service-oriented architectures for flexible enterprise systems driven by business requirements, it does not suffice to compose IT-driven web services into processes and run them on an Enterprise Service Bus. This would only entail a not so new form of system integration, instead of bridging the gap between business and IT as it was propagated for SOA. To reach the very SOA vision, one must rather think how business requirements can be possibly seamlessly transferred. As outline above, BPM can be identified as a requirements engineering approach in the business domain but highly related to information technology. Thus, it provides a solid starting point for IT development in general and SOA development in particular. Business processes as defined above serve as the very business context needed for web services and service processes to form a truly business-driven service-oriented architecture. Service orientation of an organization means that functions and subprocesses needed by numerous organizational units are provided by a single unit towards multiple units in order to reduce costs and complexity. We define such functions as business services. Due to their close relationships to functions of business processes they can be derived from business process models and rely on web service interfaces. Thus, business services act as an abstraction layer between business and IT. However, due to their content and design directives, they belong to the business layer, that is defined and reworked by business users (in contrast IT people is in charge of the technical layer). Figure 1 illustrates this relationship.

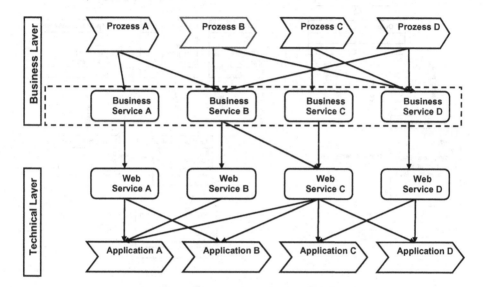

Fig. 1. Business services acting as mediation layer

Business Services are specified through their business relevant inputs and outputs but their internal operating is not visible to the outside i.e. the consuming world. Inputs and outputs can also be considered to be products that are either composed to more complex products or a single product of the types service, goods or information. Organizational units consume and provide products. In this context, they are responsible for creating certain business services and/or using them. Functions are business activities that are hierarchically structured, supported by information systems and – as a logically and timely ordered set – form a business process. As outlined above business services execute processes and functions. For quality reasons, the usage of a business service is subject to so-called service-level-agreements (SLA) that determine exact quality targets for its execution. From a technical point of view, each business service is assigned to a WSDL-operation, i.e. an operation of a Web Service described in a WSDL file. Though, due to its additional business semantics it goes beyond a web service. An excerpt from the information model of business services is presented in figure 2.

Given this close connection between business processes on the one hand side and web services on the other, business services are the very building blocks propagated by the SOA paradigm that flexibly implement a company's business strategy. However, as

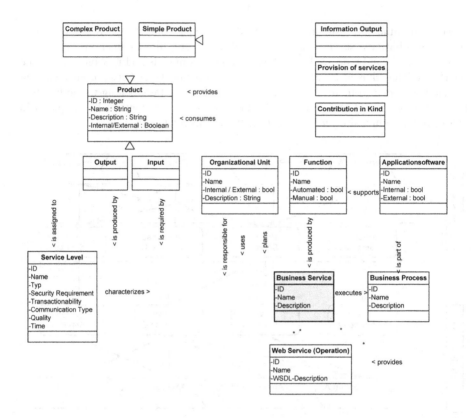

Fig. 2. Information model for business services

an additional layer of such functional modules (business services) between business processes and IT complexity rises and risks to give way to chaos and complexity instead of transparency. To counter this risk, a coherent concept to manage the business service layer based on business processes and IT resources is needed.

3.2 Process-Driven Business Service Management

Embedded in the business process logic on the one hand and in the SOA interfaces on the other hand, the business service layer must be understood as linkage between both. The challenge resides in the way business services are identified, described, composed, maintained, and controlled. The former being the currently most intricate issue since business services must be tailored in such a way that they comply with business process requirements as well as SOA postulations such as reusability, effectiveness, sustainability, transactionality, etc. and meet corresponding business needs. In order to ensure business effectiveness of these business services, the data structure proposed embeds their semantics in a business process context while linking it to technical entities of Web Service languages like WSDL and BPEL. Beyond the design of business services, there is the need for methodologies to manage business services during their run time, i.e. to deploy them to tackle new business challenges along new business processes, to compose them to form new services, to communicate their semantics towards all stakeholders, to align them vertically with given system functionalities and horizontally across departments and business units. This is vital for ripping off the potential of service outsourcing pictured by service-orientation: Only clearly, i.e. from a business perspective described services (business services) can be offered to external customers or bought in from external providers. Business service management aims to administer the alignment between business and IT. Hereby the concept of business services incorporates the interdependences between business strategies expressed in business processes and IT infrastructures. It connects business-driven web services dynamically with underlying software systems and business-level processes. Business service management is made up of a set of activities that can be ordered as figure 3 outlines. One can roughly distinguish four phases: Analysis, Design, Execution, and Controlling. In the analysis phase three steps are necessary. The business foundation of all subsequent tasks is formed by a business process analysis that defines semi-formalized representations of an enterprise from a business domain view. Secondly, the IT view on an enterprise with the running application systems, their components and responsible organizational units are examined to explore the system landscape in place. Having analyzed both business and IT constraints, this information is evaluated and scoped with regard to their quality and ability to be transformed into business services. In the subsequent phase, the design phase, these parts of the new business layer, the business services and their interactions, are identified and described. Therefore various (semi-)automatic algorithms are applied to the input data to find good candidates of EPC parts, organizational units and IT components that possibly form together a new business service.

To confirm these business service candidates, they must be aligned vertically, i.e. between business activities and IT functionalities, as well as horizontally, i.e. across

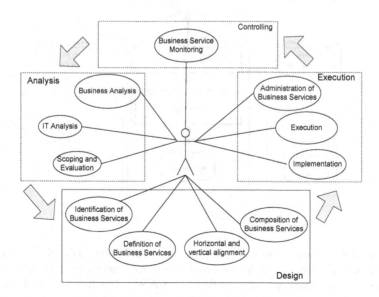

Fig. 3. The lifecycle of business services

organizational units that are to use them. Finally the newly defined services are composed to a BPEL process on the basis of business processes to support the course of business in the enterprise. The conceptual analysis and design phases (build-time) are followed by the execution and controlling phases (run-time). The execution phase establishes the connection between the business services and underlying technical web services (described in WSDL) that again access system functionalities via communication protocols such as SOAP. Hence, the SOA implementation is initiated but not finalized before having implemented a whole SOA infrastructure including Enterprise Service Bus which is responsible for instantiating and executing the services. Last but not least, the final phase, the controlling phase, of the business service management lifecycle controls the success of the business services definitions measured against business objectives. Different run-time attributes are extracted from the operating SOA, aggregated to key performance indicators and used to reconvene with the initial analysis to redesign the business service definitions and improve their fit to upcoming business requirements and new information systems.

4 Tool-Support

In real business environments, a concept as presented in this paper cannot be used without a comprehensive tool support. The very fact that there are hundreds or thousands of processes and services to be managed underlines the need for an IT solution.

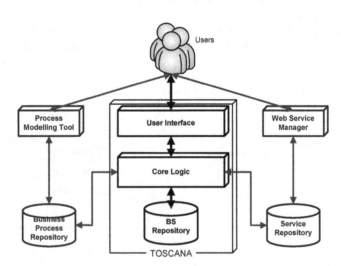

Fig. 4. Technical architecture of Toscana

To deploy our concept in practical scenarios we are going to develop a toolkit that can support all lifecycle tasks of business service management. This toolkit for business service management is called TOSCANA. The technical architecture of Toscana is shown in figure 4. It follows a classical 3 tier architecture pattern.

However, as we initially explained within the concept of business service management, BSM acts as the intermediator between BPM and SOA. Consequently, Toscana is not an insolated application, but it is intended to intensively interact with business process management systems on the one hand and with service management application on the other. Therefore, we try to prototypically connect Toscana to the ARIS Toolset (world marked leader in business process modeling) and to the Oracle Web Service Manager (commercial SOA management suite).

5   Related Work

The approach presented in this paper originates in two major fields of the information systems discipline: Business Process Management and IT Management. As this paper will reveal, the abstract service construct is very much related to existing concepts of business process management. As software functionality, a service features a very functional nature with input being transformed into output. Thus it corresponds to the artefacts of activities, functions, or actions as they have been used in enterprise modelling for decades (e.g. [4], [11]). Analogously to these artefacts, services may be composed to processes. Such service processes again can be offered as – more coarse-grained – services. Thus, it is vital to understand the central role of business process management for service-oriented architectures.

This goes hand in hand with the notion of SOA not so much being based on new technological design principles but rather on the vision to accomplish a business-driven design of IT resources. Thus, Pullier and Taylor [12] consider the effectiveness of service design depending more on business processes than on technology. Accordingly, they define service quality based on reusability of resources "that serve the needs of processes". Frankel [13] considers Web Services in the context of enterprise architecture and defines the notion of business services as "composed from lower level, finer-grained business functions and information entities." Krafzig et al. [14] shifts the focus of enterprise SOA on taking advantage of business logic and data maintained in many applications, databases and legacy systems in order to flexibly adapt IT systems to changes in business requirements. Krafzig et al. also emphasize the importance of mapping services directly to business entities, promoting SOA as a mean for enterprise integration on a business not so much on a technical level. Hagel III [15] also calls for web services that deliver "mission critical functionality" and are based on shared meaning not only on shared formats. Understanding that business-relevant service design is not the only requirement for a business-centric SOA, he develops a Service Grid consisting on Service Management, Resource Knowledge Management and Transport Management. Unfortunately, Hagel III's thoughts never get any specific but remain sketchy. Nevertheless, his and other authors' recognition of managerial perspectives on a SOA is the basis for our Business Service Management approach.

On the industrial side, there are multiple approaches on service management. However, most of them are technically motivated and aiming to manage an IT-infrastructure based on WebServices (e.g. [14], [16], [17]). They provide functionalities to assess, store and query service resp. interface specifications (mostly on data level) in order to ensure a certain quality of service and to simplify the maintenance of the it-environment. The approach of SAP is going beyond [18]. It tries to leverage the technical service descriptions on a business level. However, in contrast to this business-driven approach, it is also technology driven. SAP relies on their BAPI specifications, describing interfaces to the R/3 ERP system and it is extending these interfaces to describe business activities. Due to this procedure, the services are fully aligned with the IT-systems, but may strongly differ from the business operations and strategic objectives.

6 Conclusion

We have presented business service management as an approach to leverage the beneficial characteristics of web services and service-oriented architectures in order to flexibly align business strategy and supporting information technology. Business processes have been chosen as the very context representing business requirements for SOA, i.e. an enterprise's static and dynamic structuring and its activities. The lifecycle of business service management includes the interdependent tasks that are to be performed in order to align business process and SOA via business services. Being a cycle, it emphasizes the fact that automating business processes through services leads to a continuous improvement of both business processes and information technology: The former is subject to optimization due to previous performance and subject to change due to external economical influences. The later also needs to evolve continuously given ongoing innovations in software, hardware, and services and ever increasing quality requirements. Given these freely flowing economical and technological variables, the layer of business services is to provide the very stability and transparency needed. As business success depends on the quality of business services, their design and maintenance must be thoroughly managed. We consider research questions how to identify and tailor business services most optimally most decisive for success or failure of the enterprise SOA. Upcoming research therefore must focus on the design phase of business service management. At the moment a prototype is being developed to demonstrate feasibility and advantages of the business service management idea, especially focusing on the analysis and design phase. It is designed as a wizard to support the equally business analysts and IT specialists. By integrating the approach into business process management concepts, we propagate a comprehensive solution that bridges the gap between existing business management and the upcoming challenge of SOA administration.

This concept was developed at the Competence Centre Business Integration (CCBI), Institute for Information Systems (IWi) at the German Research Center for Artificial Intelligence (DFKI), Saarbruecken. It addresses current research problems in the area of process integration and networked businesses by bringing together the business-oriented and the IT-views. The work is performed by clustering national and international funded research projects (esp. ArKoS, ATHENA, INTEROP, P2E2, VIDE), intending the development of solutions for a better interoperability in business networks.

References

1. Papazoglou, M.P., Georgakopoulos, D.: Service-oriented computing. Communications of the ACM 46(10), 25–28 (2003)
2. Davenport, T.H.: Process Innovation. Reengineering Work through Information Technology. Harvard Business School Press, Boston (1993)
3. Hammer, M., Champy, J.: Reengineering the Corporation. A Manifesto for Business Revolution. Collins Business Essentials, New York (1993)
4. Scheer, A.-W.: Business Process frameworks, 3rd edn. Springer, Heidelberg (1999)
5. Röhricht, J., Schlögel, C.: cBusiness: Erfolgreiche Internetstrategien durch Collaborative Business am Beispiel mySAP.com. Addison-Wesley, München (2001)
6. Werth, D.: Kollaborative Geschäftsprozesse. Logos, Berlin (2006)
7. Leymann, F., Roller, D., Schmidt, M.: Web Services and Business Process Management. IBM Systems Journal 41(2) (2003)
8. Vanderhaeghen, D., Kahl, T., Werth, D., Loos, P.: Service- and Process-Matching – An Approach towards Interoperability Design and Implementation of Business Networks. In: Doumeingts, G., Müller, J., Morel, G., Vallespir, B. (eds.) Enterprise Interoperability: New Challenges and Approaches, pp. 187–198. Springer, Heidelberg (2007)
9. Parnas, D.L.: On the Criteria to be used in Decomposing Systems in Module. Communications of the ACM 15(12), 1053–1058 (1972)
10. Ziemann, J., Mendling, J.: Transformation of EPCs to BPEL – A Pragmatic Approach. In: 7th International Conference on the Modern Information Technology in the Innovation Processes of the Industrial Enterprises, Genoa (2005)
11. White, S.A.: Business Process Modeling Notation. Business Process Management Initiative, Version 1.0 (2004), http://www.bpmi.org/downloads/BPMN-V1.0.pdf
12. Pulier, E., Taylor, H.: Understanding Enterprise SOA. Manning Publications, New York (2005)
13. Frankel, D.S.: Model Driven Architecture - Applying MDA to Enterprise Computing. John Wiley & Sons, Chichester (2003)
14. Krafzig, D., Banke, K., Slama, D.: Enterprise SOA: Service-Oriented Architecture Best Practices. Prentice Hall, Englewood Cliffs (2004)
15. Hagel III, J.: Out of the Box - Strategies for Achieving Profits Today and Growth Tomorrow through Web Services. Harvard Business School Press, Boston (2005)
16. Dostal, W., Jeckle, M., Melzer, I.: Zengler: Service-Orientierte Architekturen mit Web Services – Konzepte, Standards, Praxis. Spektrum Akademischer Verlag (2005)
17. Bieberstein, N., Bose, S., Fiammante, M., Jones, K., Shah, R.: Service-Oriented Architecture Compass: Business Value, Planning and Enterprise Roadmap. IBM Press, Indianapolis (2005)
18. Woods, D., Mattern, T.: Enterprise SOA - Designing IT for Business Innovation. O'Reilly, Sebastopol (2006)

Reliable Scientific Service Compositions*

Bruno Wassermann and Wolfgang Emmerich

University College London
Dept. of Computer Science
Software Systems Engineering Group
Gower Street, London, WC1E 6BT, UK
{b.wassermann,w.emmerich}@cs.ucl.ac.uk
http://sse.cs.ucl.ac.uk

Abstract. Distributed service oriented architectures (SOAs) are increasingly used by users, who are insufficiently skilled in the art of distributed system programming. A good example are computational scientists who build large-scale distributed systems using service-oriented Grid computing infrastructures. Computational scientists use these infrastructure to build scientific applications, which are composed from basic Web services into larger orchestrations using workflow languages, such as the Business Process Execution Language. For these users reliability of the infrastructure is of significant importance and that has to be provided in the presence of hardware or operational failures. The primitives available to achieve such reliability currently leave much to be desired by users who do not necessarily have a strong education in distributed system construction. We characterise scientific service compositions and the environment they operate in by introducing the notion of global scientific BPEL workflows. We outline the threats to the reliability of such workflows and discuss the limited support that available specifications and mechanisms provide to achieve reliability. Furthermore, we propose a line of research to address the identified issues by investigating autonomic mechanisms that assist computational scientists in building, executing and maintaining reliable workflows.

1 Introduction

Achieving reliability is a key concern in the design of distributed software systems. In this paper we argue that the service-oriented Grid computing infrastructures that have attracted computational scientists as a new set of non-expert users currently only provide inadequate support at both design and runtime to cater for reliability. As we demonstrate, this gap is increased by the fact that scientific service compositions suffer from challenging threats to their reliability. Due to the proliferation of scientific service-oriented applications, it is important to investigate what kind of additional support can be offered to their developers and users.

* This research has been funded by the UK EPSRC through grants GR/R97207/01 (e-Materials) and GR/S90843/01 (OMII Managed Programme).

D. Georgakopoulos et al. (Eds.): ICSOC 2006 Ws, LNCS 4652, pp. 14–25, 2007.
© Springer-Verlag Berlin Heidelberg 2007

If computational scientists are not provided with more effective means to tackle issues of reliability, then this will present a serious impediment to the successful use of service-oriented technologies in scientific computing and thereby limit the realisation of its benefits. We therefore want to raise awareness, characterise the problem, and propose a line of research to build autonomic mechanisms that can enable non-expert users to build and execute reliable service compositions by handling failures automatically whenever possible and through meaningful interaction with human users in any other cases.

The main contribution of this paper is the characterisation of scientific service compositions and the environment they operate. We outline the ample threats to their reliability. We do this by introducing the notion of global scientific BPEL workflows (section 2) to get a clearer picture of what computational scientists need to be enabled to deal with. Then, we briefly present a typical instance of a scientific service composition and the failures it suffers from (section 3). In order to demonstrate that current mechanisms and specifications have failed to address the issue of reliability successfully, we review existing approaches (section 4). The second contribution of this paper lies in a proposal outline to investigate the application of autonomic mechanisms to achieve reliability and ways of effective interaction between these mechanisms and human users to achieve better coverage (section 5), before discussing closely related work (section 6).

2 Global Scientific BPEL Workflows

2.1 Scientific Workflows

Computational sciences have increasing demands on compute power, data storage capacity and collaboration across organisational boundaries. These requirements are satisfied by modern Grids, which have evolved into service-oriented computing environments comprised of collections of basic Web services. In order to express scientific experiments, these basic services need to be composed into larger orchestrations. In prior work, we have shown that the Business Process Execution Language (BPEL) as the industry standard for Web service orchestrations has shown to be suitable for this task and it is desirable for faster turnaround of ideas for experiments for computational scientists to take control of their own orchestrations. Computational scientists have been enabled to model scientific workflows through the tool offering developed by the OMII-BPEL project [1] and [2]. In this section, we briefly characterise the key elements of such compositions, or workflows, to identify their impact on reliability.

Scientific workflows display some interesting properties. They operate on a large scale, both in terms of the number of operations they invoke, the degree of parallelism, the size and number of messages they exchange with service partners and the amount of data they handle. Consequently, and given the nature of the computations they are designed to handle, scientific workflows are resource-intensive and long-running, which makes them prone to resource exhaustion (i.e. memory, threads, file descriptors,) and increases the likelihood of internal or latent errors from various components materialising themselves as critical failures. Furthermore, scientific workflows often operate and employ resources in a wide-area setting, which introduces further issues with respect to their stability. This state of affairs is not helped by the heterogeneity of the underlying operating systems and hardware and the fact that resource schedulers, such as Condor are explicitly addressing the scavenging of unused CPU cycles, which results in termination or relocation of computation when nodes are beginning to be used again or when nodes are actually switched off.

Computational scientists are certainly computer literate and may posses some excellent programming skills in certain languages (most notably FORTRAN, C and C++). However, they should by no means be regarded as experts in distribution middleware and the underlying technologies used in service-oriented Grid computing and BPEL enactment environments. Therefore, they will benefit from simple to use mechanisms that provide support for ensuring the reliability of scientific service compositions.

2.2 Global Computing

Research collaborations are increasing in size and often involve participating organisations, which are geographically widely dispersed. Wide-area distribution enables such collaboration and increases the capacity to handle larger computational loads. Scientific workflows must integrate resources that are distributed over wide-area settings for various reasons. First, the computations exposed by scientific services are typically resource-intensive and their compositions require the exchange of large numbers of SOAP messages. Provisioning all required resources within a single organisation could easily become prohibitively expensive. Second, some services and the expertise they encapsulate are developed and maintained by individual organisations, which then make such services available for invocation via the Internet, but may not release the source. A third instance of resource sharing arises out of the need to pool Grid compute nodes. In such a setting the resource managers (exposed as Web services) responsible for job scheduling are local to the actual compute nodes and will have to be accessed by their clients over a wide-area network.

This makes scientific workflows expressed in a service-oriented computing environment a prime example of global computing, in which the components of an application are distributed across the Internet. Cardelli asserts that wide-area computing systems are fully asynchronous distributed systems making several new phenomena visible that could previously be hidden to a sufficient extent on LANs [3]. These observables include barriers (e.g., firewall) introduced due to the involvement of separate administrative domains and unpredictably fluctuating network conditions making long delays indistinguishable from failures. This is the category of applications scientific service compositions are a part of.

Being an instance of global computing systems has an impact on the available options for ensuring the reliability of scientific workflows. We cannot rely on timeouts to determine process failures and even if we were to ignore the impossibility result of reaching consensus in an asynchronous distributed system [4], relying on mechanisms such as fault detectors may be prohibitively expensive.

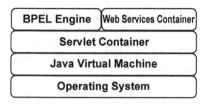

Fig. 1. Stack of high-level middleware components involved in hosting and running BPEL workflows

Techniques primarily developed for mobile networks, such as for example probabilistic broadcasts have no direct feasible application as they may rather resemble a DDoS attack (but see [5]).

2.3 Middleware Components

Compositions need to be modelled using the tools of a buildtime in such a way as to ensure subsequent reliable execution in a runtime. In OMII-BPEL, this buildtime involves graphical modelling environments whose features assist users in designing, validating, debugging and deploying a workflow in an executable format. There is merit to briefly examine what a typical runtime consists of.

We consider middleware components as they occur in a typical Java environment, shown in Fig. 1. Distributed scientific applications may rely upon some or all of these middleware components in order to provide correct service. However, a considerable degree of complexity arises from the various middleware components and their interactions with each other, which can give rise to various failures. For example, the limitations on the number of sockets, threads or size of memory per process imposed by the operating system can lead to conditions causing the servlet container to crash. This then causes the subsequent failure of one or more parts of a workflow. Or, some problem in the servlet container preventing clients from accessing a particular resource (e.g., an XML Schema), may, via a chain of dependencies, cause a remote service to terminate abnormally. Such failures are extremely difficult to debug as none of the components involved provides much useful information.

Each of the middleware components contributes independent failure modes and each application may exercise different parts of these components under varying conditions. Hence, in order to ensure the reliable execution of a composition, a process modeller must reason about how potential failures in the middleware may influence their applications' ability to provide correct service. This may be a formidable challenge for software engineers, but presents a wholly unacceptable burden on computational scientists.

3   Example: Failures in the Polymorph Search Workflow

Scientific workflows are subject to many different failures. These failures often have no direct obvious cause and can have complex effects, such as cascading

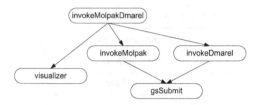

Fig. 2. Abstract overview of the polymorph search workflow illustrating its component sub-workflows. For simplicity, omits details of the services involved and distribution of services and sub-workflows.

failures of components. In this section we briefly present a typical scientific BPEL workflow and discuss some of the failures that it experiences in practice. We refer the reader to [1] for a more detailed account of this workflow.

The domain of the polymorph search workflow is Theoretical Chemistry and its application is the computational prediction of organic crystal structures. Its characteristics are typical of a realistic scientific workflow. It involves massively parallel computations, at times executing up to 7, 600 service invocations concurrently. The individual compute jobs resulting from these invocations take anything between two minutes and several hours to complete. The total data volume resulting from a single polymorph search is in the region of 6 GB and parts of this data will be exchanged among sub-workflows and other services in a large number of SOAP messages.

In order to conquer the size and complexity of the polymorph search workflow, it has been designed and built as several BPEL processes, which are hierarchically composed so that a main process coordinates among several sub-workflows. An abstract overview is shown in figure 2. The invokeMolpakDmarel workflow (top-level) starts by gathering some input data and then invokes a number of instances of the invokeMolpak sub-workflow in parallel. As results become available from this, they are fed to a large number of concurrently executing instances of invokeDmarel. Both of these workflows make use of the gsSubmit sub-workflow, which encapsulates the steps necessary to submit compute jobs to a Grid via the GridSAM job submission and job monitoring services [6]. As the results of individual invokeDmarel invocations are returned, the top-level workflow submits them to the visualizer sub-workflow. Visualizer uses a Web service hosted by Southampton University to present molecule data in a standard tabular format and to render results on a scatter plot.

A selection of the failures experienced with the polymorph search workflow helps to illustrate the brittleness such compositions suffer from.

Omission failures. Some omission failures may go undetected and therefore result in corrupted results. For example, an instance of the visualizer process may fail due to its partner service in Southampton being temporarily unavailable, exhaustion of disk space, etc. As the visualizer sub-workflow provides for one-way invocation through its interface, such a failure will go undetected. A user would be left to manually inspect the resulting data for this omission as no part of the system capable of resolving the issue may have become aware of it.

Cascading failures. There are various scenarios that cause cascading failures to occur. One example for this is when an invoked service tries to reply to its caller after the latter has failed. The invoked service will fail as well and it is easy to see how this may lead to further cascading failures in a system of hierarchically composed sub-workflows. Furthermore, the Web service container of the invoked service may merely report the caller's failure as a broken connection.

Application-specific failures. A service being faced with a compute job which will never complete has little information available to decide how to handle this job and will itself never terminate (unless through resource exhaustion). A user however could in theory inspect this job and decide that it is an irrelevant outlier and should be discarded. However, there is currently no automated mechanism to establish this link from detection of the problem to making a human operator attentive to it and supplying further information.

4 Existing Approaches

In this section we present a brief survey of the key facilities made available by BPEL and various Web service specifications for handling failures.

4.1 Transactional Mechanisms

The traditional transaction model based on the four properties of atomicity, consistency, isolation and durability (ACID) has been applied with great success in database management systems (DBMS). Its success for short-lived transactions is, to a large extent, due to the fact that it effectively handles concurrency and failures on behalf of a programmer. It would therefore seem to also afford a convenient implementation of backward error recovery in the context of scientific workflows.

However, whilst ACID transactions are necessary and useful for certain cases in service-oriented applications, it is well known that they are of limited use in large-scale, long-running processes [7] and advanced transactions models (ATMs) have been devised that relax some of the properties of ACID transactions. ATMs allow programmers to focus on business logic rather than reason about exceptional executions by providing runtime support for handling failures and concurrency similar to the one afforded by ACID transactions.

Concepts from various ATMs have found application in workflow management systems (WFMS). For example, [8] has applied the concepts developed to preserve reliability in multidatabase systems [9] to WFMSs. In [8] a single workflow/process represents a global transaction and its individual activities represent sub-transactions. Consequently, process modellers need to equip activities with transactional characteristics, such as compensatable (effects can be undone), retriable (will eventually commit) and pivot (either commits or fails) [9]. This affords the definition of a well-formed process, in which a single pivot activity is preceded only by compensatable activities and followed by retriable activities. In case the pivot activity fails, all previous ones can be undone, and in case it succeeds, all following activities are guaranteed to succeed eventually. Therefore, processes which are structured so as to adhere to the concept of well-formedness, can then achieve semi-atomicity, which affords preservation of the local autonomy of participants, whilst still preserving consistency in the presence of failures.

Although these concepts solve some of the issues we identified with the use of ACID transactions, there are a number issues when applied in our context. First, for computational scientists, the execution characteristics of individual activities in their workflows are far from obvious and reasoning about this is complex. Second, the constraints imposed by the property of well-formedness are too restrictive in practice when applied to large scientific workflows. The primary reason for this is that scientific workflows make use of hierarchical composition of a number of sub-workflows in order to conquer the complexity of large compositions during design and maintenance. Third, even if we were to relax the property of well-formedness, as shown in [10] in the context of MDBMs by introducing flexible transactions with retriable alternatives, the resulting guarantee of *eventual* reliability, that is, a guarantee that an activity will succeed at some point in the future, may introduce considerable delays. Instead, it would be preferable to detect and resolve an issue sooner rather than later, possibly by notifying a human operator.

4.2   BPEL Compensation-Handling

BPEL provides process modellers with various tools to build reliable workflows. It comes equipped with constructs to handle faults similar to the exception handling constructs in modern programming languages. It furthermore offers constructs to carry out compensation.

The concept of compensation as implemented in BPEL is restrictive and complex. In [11] the authors identify the combination of explicit and implicit compensation in BPEL as a main source of this complexity and question whether this added complexity is actually justified by any benefits. The lack of control for steering compensation provided to process modellers is criticised in [12]. It is furthermore noted that there is no support for reasoning about the correctness of an overall workflow in case compensation has been applied. It is also not the case that services usually come equipped with compensating operations, which is a problem in cross-organisational compositions where a developer may have no control over another organisation's services. In our experience, implementing forward error recovery in BPEL is complicated by the assumptions its relevant constructs are based on; immediate termination and backward error recovery. This restriction is revealed in the BPEL specification, which states that the sole aim of fault handling in BPEL is to undo the effects of an unsuccessful scope. Yet, achieving forward error recovery whenever possible is of utmost importance in scientific workflows and should be made as simple as possible.

4.3   WS-Reliability

A number of specifications have been defined in order to increase the reliability of Web services. A crucial component of reliable distributed systems is reliable message delivery. There are two competing, but rather similar, specifications in the area of WS-Reliability (WS-R) area ([13,14]). WS-R supports the reliable exchange of SOAP messages between endpoints and allows applications to configure parameters such as message delivery semantics and timeouts. Message queuing systems suggest themselves as an implementation of WS-R.

Whilst the service offered by WS-R provides an important component to maintain reliability, two issues become apparent in practice. First, the cost that arises from maintaining message queues does not bode well for scientific workflows. This cost arises from persisting messages in some form of database and includes storing additional message histories in the case exactly-once semantics are required. During a single run, a scientific workflow may make thousands of service invocations and may consequently send and receive in the region of tens of thousands of SOAP messages. Second, WS-R guarantees that a message will be delivered eventually. In a loosely-coupled, highly distributed environment involving different administrative domains it becomes difficult to predict for how long a particular set of services may be unavailable to process an incoming message. That is, the delay introduced by the concept of eventual reliability can be significant and an opportunity to detect and resolve a failure is missed.

In summary, we find that even though there are mechanisms to address reliability, they cannot be easily applied to scientific service compositions. The main characteristics of such compositions (long-running, resource-intensive, highly distributed) make the use of ACID transactions impractical. ATMs impose restrictions on the structure of workflows, which are difficult to adhere to in practice. Due to the demand for forward error recovery whenever possible and due the described complexity, which makes it difficult to anticipate all possible failures, BPEL's compensation constructs often fail to provide adequate support. The cost incurred by WS-R may actually be prohibitive and the range of failures encountered by scientific service compositions cannot be solved by reliable messaging alone. This leads us to the question what is actually needed to enable computational scientists to build reliable, fault-tolerant service compositions.

5   Making Reliability Useable

Making service-oriented Grid computing infrastructures directly 'programmable' by computational scientists has a number of benefits to offer that can advance scientific computing.

However, current mechanisms to address reliability are lacking in various respects. This forces computational scientists who develop complex compositions to engage in a lengthy, time-consuming and often frustrating process of trial-and-error where vulnerabilities are discovered through numerous runs of a workflow and protected against by piecemeal modifications. This process of 'design-by-trial-and-error' is not acceptable. The aim of our proposed research is therefore to enable computational scientists to design and execute global scientific BPEL workflows with reasonable trust that the composition will handle any failures and progress forward to completion.

We can derive a number of key features that any reasonable solution should offer. It is desirable to detect failures as soon as possible so that they can be handled and the overall workflow is able to progress forward. This is in contrast to notification of failures by timeouts and undoing a great deal of work in light of failures. In cases where it may be impossible to avoid undoing already completed computations, the least amount of work that needs to be undone in order to proceed to completion should be identified. Of course, any automated handling of failures should be efficient and above all lead to correct behaviour of the system. Achieving correct behaviour is complicated in the case of application-specific failures. Last but not least, it is of crucial importance to allow computational scientists to interact with any autonomic fault handling mechanisms in an intuitive manner so as to be able to indicate desired behaviour and possibly to increase coverage. Amongst other things, this means that autonomic failure handling must be able to operate satisfactorily with the least amount of input from users.

Our proposed solution for achieving our stated objective consists of three major parts.

Failure investigation service. Failure investigation is a crucial element in enabling clever(er) handling of failures. Our experience with scientific BPEL workflows suggests that it may often be possible to handle otherwise fatal failures successfully, if only there was more information available to drive autonomic failure handling mechanisms. The design and implementation of a failure investigation service pose a number of interesting questions to be addressed. One question is what kind of infrastructure is actually needed and what kind of information such an infrastructure should provide. Another issue is to determine what level of support can be achieved without being concerned about providing a global view of system state.

Autonomic recovery strategies. In order to handle failures and enable forward progress, autonomic recovery strategies need to monitor the various components involved in scientific workflows and then take action to prevent the various parts of a workflow from terminating abnormally. There are a number of complications. First, there are many components which may suffer under very different kinds of conditions and therefore require specialised failure investigation and recovery. Second, given the limited degree of software engineering expertise of our users, we cannot expect them to inform such recovery strategies through, for example, sophisticated architectural models. This raises the question of how such strategies should be expressed? Should they be hard-coded and added to a system by some kind of plug-in mechanism? Or can we enable computational scientists to inform these strategies in an intuitive manner? We are furthermore interested to determine the coverage such strategies can achieve, how to ensure recovery leading to correct system behaviour and to find out limits of such autonomic strategies.

Division of Responsibility. The final part of our research deals with opportunities for interaction between computational scientists and autonomic recovery strategies. There are two main elements to this. For the sake of accountability of autonomic recovery strategies, it will be necessary to make reports available to human users about any incidents and actions taken during a run of a workflow. By identifying failures that cannot be addressed automatically, it will furthermore become possible to determine when human users should be involved in decisions about which actions to take in order to handle such failures successfully. Autonomic strategies could then guide users in resolving issues and make their repository of actions available to be steered by users. The question here is in how far support for dividing responsibility between human users and autonomic mechanisms can be used to overcome any limitations of the latter.

We believe that the combination of informed autonomic recovery strategies and meaningful interaction with human users provides a promising avenue for resolving some, if not many, of the reliability challenges computational scientists are currently confronted with.

6   Related Work

There are a number of related efforts taking place at Cornell. Services to monitor system health in support of high-availability in mission-critical Web service applications have been proposed in [15]. Astrolabe [5] has been proposed as a monitoring standard applications could use to implement autonomic behaviour [16]. And finally, [17] discusses services for tracking of process group membership, failure detection and reaching consensus.

Our work differentiates itself from these efforts in various respects. Our failure investigation service does not aim to support process group semantics or achieve a global view of system state. We prefer to avoid the added cost and complexity of establishing a strong notion of consistency and are instead interested to determine the capabilities and limits of mechanisms built on a simple infrastructure that makes additional system information available on request. In cases where achieving consensus may be required, we will investigate the use of resolution schemes [18]. Defining our main target group to be computational scientists means that we cannot expect them to use the features of a monitoring service directly to implement autonomic behaviour in their workflows and that we must limit the necessary setup and configuration activities. Another difference is our interest in investigating how the coverage achieved by such recovery strategies can be increased through cooperation with human users.

An interesting first step in the context of scientific grid applications is represented by OPERA-G [19]. However, the autonomic behaviour OPERA-G was able to achieve is limited. We propose to develop autonomic recovery strategies based on a richer set of information.

The issue of accountability of autonomic computing mechanisms has been raised in [20] and [21].

7   Conclusion

In this paper we discussed the notion of global scientific BPEL workflows and the environment they operate in. The examples of typical failures of global workflows that occur in practice and their consequences provide an insight into the variety and complexity of failures. This helps to confirm our experience. Namely, that tackling the threats to a scientific workflow's reliability is a challenging task, even for experienced software engineers. Our brief examination of existing reliability mechanisms and language constructs lets us conclude that neither do the proposed techniques address the breadth of threats effectively nor do they provide an interface that allows for sufficiently simple interaction with computational scientists.

For solving many of the identified issues, we proposed a solution consisting of three main parts. We aim to build an environment that can make basic information about failures available in order to enable informed autonomic recovery strategies. Furthermore, we will investigate how to achieve useful interaction between human users and these mechanisms to overcome any limitations. The proposed research seems promising and its components raise a number of interesting questions which we look forward to addressing and examining more closely.

References

1. Emmerich, W., Butchart, B., Chen, L., Wassermann, B., Price, S.L.: Grid Service Orchestration using the Business Process Execution Language (BPEL). J. Grid Comp. 3(3-4), 283–304 (2005)
2. Wassermann, B., Emmerich, W., Butchart, B., Cameron, N., Chen, L., Patel, J.: Sedna: A BPEL-based environment for visual scientific workflow modelling. In: Taylor, I.J., Deelman, E., Gannon, D., Shields, M.S. (eds.) Workflows for eScience - Scientific Workflows for Grids, Springer, Heidelberg (2006)
3. Cardelli, L.: Wide Area Computation. In: Wiedermann, J., van Emde Boas, P., Nielsen, M. (eds.) ICALP 1999. LNCS, vol. 1644, pp. 10–24. Springer, Heidelberg (1999)
4. Fischer, M.J., Lynch, N.A., Paterson, M.S.: Impossibility of distributed consensus with one faulty process. JACM 32(2), 374–382 (1985)
   Vogels, W.: technology for distributed system data mining. (2003) 164–206
5. Renesse, R., Birman, K., Vogels, W.: Astrolabe: A robust and scalable technology for distributed system monitoring, management, and data mining. ACM Tran. Comp. Sys 21(2), 164–206 (2003)
   Darlington, J.: submission through web services. Proc. of the UK e-Science All Hands Meeting, EPSRC (2004) 901–905 ISBN 1-904425-21-6.
6. Lee, W., McGough, S., Newhouse, S., Darlington, J.: A standard based approach to job submission through web services. In: Cox, S. (ed.) Proc. of the UK e-Science All Hands Meeting, Nottingham. pp. 901–905. EPSRC (2004) ISBN 1-904425-21-6
7. Barghouti, N.S., Kaiser, G.E.: Concurrency Control in Advanced Database Applications. ACM Computing Surveys 23(3), 269–317 (1991)
8. Hagen, C., Alonso, G.: Exception handling in workflow management systems. IEEE TSE 26(10), 943–958 (2000)

9. Mehrotra, S., Rastogi, R., Silberschatz, A., Korth, H.: A transaction model for multidatabase systems. In: Proc. of the 12th Intl.Conference on Distributed Computing Systems, pp. 56–63. IEEE Computer Society Press, Los Alamitos (1992)
10. Zhang, A., Nodine, M., Bhargava, B., Bukhres, O.: Ensuring relaxed atomicity for flexible transactions in multidatabase systems. In: Proc. of the 1994 ACM SIGMOD Intl. Conference on Management of Data, pp. 67–78. ACM Press, New York (1994)
11. Butler, M., Ferreira, C., Ng, M.: Precise Modelling of Compensating Business Transactions and its Application to BPEL. Journal of Universal Computer Science 11(5), 712–743 (2005)
12. Greenfield, P., Fekete, A., Jang, J., Kuo, D.: Compensation is Not Enough [fault-handlng and compensation mechanism]. In: Proc. of the 7th IEEE Intl. Enterprise Distributed Object Computing Conference, Brisbane, Australia, pp. 232–239. IEEE Computer Society Press, Los Alamitos (2003)
13. Evans, C., Chappell, D., Bunting, D., Tharakan, G., Shimamura, H., Durand, J., Mischkinsky, J., Nihei, K., Iwasa, K., Chapman, M., Shimamura, M., Kassem, N., Yamamoto, N., Kunisetty, S., Hashimoto, T., Rutt, T., Nomura, Y.: Web Services Reliability (WS-Reliability 1.0) (2003)
Services Reliable Messaging Protocol (WS-ReliableMessaging). Software (2005)
14. Ferris, C. (ed.): Web Services Reliable Messaging Protocol (WS-ReliableMessaging). BEA Systems. IBM, Microsoft Corporation, TIBCO Software (2005)
15. Birman, K., Renesse, R., Vogels, W.: Adding high availability and autonomic behavior to web services. In: Proc. of the 26th Intl. Conference on Software Engineering, Washington, DC, pp. 17–26. IEEE Computer Society Press, Los Alamitos (2004)
16. Birman, K., Renesse, R., Vogels, W.: Navigating in the storm: Using Astrolabe to adaptively configure web services and their clients. Journal of Cluster Computing 9(2), 127–139 (2006)
17. Vogels, W.: Tracking Service Availability in Long Running Business Activities. In: Gschwind, T., Aßmann, U., Nierstrasz, O. (eds.) SC 2005. LNCS, vol. 3628, pp. 395–408. Springer, Heidelberg (2005)
18. Kermarrec, A.-M., Rowstron, A., Shapiro, M., Druschel, P.: The icecube approach to the reconciliation of divergent replicas. In: Proc. of the 20th annual ACM Symposium on Principles of Distributed Computing, pp. 210–218. ACM Press, New York (2001)
19. Bausch, W.: OPERA-G: a microkernel for computational grids. PhD thesis, ETH Zürich (2004)
20. Anderson, S., Hartswood, M., Procter, R., Rouncefield, M., Slack, R., Soutter, J., Voss, A.: Making autonomic computing systems accountable: the problem of human computer interaction. In: Mařík, V., Štěpánková, O., Retschitzegger, W. (eds.) DEXA 2003. LNCS, vol. 2736, pp. 718–724. Springer, Heidelberg (2003)
21. Ibrahim, M.T., Telford, R., Dini, P., Lorenz, P., Vidovic, N., Anthony, R.: Self-adaptability and man-in-the-loop: A dilemma in autonomic computing systems. In: Proc. of the 15th Intl. Workshop on Database and Expert Systems Applications, Washington, DC, pp. 722–729. IEEE Computer Society Press, Los Alamitos (2004)

A Service-Oriented Architecture for Electric Power Transmission System Asset Management*

Jyotishman Pathak[1], Yuan Li[2], Vasant Honavar[1], and James McCalley[2]

[1] Department of Computer Science
[2] Department of Electrical & Computer Engineering
Iowa State University
Ames, IA 50011-1040 USA
{jpathak,tua,honavar,jdm}@iastate.edu

Abstract. In electric power transmission systems, the assets include transmission lines, transformers, power plants and support structures. Maintaining these assets to reliably deliver electric energy at low prices is critical for a nation's growth and development. Towards this end, we describe a novel service-oriented architecture for sensing, information integration, risk assessment, and decision-making tasks that arise in operating modern high-voltage electric power systems. The proposed framework integrates real-time data acquisition, modeling, and forecasting functionalities provided by relatively autonomous, loosely coupled entities that constitute the power industry to determine operational policies, maintenance schedules and facility reinforcement plans required to ensure reliable operation of power systems.

1 Introduction

Modern electric power systems comprising of power transmission and distribution grids consist of a large number of distributed, autonomously managed, capital-intensive assets. Such assets include power plants, transmission lines, transformers, and protection equipment. Over the past 15 years, the investment in acquiring new assets has significantly declined causing many such assets to be operated well beyond their intended life with unavoidable increase in stress on the system. Typically, a single power transmission company has its own centralized control center and is responsible for maintaining different types of equipment. The failure of critical equipment can adversely impact the entire distribution grid and increase the likelihood of additional failures.

Avoiding catastrophic failures and ensuring reliable operation of such a complex network of assets presents several challenges in data-driven decision making related to the operation, maintenance and planning of assets. Specifically, decision-makers must anticipate potential failures before they occur, identify alternative responses or preventive measures, along with their associated costs, benefits and risks. Effective decision-making in such a setting is critically dependent on gathering and use of information characterizing the *conditional, operational* and *maintenance* histories of the

* This research is funded in part by the NSF DDDAS-TMRP grant# 0540293 and the ISU Center for CILD (http://www.cild.iastate.edu).

assets, e.g., equipment *age* and *time* since the last inspection and maintenance. Recent advances in sensing, communications, and database technologies have made it possible, at least in principle, for decision-makers to access operating/maintenance histories and asset-specific real-time monitoring data, which can be used to ensure reliable and cost-effective operation of modern power systems so as to reduce (if not eliminate) the frequency and severity of catastrophic failures such as blackouts[1].

However, effective acquisition and use of condition data, operating and maintenance histories, and asset-specific real-time monitoring data presents several challenges in practice: (i) the assets that constitute a modern power system are geographically distributed (ii) the data sources differ in terms of data semantics (due to differences in *ontologies*), and spatial and temporal granularity of data (iii) the development of models that use this information to reliably predict the ways the asset may deteriorate and fail (and recommend counter-measures) requires integration of results of several types of analysis.

Service-Oriented Architecture (SOA) [2] and Web services [3] offer a flexible and extensible approach to integration of multiple, often autonomous, data sources and analysis procedures. The recent adoption of Web services in the power industry [4,5,6,7] and the support for interoperability with other frameworks (e.g., SCADA) through the use of emerging Web services standards make SOA an especially attractive framework for designing software infrastructure to address the challenges outlined above. Against this background, we propose a service-oriented software architecture for power systems asset management. The design of this architecture which is being outlined in this paper is currently being implemented.

The rest of the paper is organized as follows: Section 2 presents an overview of the electric power system asset management problem along with our proposed solution; Section 3 discusses the proposed service-oriented architecture for power systems asset management; Section 4 describes some of the modules (services) comprising the proposed system; Section 5 briefly discusses related work; and Section 6 concludes with a summary and an outline of some directions for further research.

2   Electric Power System Asset Management

In electric power systems, asset management decision problems are characterized by: (1) strong interdependencies between physical performance of individual assets, physical performance of the overall system, and economic system performance; (2) limited resources; (3) important uncertainties in individual component performance, system loading conditions, and available resources; (4) multiple objectives. These problems can be classified into one of four types which involve resource allocation with the objective to minimize cost and risk. These specific asset management decision problems include (a) Operations, (b) Short-term maintenance selection and scheduling, (c) Long-term maintenance planning, and (d) Facility planning. The problems differ primarily in their time scale but are linked by a common focus on the interactions between the equipment condition and the decisions taken. The operational decision problem of how to meet demand in the next hour to week treats facilities available and their deterioration levels as given (though the deterioration is not known precisely).

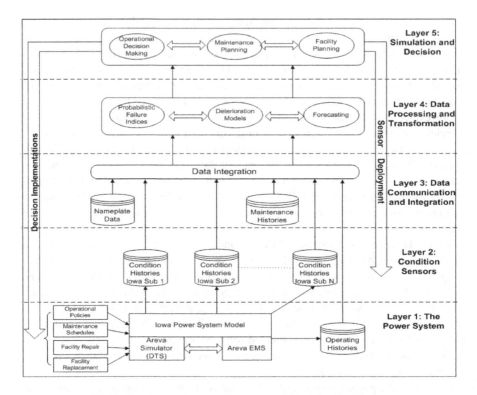

Fig. 1. Structure of the Asset Management Decision Problem [8]

Figure 1 illustrates the structure of the asset management problem and facilitates description of how we intend to address the problem. Essentially, our approach focuses on the use of equipment condition measurements to estimate short-term failure probabilities along with the deterioration effects of loading each piece of equipment at various levels, and the use of such estimates to guide dispatch and unit commitment decisions.

Layer 1, The Power System: This layer consists of a continuously running model of the Iowa power system with network data provided by local utility companies using a commercial-grade (Areva[1]) Dispatcher Training Simulator (DTS) and Energy Management Software (EMS). The DTS and EMS were developed to simulate the environment as seen by a control center operator.

Layer 2, Condition Sensors: This layer consists of databases (one for each substation) that capture condition data and operational and maintenance histories of equipment in substations. Different substations may be owned by different utility companies.

Layer 3, Data Communication & Integration: This layer models communication between each substation and the respective substation server (typically through wireless links) together with integration of data. This layer needs to provide dependable, efficient and secure mechanisms for connecting the data sources with analysis mechanisms (Layer 4).

---

[1] http://www.areva.com

Layer 4, Data Processing & Transformation: This layer operates on the integrated data from Layer 3 to produce, for each piece of equipment, an estimate of the short-term probability of failure at any given time. The estimation of such failure probabilities relies on deterioration models (e.g., models [9] of chemical degradation processes in power transformer insulating materials such as oil and cellulose), driven by on-line sensors which measure levels of certain gases in the oil, gases that are produced by these deterioration processes.

Layer 5, Simulation & Decision: This layer utilizes the component probabilistic failure indices from Layer 4 together with short and long-term system forecasts to drive stochastic simulation and decision models. The resulting operational policies, maintenance schedules, and facility reinforcement plans will then be implemented in the power system (as modeled by the Areva simulator).

In what follows, we describe a service-oriented software architecture for power systems asset management that realizes the framework outlined above.

3   SOA-Based Framework for Power System Asset Management

A Service-Oriented Architecture (SOA) is a component model that supports interaction between multiple functional units, called *services*. A service is a software module that has a well-defined interface specifying a set of named operations that the service provides and a set of messages that the service receives/sends, an implementation of the interface, and if deployed, a binding to a documented network address [2]. An SOA can be implemented using several alternative technologies including Web services [3]. A Web service is a service that defines its interface using the Web Services Description Language[2]. Such a service can be accessed using a protocol that is compliant with the Web Services Interoperability[3] standards. Web service interfaces are platform and language independent, thereby allowing Web services running on different platforms to interoperate.

Our framework, PSAM-s, for Power System Asset Management shown in Figure 2 employs a Web services-based SOA . The core of the framework[4] is the PSAM-s engine comprising of multiple services that are responsible for enabling interaction between the users and other services that offer specific functionality (e.g., prediction of power transformer failure-rates). These services can be broadly categorized into *internal* and *external* services.

3.1   PSAM-s Internal Services

These are the services which are part of the PSAM-s engine. They include:

Submission Service. This service is responsible for handling job requests from the user. Such a request would typically initiate the execution of one or more *information processing services* (described in Section 3.2), and the results after the execution will be

---

[2] http://www.w3.org/TR/wsdl

[3] http://www.ws-i.org

[4] In the context of PSAM-s, we use the terms "service" and "Web service" interchangeably.

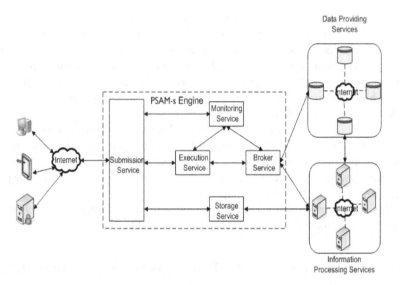

Fig. 2. PSAM-s System Architecture

returned to the user as well as stored in a repository via the *storage service* (described below). The submission service expects the job requests to be defined using the Web Services Business Process Execution Language (WS-BPEL[5]). WS-BPEL specifies a model and a grammar for describing the behavior of a process based on its interactions with other processes (also called partners in WS-BPEL terminology). The interaction with the partners happens through the Web service interfaces and the WS-BPEL process defines the coordination, along with the state and logic necessary for the coordination, to realize a specific goal or requirement. We assume that there exists an "integration specialist" in PSAM-s who is responsible for assembling WS-BPEL process templates/documents for some of the routinely requested user jobs in power system asset management (e.g., failure-rate prediction) that could be used by a common user (e.g., a control center operator). Over time, new templates could be designed or the existing ones modified depending on the user requirements.

Execution Service. Once the user submits a job request (i.e., a WS-BPEL document) to the submission service, the job is sent to the execution service which is responsible for executing the *information processing service(s)* specified in the WS-BPEL document to fulfill the user job requirement. Usually, this document will specify a composition of multiple services whose execution needs to be orchestrated according to a specified control flow (defined as part of the workflow). For example, executing a composite service might involve executing an information processing service that will predict the failure-rate indices for a particular equipment (Layer 4 in Figure 1) which in turn is used by another information processing service to determine if short-term maintenance is required for the equipment under consideration (Layer 5 in Figure 1).

---

[5] http://www.oasis-open.org/committees/tc_home.php?
wg_abbrev=wsbpel

Broker Service. The information processing services mentioned above use equipment condition and historical data to determine the information needed to improve maintenance scheduling. To facilitate the access to this data, we introduce a broker service that is responsible for establishing "dynamic data links" between the information processing and the data providing services (described in Section 3.2). The broker service enables the information processing services dynamically access and interact with the data providing services that are online and contain information that is of interest.

The broker service is based on the WS-Brokered Notification (WSN) specification [10]. It implements an event-driven publish/subscribe protocol. Here, an event represents an occurrence or something that has happened, e.g., a database being updated with new data; resulting in event-messages that are produced and consumed explicitly by the applications. The broker service acts as an intermediary which allows potential message publishers and consumers to interact. In our context, the message publishers correspond to the data providing services and the consumers correspond to the information processing services. Essentially, a data providing service sends an one-way notification message to the broker whenever an event occurs (e.g., a database update). These messages are wrapped in the WSN notify message and are associated with a *topic*, which corresponds to a concept (e.g., `DatabaseStatus`) used to categorize kinds of notification. These topics belong to the same topic namespace (a combination of an unique uniform resource identifier and the topic name), which also contains the meta-data associated with the topics. This meta-data includes information about the type or types of messages that the notification publisher will send on a given topic.

The notification consumers (in our case, the information processing services), are registered with the broker service that is capable of distributing the information provided by the notification producers. Thus, the broker acts as a 'matchmaker service' and identifies the consumers that have registered for specific types of notifications (or topics) and disseminates the relevant information when available (from the publisher). Since the consumer recognizes the topic and its associated meta-data, it knows how to handle the notification. Thus, depending on the message contained in the notification message, the consumer (information processing services) may or may not interact (or establish a 'data link') with the producer (data providing services).

Monitoring Service. Once the job has been submitted, the user can monitor its status via the monitoring service. The idea is to allow users to observe the behavior of the information processing services (during execution) for purposes such as fixing problems or tracking usage. Essentially, the monitoring service maintains an index which automatically registers all the information processing services (notification consumers) that are registered with the broker service mentioned above. These information processing services are WSRF-compliant [11], and thereby readily make their status and state information available as WSRF resource properties (more details in Section 3.2). Whenever the values of these properties change (e.g., the status of a service changing from `idle` to `active`), a notification is pushed via WSN [10] subscription methods to the monitoring service. This information is provided to the user dynamically at run-time.

Storage Service. The results of the computations done by the information processing services are stored in the storage service along with additional meta-data about the computations themselves (i.e., the workflow-related information stating which services were executed and in what fashion). The computation results are provided to the user, whereas the meta-data is used by the storage service as follows: in many scenarios, the users might be interested in executing a workflow, comprising of a set of information processing services, multiple times in a periodic fashion. Obviously, this is a very compute- and I/O-intensive process. Hence, when a job is first submitted by the user via the submission service, the description of the job is matched with the computational meta-data (previously stored) by the storage service. If there is no match (i.e., this job or workflow has not been executed yet), the job is sent to the execution service as described above. However, if there is a match (i.e., the same job has been executed before), the storage service communicates with the broker service to identify the relevant data providing services that will potentially take part during the execution of the job under consideration, and then analyzes to determine if there has been any change/update to the data represented by these services since the previous execution of the job. If not, then the results from the previous computations are returned to the user, otherwise, computations are executed on this new/updated data. We believe that such an optimization approach will potentially result in saving significant time and computational power, specially for periodically executed jobs. However, in principle, this approach can be substituted by more sophisticated sampling techniques that are used to scale the performance of traditional data-driven decision making algorithms [12].

3.2 PSAM-s External Services

These services interact with the PSAM-s internal services to do useful analysis, and in principle, can be provided by external vendors. These external services include:

Data Providing Service. As mentioned earlier, analysis of equipment-related data play an important role in the decision-making process, and in our framework, this data is provided by the components in layers 2 & 3 (Figure 1). There are at least 4 types of information that is captured in these two layers: *equipment data* consists of "nameplate" information including manufacturer, make, model, rated currents, voltages and powers etc.; *operating histories* refer to the loading and voltage conditions, and through faults, to which the equipment has been subjected in the past; *maintenance histories* records inspections and maintenance activities performed on each piece of equipment; and finally *condition histories* are comprised of measurements providing information about the state of the equipment with respect to one or more failure modes. For example, common condition data information for a transformer includes tests on: oil (dissolved gas, moisture, hydrogen, and furan), power factor, winding resistance, partial discharge (acoustic emissions, spectral decomposition of currents), and infrared emissions.

Except the condition data, all the above data are usually collected manually and recorded in multiple database systems distributed across the substation and corporate headquarters of the utility companies. For our PSAM-s project, we are collaborating with few such companies[6] across the mid-western US, and Iowa in particular, for accessing these databases. At the same time, for the equipment condition data, we have

---

[6] The company names are withheld due to confidentiality issues.

deployed multiple sensors in one of the substation test sites in central Iowa to monitor: (i) anomalous electrical activity within transformer via its terminals, (ii) anomalous chemical changes within the transformer oil, and (iii) anomalous acoustic signals generated by partial discharge events within the transformer. The data collected by the sensors is fed at regular intervals in multiple condition-monitoring databases maintained at our university.

To model the various databases as data providing services, we "wrap" the databases into WSRF-compliant [11] (Web Services Resource Framework) Web services. WSRF provides a generic framework for modeling and accessing persistent resources (e.g., a database) using Web services. WSRF introduces the notion of *Resource Properties* which typically reflect a part of the resource's state and associated meta-data. For example, one of the resource properties for PSAM-s data providing services is DBstatus, which has sub-topics offline, online and updated, that can be assigned a value true/false. Whenever there is a change in the value of the resource property[7], an appropriate notification associated with a particular topic is sent to the broker service mentioned above. This information is appropriately handled by the broker to establish "dynamic data links" between the data providing and information processing services.

Information Processing Service. The information processing services are the most important set of components in PSAM-s as they provide insights into the asset management decision problem. Similar to the data providing services, they are also WSRF-complaint and publish various resource properties (e.g., whether a service is idle or active) that are monitored by the monitoring service. Furthermore, the dynamic data links (with the data providing services) that are established by the broker service, allow the information processing services to communicate with them in a *federated* fashion [13], where the information needed (by the information processing services) to answer a query is gathered directly from the data sources (represented by the data providing services). There are two advantages of such an approach: (a) the information is always up-to-date with respect to the contents of the data sources at the time the query is posted; (b) the federated approach avoids a single point-of-failure in query answering, as opposed to a centralized architecture (e.g., a data warehouse), where once the central data warehouse fails, no information can be gathered. We divide the set of information processing services modeled in PSAM-s into two categories corresponding to layers 4 & 5 in Figure 1: (i) data transforming services, and (ii) simulation & decision-making services.

The data transforming services (part of Layer 4) interact with the data providing services to gather and utilize equipment condition information collected from inspections, testing and monitoring, as well as maintenance history to estimate probabilities of equipment failure in some specified interval of time [9]. The underlying probabilistic model captures the deterioration in equipment state as influenced by past loading, maintenance and environmental conditions.

The simulation & decision-making services (part of Layer 5) utilize the failure probabilities determined by the data transforming services together with the short and long term system forecasts to drive integrated stochastic simulation and decision models [14,15]. The resulting operational policies, maintenance schedules, and facility

---

[7] The topics offline and online cannot have similar values at the same time.

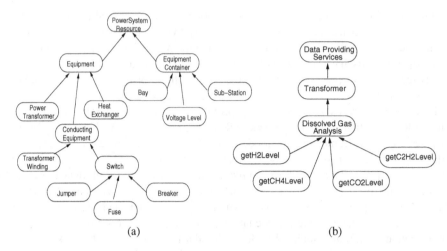

Fig. 3. (a) A Partial Data Ontology (b) A Partial Process Ontology

reinforcement plans are then implemented on the power system (as represented by the Areva simulator in Figure 1). Furthermore, the decision models help discover additional information which drive the deployment of new as well as re-deployment of existing sensors in Layer 2.

3.3 Semantic Interoperability in PSAM-s

As noted earlier, the data providing services in PSAM-s model multiple data repositories (e.g., condition data, maintenance histories) as WSRF-compliant Web services. Typically, these data repositories are autonomously owned and operated by different utility companies. Consequently, the data models that underlie different data sources often differ with respect to the choice of attributes, their values, and relations among attributes (i.e., data source ontologies). Thus, effective use of this data (by the information processing services) requires flexible approaches to bridging the syntactic and semantic mismatches among the data sources. To address this issue in PSAM-s, we model two different types of ontologies: *data ontology* and *process ontology*.

The *data ontology* provides a reference data model that will be used by the software entities and applications, and is based on the Common Information Model (CIM) [16]—a widely used language for enabling semantic interoperability in the electric energy management and distribution domain. The basic CIM data model comprises of twelve different packages structuring the data model and allows representation of various power system related information (e.g., dynamic load data, flow of electricity). In PSAM-s, all the services provide their internal data according to this data ontology and expose CIM-compliant interfaces (based on the *process ontology* described below) thereby allowing multiple services to exchange system data. For example, Figure 3(a) shows a partial data ontology which corresponds to the equipment class hierarchy adopted from the CIM. Each node in this ontology corresponds to an equipment (or an equipment category) and the edges represent sub-class/category relationships. However, in certain cases, it may not be possible to readily map the system's internal data into the common model. In such cases, we propose to use custom-adapters or mappings [13] for the required translation.

The *process ontology* provides a reference functional model that focuses on the interfaces that the compliant services have to provide. This ontology is also based on CIM and specifies the functionalities that the services must deliver, where the formal definition of those functions is understood in terms of CIM semantics. The process ontology allows us to create a standardized service interface that is insulated from the change in the implementation of the service itself. This provides significant flexibility in terms of system integration and pragmatic advantage in the modeling of existing large systems (e.g., SCADA) as services in PSAM-s, which are predominantly non-CIM at their core. For example, Figure 3(b) shows a partial process ontology corresponding to the data providing services which expose information about transformers, and in particular, the dissolved gas concentrations in the transformer oil. Thus, any data providing service that complies to provide this information must implement an interface that defines functions such as $getH_2Level$ and $getCH_4Level$ to extract the hydrogen and methane concentrations in the transformer oil, respectively.

4   Implementation Status

We have implemented an early prototype of the proposed PSAM-s framework for the problem of power transformer failure rate estimation based on condition monitoring data [9], a sub-problem of the larger power systems asset management problem (Figure 1). The prototype [9] integrates power transformer data from multiple sources to train Hidden Markov Models [17] for predicting the failure rate of transformer oil deterioration.

A more complete implementation of the PSAM-s framework is currently underway. A major part of this effort lies in modeling the needed data analysis services. We are currently porting our code for transformer failure rate prediction [9] to WSRF-compliant information processing services. We are developing WSRF-compliant data providing service models based on condition, maintenance and operational data repositories for transformers. The development of the data and process ontologies as well as inter-ontology mappings needed for semantic interoperability between multiple services is also underway [13].

5   Related Work

In recent years, service-oriented architectures for solving problems in electric power systems are beginning to receive attention in the literature. Lalanda [4] have proposed an e-Services based software infrastructure for power distribution. This infrastructure is based on the Open Services Gateway Initiative (OSGi) model and comprises of various components that are integrated and correlated to enable effective monitoring and management of electrical equipment and optimization of power usage. Marin et al. [5] have outlined an approach for adopting e-Services for power distribution. Their proposal involves designing a meta model containing the business logic for services-based power distribution which is then used to generate the code needed to realize the model, thereby providing an increased flexibility in building the underlying software infrastructure. Morante et al. [6] have proposed a framework for power system analysis based on Web and Grid services. Their architecture integrates a set of remotely based controlled units responsible for acquisition of field data and dynamic loading of power equipments, a grid computing based solution engine for on-line contingency analysis, and an interface for reporting the results of analysis. Later, the authors in [6] also present a Web services based framework for power system security assessment [7]. Here, the proposed approach integrates multiple services such as real-time data acquisition, high performance computational and storage services to efficiently perform complex on-line power system security analysis.

Our work on PSAM-s, is focused on a flexible, distributed software architecture for determining operational policies, maintenance schedules and facility reinforcement plans for power systems assets management. The framework builds on and extends our previous work [14,15] on the use of transformer condition data to assess probability of failure [9]. A major focus of PSAM-s is on integrating disparate information sources and analysis services, drawing on our work on data integration [13] and service composition [18] to advance the current state-of-the-art in electric power system asset management.

6   Summary and Discussion

We have described PSAM-s, a service-oriented software architecture for managing operations, maintenance and planning in modern high-voltage electric power transmission systems. The adoption of the service-oriented architecture in PSAM-s provides for interoperability of multiple, autonomously operated data sources and analysis services along with the much needed flexibility and agility to respond to changes in the power transmission and distribution network that call for new data sources or analysis services to be incorporated into the system.

We have completed implementation of an initial prototype of the proposed framework (focused on condition assessment and failure prediction of transformers). Work in progress is aimed at a more complete implementation, incorporating additional data sources and services needed to support a more comprehensive approach to power systems assets management.

Some directions for future work include: (a) development of approaches that allow incremental update of analysis results and predictions based on new data (as opposed to calculating the predictions from scratch); (b) better support for service selection and composition, e.g., incorporation of non-functional attributes of the services (such as Quality of Service) during the process of selection and establishment of dynamic data links by the broker service, and (c) performance evaluation of PSAM-s under a range of operational scenarios.

References

1. Pourbeik, P., Kundur, P., Taylor, C.: The Anatomy of a Power Grid Blackout - Root Causes and Dynamics of Recent Major Blackouts. IEEE Power and Energy Magazine 4(5), 22–29 (2006)

2. Ferguson, D., Stockton, M.: Service-Oriented Architecture: Programming Model and Product Architecture. IBM Systems Journal 44(4), 753–780 (2005)
3. Alonso, G., Casati, F., Kuna, H., Machiraju, V.: Web Services: Concepts, Architectures and Applications. Springer, Heidelberg (2004)
4. Lalanda, P.: An E-Services Infrastructure for Power Distribution. IEEE Internet Computing 9(3), 52–59 (2005)
5. Martin, C., Lalanda, P., Donsez, D.: A MDE Approach for Power Distribution Service Development. In: Benatallah, B., Casati, F., Traverso, P. (eds.) ICSOC 2005. LNCS, vol. 3826, pp. 552–557. Springer, Heidelberg (2005)
6. Morante, Q., Vaccaro, A., Villacci, D., Zimeo, E.: A Web based Computational Architecture for Power System Analysis. In: Bulk Power System Dynamics and Control - VI, pp. 240–246 (2004)
7. Morante, Q., Ranaldo, N., Zimeo, E.: Web Services Workflow for Power System Security Assessment. In: IEEE International Conference on e-Technology, e-Commerce and e-Service, pp. 374–380. IEEE Computer Society Press, Los Alamitos (2005)
8. McCalley, J., Honavar, V., Ryan, S., et al.: Auto-Steered Information-Decision Processes for Electric System Asset Management. In: Alexandrov, V.N., van Albada, G.D., Sloot, P.M.A., Dongarra, J.J. (eds.) ICCS 2006. LNCS, vol. 3993, pp. 440–447. Springer, Heidelberg (2006)
9. Pathak, J., Jiang, Y., Honavar, V., McCalley, J.: Condition Data Aggregation with Application to Failure Rate Calculation of Power Transformers. In: 39th Annual Hawaii Intl. Conference on System Sciences, IEEE Computer Society Press, Los Alamitos (2006)
10. Niblett, P., Graham, S.: Events and Service-Oriented Architecture: The OASIS Web Services Notification Specifications. IBM Systems Journal 44(4), 869–886 (2005)
11. Snelling, D.: Web Services Resource Framework: Impact on OGSA and the Grid Computing Roadmap. GridConnections 2(1), 1–7 (2004)
12. Ghoting, A., Otey, M.E., Parthasarathy, S.: LOADED: Link-Based Outlier and Anomaly Detection in Evolving Data Sets. In: 4th IEEE International Conference on Data Mining, pp. 387–390. IEEE Computer Society Press, Los Alamitos (2004)
13. Caragea, D., Zhang, J., Bao, J., Pathak, J., Honavar, V.: Algorithms and Software for Collaborative Discovery from Autonomous, Semantically Heterogeneous, Distributed Information Sources. In: Balcázar, J.L., Long, P.M., Stephan, F. (eds.) ALT 2006. LNCS (LNAI), vol. 4264, pp. 13–44. Springer, Heidelberg (2006)
14. Dai, Y., McCalley, J., Vittal, V.: Annual Risk Assessment for Overload Security. IEEE Transactions on Power Systems 16(4), 616–623 (2001)
15. Ni, M., McCalley, J., Vittal, V., Greene, S., et al.: Software Implementation of On-Line Risk-based Security Assessment. IEEE Transactions on Power Systems 18(3), 1165–1172 (2003)
16. McMorran, A., Ault, G., Morgan, C., Elders, I., McDonald, J.: A Common Information Model (CIM) Toolkit Framework Implemented in Java. IEEE Transactions on Power Systems 21(1), 194–201 (2006)
17. Rabiner, L.R., Juang, B.H.: An Introduction to Hidden Markov Models. IEEE ASSP Magazine 3(1), 4–15 (1986)
18. Pathak, J., Basu, S., Honavar, V.: Modeling Web Services by Iterative Reformulation of Functional and Non-Functional Requirements. In: Dan, A., Lamersdorf, W. (eds.) ICSOC 2006. LNCS, vol. 4294, pp. 314–326. Springer, Heidelberg (2006)

A Language for Quality of Service Requirements Specification in Web Services Orchestrations

Fabien Baligand[1], Didier Le Botlan[2], Thomas Ledoux[2], and Pierre Combes[1]

[1] France Telecom - R&D / MAPS / AMS,
38-40 rue du general Leclerc, 92794 Issy les Moulineaux, France
`firstname.name@orange-ftgroup.com`
[2] OBASCO Group, EMN / INRIA, Lina
Ecole des Mines de Nantes,
4, rue Alfred Kastler, F - 44307 Nantes cedex 3, France
`firstname.name@emn.fr`

Abstract. Service Oriented Architectures industry aims to deliver agile service infrastructures. In this context, solutions to specify service compositions (mostly BPEL language) and Quality of Service (QoS) of individual services have emerged. However, architects still lack adapted means to specify and implement QoS in service compositions. Typically, they use ad-hoc technical solutions that significantly reduce flexibility and require cost-effective development. Our approach aims to overcome this shortcoming by introducing both a new language and tool for QoS specification and implementation in service compositions. More specifically, our language is a declarative domain-specific language that allows the architect to specify QoS constraints and mechanisms in Web Service orchestrations. Our tool is responsible for the QoS constraints processing and for QoS mechanisms injection into the orchestration. A key property of our approach is to preserve compatibility with existing languages and standards. In this paper, we present our language and tool, as well as an illustrative scenario dealing with multiple QoS concerns.

1 Introduction

A Web Service is a component accessible over the Web that aims to achieve loose coupling between platforms through the use of XML documents and standardized protocols. As a platform neutral technology, Web Services bring a relevant solution to companies that wish to open their Information System and to allow other businesses to connect to their services. Quality of Service (QoS) is an essential criterion for customers seeking a service. A way to specify the customer-provider relationship is to enrich Web Services with QoS documents that aim to provide some guarantees (*e.g.* throughput, response time, price). For the time being, several approaches [7,3,12,4] allow to publish service QoS so that both customers and providers can agree to a certain QoS level.

Additionally, because of their loose coupling property, Web Services can be easily assembled. This feature is especially useful for business companies that want to

D. Georgakopoulos et al. (Eds.): ICSOC 2006 Ws, LNCS 4652, pp. 38–49, 2007.

integrate several services from different sources. For instance, telecommunication companies plan to provide their products (cell phones) with integrated services, built on top of other services delivered by external businesses. Multiple tools and languages [1,2] are available for Web Service composition purpose.

When composing services, some issues dealing with QoS arise. First, a crucial issue is to guarantee global properties of the assembly. Architects need methods or tools either to deduce the global QoS of a composition where each service QoS is known, or to enforce QoS requirements over the composition. For now, architects still have to deal manually with SLA combinatory of services involved in their composition. The second issue relates to the complexity of adapting a composition to a specific context. At deployment time, the system architect has to ensure that the workflow fits to some specific QoS requirements. Dealing with security, reliability and other QoS mechanisms (e.g. load balancing or message queuing) requires a consequent expertise of the platform and of WS-* standards (e.g. WS-Security, WS-Reliability). System architects lack abstractions to address such QoS requirements.

In this paper, we present a new approach aiming to provide the architect with adequate means to specify QoS requirements in Web Service compositions. To this end, we design a language, named "QoSL4BP" (Quality of Service Language for Business Process) or "QoSL" for short, that abstracts QoS concerns from the low-level details of Web Services compositions. Additionally, we propose a tool, named "ORQOS" (ORchestration Quality Of Service) that interprets QoSL4BP and that produces an orchestration enhanced with QoS concerns. We illustrate the whole approach with a scenario.

The remainder of the paper is organized as follows: Section 2 gives a brief introduction of Web Service QoS and composition, before we talk about the issues that result from the intersection of these two topics. Section 3 describes the approach we propose to overcome these shortcomings, introducing both the language and the mechanisms related to the implementation of QoS specifications. Section 4 illustrates our approach through an illustrative use case. Section 5 discusses of related works while Section 6 concludes and outlines future work.

2   Background

2.1   Quality of Service in Web Service World

Web Services are built on standards widely adopted. Best known among these standards are WSDL (interface specification), SOAP (communication protocol), and UDDI (service description and discovery). There also exist multiple WS-* standards that address non functional properties (e.g. WS-Security or WS-Addressing). Although most of these definitions have resulted into solid standards, there still is no consensus to the question of how one should publish the QoS of Web Service.

Among different approaches to predict the QoS of a service, current works focus on promoting the use of Service Level Agreement (SLA). SLA consists in a prescription concerning QoS between a consumer and its provider. For the time being, there is no standard SLA definition and each vendor has designed and implemented its platform specific solution (IBM Web Service level Agreement, HP Web Service Management Language, Web Service Offering Language, WS-Agreement).

2.2   Web Service Composition

Using several Web Services as building blocks, architects may design more elaborated Web Services by composing them. A possible way to achieve Web Service composition is to design a message workflow and specify the services to be called within the workflow. Such a composition is called an orchestration. Orchestration processes are centralized and one entity is responsible for the execution logic of the whole workflow. This method is convenient for maintenance and evolution since the architect can design the workflow in the boundaries of his own business.

To design such orchestrations, many languages have merged into a standard and widely agreed language named "Business Process Execution Language for Web Services" (BPEL4WS or BPEL for short) [2]. This language is based on a small set of primitives (*e.g.* invoke, receive, reply, flow, throw), hence allowing any architect to specify the structure of his orchestration.

2.3   Current Issues

At pre-deployment time, the SLA of local services (*i.e.* services that take part in the composition) is computed to deduce the SLA of the composite service (bottom-up approach), or, conversely, the architect must resolve a set of local services whose SLA aggregation match the SLA of the composite service (top-down approach). However, both approaches do not take into account architects advanced QoS requirements. For instance, the architects may want to guaranty the SLA of their orchestrations, while specifying QoS of some parts of their orchestrations and requiring that some local services are discovered to match the global SLA. In this case, SLA documents do not provide expressivity to address such QoS requirements. Furthermore, being able to specify QoS mechanisms, such as security, over parts of the orchestration is a major concern that SLA cannot address either.

Because BPEL language does not provide expressivity for QoS management, and since SLA are limited, architects cannot easily declare QoS requirements and logic in their orchestrations. Instead, they specify QoS management at the message level, using multiple frameworks and languages. Making all these frameworks work together leads to code that lacks flexibility and portability, that decreases loose coupling nature of the composition, and which is error-prone.

3   Quality of Service Requirements Specification

3.1   Motivation

BPEL is a language allowing the architect to design orchestrations. From the outside, an orchestration can be seen as a composite service with a WSDL functional interface. A SLA document can be associated to a service or a composite

Table 1. Web Services related Languages

	Functional Description	QoS Description
External Interface	WSDL	SLA
Composition Implementation	BPEL	Lack of expressivity

service to specify its QoS properties. However, there is a lack of expressivity for architects willing to specify QoS objectives and mechanisms in the orchestration (*e.g.* the architect may want to specify security, performance or even pricing requirements over parts of his orchestration). We give an illustration of this discussion in Table 1.

To overcome this lack of expressivity, we can consider several guidelines, such as specifying a QoS extension for BPEL, or implementing a QoS-aware BPEL engine, or designing a specific language and platform for QoS requirements specification and enactment in BPEL. Because a key decision of our approach was not to be intrusive, in order to preserve existing infrastructures and languages, we choose not to extend BPEL language or to implement a new BPEL engine. Moreover, because languages improve reusability and portability, we decided to provide an appropriate language, namely "QoSL4BP" (Quality of Service for Business Process) or QoSL for short, for QoS requirements specification in Web Service compositions. More specifically, QoSL allows to specify QoS constraints and mechanisms in Web Service orchestrations.

3.2 Design

To design the QoSL language, we focussed on a couple of properties that seem relevant to our application domain:

- QoSL is a domain-specific language (DSL) [9]. Domain expertise is captured in the language implementation rather than being coded explicitly. The domain of QoSL corresponds to "Quality of Service applied to Web Service Orchestrations", encompassing sub domains (*e.g.* security or performance).
- QoSL is a declarative language [10] as it meant to be goal driven. Control is not the concern of the architect who does not need to provide a fully detailed list of instructions to specify QoS objectives and mechanisms.
- QoSL is modular. Separation of concerns is the process of breaking a program into distinct features, hence increasing code clarity and evolutivity. In order to separate concerns, the QoSL language isolates the code into several modules (policies), each of them capturing one particular QoS concern.

3.3 Specification

Policies are the basis of QoSL language structure. A policy represents a single QoS concern of the service and contains a set of rules, which are composed of QoS constraints and mechanisms. In QoSL, a policy has a name, targets a scope of the orchestration (a scope represents a single activity, multiple activities or

Table 2. QoSL Language Entities

Language Entity	Meaning
scope (Where)	abstracts away an orchestration subset. represents a single activity, multiple activities, or even the whole orchestration.
concern (What)	specifies which QoS concern is addressed in a specified scope. enforces separation of concerns.
policy (How)	consists in a module encompassing QoS constraints and mechanisms in a scope for a specific QoS concern.

even the whole orchestration) and refers to a particular QoS concern to enforce homogeneity of the body of the policy. Since QoSL aims to bind BPEL, SLA and WS-* standards, then QoSL borrows some abstractions from these languages. Table 2 shows entities of the QoSL language.

To implement the body of policies, we focussed on adapted constructs. QoSL allows to bind variable names to values (using "let variableName = $value$"), to define constraints ("check QoSproperty > $quantitativeRequirement$") and to set mechanisms ("set QoSmechanism(parameterList)"). It allows the architect to specify essential parameters, related to the policies he defines, as well as parameters that would otherwise be inferred (*e.g.* weights for weighted round-robin load balancing algorithm). We present here a first version that will be refined and extended later on (*e.g.* to integrate policy composition primitives). Figure 1 illustrates the structure of actual QoSL language.

```
orqos orqos_name {
    policy policy_name scope BPEL_scope_name concern QoS_concern {
        // specify some variable
        let variable_name = value ;
        // specify some constraint
        check QoS_property > quantitative_requirement ;
        // specify some mechanism
        set QoS_mechanism( parameterList ) ;
    }
}
```

Fig. 1. QoSL Policy Template

It is worth noting that although our approach enables the architect to write policies, it is different of WS-Policy. WS-Policy provides a grammar for expressing the capabilities and requirements of a single entity, whereas QoSL allows to set objectives and actions over parts of a workflow.

3.4   Interpretation

Figure 2 shows the QoSL interpretation process. This process is static and occurs before the workflow is instantiated in the BPEL engine.

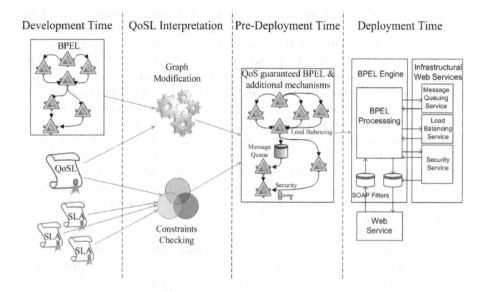

Fig. 2. QoSL Interpretation Process

At development time, the business architect is responsible for designing the workflow, using BPEL language. Then the system architect has to specify the non functional properties of the architecture. He collects SLA related to services involved in the orchestration and specifies QoS policies, using QoSL language. QoSL interpretation is performed by our tool ORQOS. The result is a new BPEL document and its associated SLA. BPEL document contains QoS mechanisms, and is ready to be deployed on a BPEL engine. Once deployed the BPEL workflow can be executed. While running, calls are made to some Web Services that contain QoS mechanism logic. For the time being, runtime monitoring and SLA violation are not handled by ORQOS.

3.5 ORQOS Process

ORQOS aims to process the QoSL policies specified by the architect. A major issue consists in dealing with policies composition to avoid possible interactions during the processing. For now, each policy is processed sequentially based on their order in the QoSL document. We plan to improve this model in our future works. So far, processing a QoSL document consists in five steps.

- First, ORQOS checks policies consistency to ensure that the code contained by a policy is homogeneous and that it addresses a single concern. For instance, a security mechanism should not be called within a policy whose concern is performance. By clearly separating the different concerns, it becomes easier to figure out how policies should be composed one with another.
- Second step corresponds to modifying the original BPEL graph in such a way that QoS mechanisms are introduced at specific places determined by

the scope of the policy (application domain). Such mechanisms are specified by the policies and are injected into the BPEL as "extra BPEL" activities. Potentially, extra BPEL activities set can include a wide range of QoS mechanisms such as traditional QoS mechanisms found in regular Web application servers, as well as mechanisms involving WS-* standards.

– Once the new workflow is generated, ORQOS sets constraints on each activity. Constraints are provided by SLA of local services and composite service, and by QoSL specifications concerning QoS requirements over scopes.

– Constraints are checked by a constraint solver. At this step, if the constraints defined by the architect cannot be satisfied, ORQOS stops and returns an exception. In the opposite case, ORQOS keeps processing and may use some of the results as parameters for QoS mechanisms settings (e.g. balance weights or capacities for message queuing) and to generate the SLA of the composition.

– Final step is the production of a BPEL document that can be read by any BPEL engine. Extra BPEL activities are refined into plain BPEL activity sequences that can involve some "invoke" activities that reach infrastructural Web Services containing mechanism logic (e.g. for security concern, an infrastructural Web service is responsible for WS-Security implementation logic). Thus, the potential boundaries of the approach correspond to the set of actions that can possibly be performed by modifying a BPEL document and calling logic contained in infrastructural Web Services.

4   Illustrative Scenario

4.1   Urban Trip Planner Scenario

Depicted in Figure 3, the "Urban Trip Planner" (UTP) scenario illustrates a Web Service orchestration. It aims to plan trips in big cities, by using transportation services. By calling the UTP service, a client gets the complete transportation route, as well as a map showing the path from the last station to his final destination.

As can be seen on Figure 3, the Urban Trip Planner Service is composed of multiple services. It requires both a destination and a device identification number as inputs. Next, the request is sent to two different services in parallel. These services belong a flow named "OrangeScope". The first service uses the device identification number and returns the client current location (for instance, using a Wifi access point location service). The second service takes the destination in input and returns the exact address, using the Yellow Pages service. Upon reception of both replies, the UTP service sends both addresses to a Transportation service that returns the route and commutes details. The final station address and the destination address are sent to a Grapher service that delivers a map of the path from the station to the destination. Eventually, both the route details and the map are returned to the user.

Let us now give an example of our approach through a scenario involving three QoS properties: throughput, capacity and authentication properties. Throughput is the number of requests by second that a service can process. Capacity

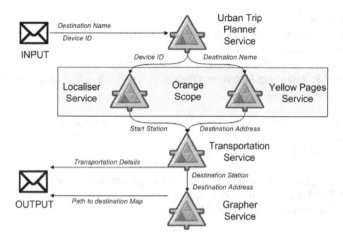

Fig. 3. Urban Trip Planner Service Workflow

relates to the limit of the number of simultaneous requests which should be provided with guaranteed performance. Authentication is the ability of a client to show credentials to access a service. To address these QoS properties, the architect would like to specify some QoS constraints and some QoS mechanisms in the UTP orchestration.

4.2 Specification of QoS Concerns

Once the business architect has implemented the workflow using BPEL, the system architect has to ensure it fits to some QoS requirements. Thus, before deploying the orchestration, the system architect reads each SLA document, then deduces and validates the global QoS of the assembly.

To adjust to services offers and requirements, he also needs to implement QoS mechanisms such as load balancing, message queuing and username token authentication. Such information can be specified using QoSL policies. For this, constraints and mechanisms targeting a same QoS concern in a same scope are gathered in a same policy. The policies corresponding to the requirements of the architect are shown on Figure 4.

- The first policy is called "IncreaseGrapherThroughput" and targets the single "InvokeGrapher" activity. It specifies that the throughput property of the Grapher service should be more than 5 000 requests/sec and introduces a load balancing mechanism using the weighted round robin algorithm over Mappy, GoogleMap, and MapQuest services with weights 3, 2 and 5.
- The second policy, called "ManageGlobalCapacity" aims to force the orchestration capacity to be more than 200 parallel requests. It specifies that a queuing mechanism can be used to increase the capacity.
- The third policy affects the security settings when calling services of the "OrangeScope" (which are the Localiser and the Yellow Pages services). The

```
orqos UTPpolicies {
    policy IncreaseGrapherThroughput scope InvokeGrapher concern Performance {
        check Throughput ≥ 5000 ;
        let $MyLinks={Mappy, GoogleMap, MapQuest} ;
        set LoadBalancing(Algorithm=WeightedRoundRobin, PartnerLinks=$MyLinks,
            Weights={3, 2, 5}) ;
    }
    policy ManageGlobalCapacity scope UTPFlow concern Capacity {
        check Capacity ≥ 200 ;
        set Queue() ;
    }
    policy OrangeAuthentication scope OrangeScope concern Security {
        let $MyToken = {ORQOSuser, mypassw} ;
        set Authentication(Token=$MyToken) ;
    }
}
```

Fig. 4. QoSL Document for UTP Orchestration

architect defines a username token (with name "ORQOSuser" and password "mypassw") and specifies the authentication mechanism to use.

4.3   Interpretation of QoSL

As said earlier, ORQOS processes QoSL documents through five steps. At first step, it takes the BPEL document of the UTP orchestration document, as well as the QoSL document stating the three policies (IncreaseGrapherThroughput, ManageGlobalCapacity and OrangeAuthentication) and the SLA of each service (Localiser, Yellow Pages, Transportation and Grapher services). These documents are translated to objects and policies homogeneity is verified.

Next, the graph describing the UTP workflow is modified. A "Load Balancing activity" replaces the Grapher invoke activity and encapsulates a Mappy, MapQuest and GoogleMap invoke activities. Each invoke activity is encapsulated in a "Message Queuing activity". The OrangeScope is encapsulated in an "Authentication Activity".

Next step consists in setting constraints on each activity of the workflow. In this example, we focus on throughput and capacity properties. Each activity encapsulates both a throughput and a capacity parameter. Simple activities (invoke activities to services involved in UTP workflow) are linked to SLA information related to these properties, while composite activities (Load Balancing activity, Message Queuing activity, Orange Scope parallel branches) aggregates encapsulated activities parameters. Eventually, it results in a constraint network that is solved by a java constraint solver (Choco constraint solver).

The solver returns solutions to determine the capacity of the Message Queues activities, as well as weights for the weighted round robin algorithm of the Load Balancing activity. It also computes the SLA of the composite service so that the service customer can get a guaranty of the service QoS.

Finally, the graph is transformed back to plain BPEL. First, the Load Balancing activity gets replaced by a sequence of two activities: an invoke activity to a load balancing infrastructural Web Service to figure which Grapher service should be called for this specific instance of the workflow, then a switch activity tests the output and calls the appropriate Grapher service. Message queuing activities get replaced by an invoke activity to a message queue infrastructural Web Service before each invoke activity of the workflow. With regards to performance issues, tests have shown that load balancer service or message queues, using a cache mechanism for state management, do not significantly impact the BPEL engine performance. Then the Authentication activity gets replaced by two invoke activities, located around the Orange Scope, to an authentication infrastructural Web Service. This security service injects a security token through the filters of the BPEL engine when the orchestration reaches the Orange Scope. Because infrastructural Web Services are located on the same server as the BPEL engine, performance overhead is minimal. The new BPEL document is eventually generated and ready to be deployed.

5 Related Works

"Aspect Oriented for Business Process Execution Language" (AO4BPEL) [6] aims to bring AOP (Aspect Oriented Programming) mechanisms to BPEL. The authors have given examples of their solution with security aspects and use deployment descriptors to generate aspects. Although very promising, AO4BPEL is an imperative language and we do not believe that architects want to deal with implementation details in the BPEL process. We also think that deployment descriptors are limited when it comes to expressing mechanisms over multiple activities of the workflow and, since AO4BPEL approach does not benefit of SLA works, they do not address QoS constraints specification. Our belief is that architects would rather use a declarative language to specify constraints and mechanisms over different scopes of their orchestrations.

In [5] the authors propose a policy assertion language, "WS-CoL" (Web Services Constraint Language), based on WS-Policy and specifically designed for user requirements (constraints) specification on the execution of Web service compositions. This language is meant to be compliant with the WS-Policy framework, and its process requires a transformation step of the BPEL document to integrate some monitoring activities. This approach is similar to ours in that it provides expressivity concerning requirements on BPEL orchestrations. However, the authors only considered security assertions, using WS-SecurityPolicy.

"Self-Serv" [11] solution includes a platform to compose Web Services, a declarative language based on state charts and a "community of service" concept (containing alternative services), to add a layer between composition level and applicative services level. Composition execution is controlled by "coordinators" components that are in charge of initializing, controlling and monitoring the composition. Although this solution brings interesting elements to QoS management, the fact that BPEL is not supported is quite limitative.

[8] offers to extend BPEL with QoS attributes in order to manage SLA data written using the WSLA language. A new tag, named "agreement", has been inserted into BPEL schema. Architect should be able to specify some QoS constraints while actual QoS properties are evaluated through Computational Quality Attributes elements. Because this work extends BPEL, it is not compliant with regular BPEL engines. Moreover, these extensions do not deal with QoS mechanism and so the architect still has to implement logic of QoS mechanisms. Also, our approach allows the orchestration logic and QoS logic to be separated, hence improving flexibility and reusability.

6   Conclusion and Future Works

We first outlined a crucial issue concerning Web Service compositions. Although solutions exist to compose Web Services and to publish the Quality of Service of individual services, there is still no solution for QoS requirements specification in Web Service compositions. For now, system architects have multiple languages and frameworks to deal with, at deployment time. They also have to check each SLA to deduce the global outcome, making it a complex task to guarantee QoS properties of an assembly.

Our solution aims to provide abstractions for system architects, so they can specify and implement QoS requirements before deployment time. Our first contribution is a language, called "QoSL4BP" (Quality of Service Language for Business Process), that allows the architect to specify QoS constraints and mechanisms in their orchestration. Secondly, a tool, called "ORQOS" (ORchestration Quality Of Service), validates these constraints (by analyzing both the QoSL document as well as the multiple SLA documents) and injects QoS mechanisms (*e.g.* security mechanisms). QoS mechanisms logic is implemented by some infrastructural Web Services that can be reached via BPEL invocations. A key decision for the design of our approach was to not modify any existing language or standard from the Web Service world.

So far, we have built a first prototype that tackles with three different QoS concerns (throughput, capacity and security) and that is able to inject load balancing, message queuing and authentication mechanisms into an orchestration. Because QoS concerns are likely to be tangled up, we plan to study composition of policies in a more formal way as we extend our approach to other concerns.

References

1. Web service choreography interface (wsci) 1.0 (2002), http://www.w3.org/TR/wsci/
2. Business process execution language for web services, version 1.1 (2003), ftp://www6.software.ibm.com/software/developer/library/ws-bpel.pdf
3. Keller, A., Ludwig, H.: The wsla framework: Specifying and monitoring service level agreements for web services. In: Journal of Network and Systems Management, March 2003, vol. 11, Plenum Publishing (2003)

4. Sahai, A., Machiraju, V., Sayal, M., van Moorsel, A., Casati, F.: Automated sla monitoring for web services. In: 13th IFIP/IEEE International Workshop on Distributed Systems: Operations and Management, DSOM, Montreal, Canada, pp. 28–41. Springer, Heidelberg (2002)
5. Baresi, L., Guinea, S., Plebani, P.: Ws-policy for service monitoring. In: Bussler, C., Shan, M.-C. (eds.) TES 2005. LNCS, vol. 3811, pp. 72–83. Springer, Heidelberg (2006)
6. Charfi, A., Schmeling, B., Heizenreder, A., Mezini, M.: Reliable, secure, and transacted web service compositions with ao4bpel. In: ECOWS. Proceedings of the 4th IEEE European Conference on Web Services, Zurich, Switzerland, December 2006, IEEE Computer Society Press, Los Alamitos (2006)
7. Li Ji Jin., et al.: Analysis of service-level agreement for web services. Technical Report HPL-2002-180 (2002)
8. Fung, C.K., Hung, P.C.K., Linger, R.C., Walton, G.H.: Extending business process execution language for web services with service level agreements expressed in computational quality attribute. In: HICSS-38. IEEE Thirty-Eighth Hawaii International Conference on System Sciences, Big Island, Hawaii, IEEE Computer Society Press, Los Alamitos (2005)
9. Mernik, M., Heering, J., Sloane, A.M.: When and how to develop domain-specific languages. csur 37(4), 316–344 (2005)
10. Sethi, R.: Programming languages: concepts and constructs. Addison-Wesley Longman Publishing, Boston, MA (1989)
11. Sheng, Q.Z., Benatallah, B., Dumas, M., Mak, E.O.-Y.: Self-serv: A platform for rapid composition of web services in a peer-to-peer environment. VLDB02 (2002)
12. Tosic, V., Patel, K., Pagurek, B.: Wsol - web service offerings language. In: Bussler, C.J., McIlraith, S.A., Orlowska, M.E., Pernici, B., Yang, J. (eds.) CAiSE 2002 and WES 2002. LNCS, vol. 2512, pp. 57–67. Springer, London (2002)

A Semi-automated Orchestration Tool for Service-Based Business Processes

Jan Schaffner[1], Harald Meyer[1], and Cafer Tosun[2]

[1] Hasso-Plattner-Institute for IT-Systems-Engineering at the University of Potsdam
Prof.-Dr.-Helmert-Strasse 2-3, 14482 Potsdam, Germany
{jan.schaffner,harald.meyer}@hpi.uni-potsdam.de
[2] SAP Labs, Inc.
3421 Hillview Ave, Palo Alto, CA 94304, USA
cafer.tosun@sap.com

Abstract. When creating service compositions from a very large number of atomic service operations, it is inherently difficult for the modeler to discover suitable operations for his particular goal. Automated service composition claims to solve this problem, but only works if complete and correct ontologies alongside with service descriptions are in place.

In this paper, we present a semi-automated modeling environment for Web service compositions. At every step in the process of creating the composition, the environment suggests the modeler a number of relevant Web services. Furthermore, the environment summarizes the problems that would prevent the composed service from being invocable. The environment is also able to insert composed services into the composition at suitable places, with atomic services producing the required data artifacts to come to an invocable composition.

Our results show that this mixed initiative approach significantly eases the creation of composed services. We validated our implementation with the leading vendor of business applications, using their processes and service repository, which spans across multiple functional areas of enterprise computing.

1 Introduction

In recent years, the fact that handcrafted service compositions are often erroneous has been serving as a rationale to automate the creation of Web service compositions ([1,2,3,4]). Academia has proposed systems that automatically create invocable plans for each individual case at runtime. This opposes the idea of creating composed services that cover as many cases as possible. The plans are produced in a fully automatic fashion, based on domain knowledge and semantic service descriptions. While automated planners are able to reduce complexity, inflexibility and error-proneness akin to the creation of composed services, several drawbacks can be identified: Automated planning relies on the availability of complete formal representations of the domain knowledge. The task of formally specifying a domain in sufficient fidelity presents a tremendous challenge. Especially for complex domains we can legitimately assume that complete ontologies will not be available in the near future. Incomplete domain knowledge, however, will often result in the situation that an automated planner fails to

D. Georgakopoulos et al. (Eds.): ICSOC 2006 Ws, LNCS 4652, pp. 50–61, 2007.

produce a plan. Erroneous domain knowledge, moreover, can result in situations where a planner finds wrong plans. In contrast, a human planner can draw upon his experience within a specific domain. This experience will often compensate for missing or erroneous ontologies. Moreover, the fact that fully automated service composition methods do not require a human in the loop poses an organizational and juridical impediment: In business reality, it is required that concrete persons are responsible for a particular business process. This fact lowers the industry acceptance of automated planning techniques; their transition from research to industry is progressing slowly.

In this paper we show that the techniques from automated planning can be used to ease the manual creation of business processes. The incorporation of matchmaking technologies used by automated planners into a semi-automated modeling tool for creating enterprise service compositions has several advantages. The problems manual service composition can be reduced or eliminated by the aid of new "mixed initiative features". This paper is organized as follows: Section 2 presents a scenario from practice, which is used in section 3 to show the usefulness of the proposed mixed initiative features. Section 3 also discusses the implementation of these mixed initiative features. In section 4 we give an overview of related work in the field of semi-automated service composition and discuss our tool from that perspective. Section 5 concludes the paper.

2   Usage Scenario: Leave Request

The following scenario is taken from Duet[1], a recent software product by SAP and Microsoft. Duet extends the reach of SAP's business processes to a large number of users by embedding them into Microsoft's Office environment. We extracted the process flow among the ERP Web services Duet is built upon. We are using the process as a case study for the semi-automated composition environment developed in Jan Schaffner's Master's thesis [5]. The leave request scenario consists of two parts: First, an employee files a leave request. Second, his manager approves or denies this request. Therefore, the two roles "employee" and "manager" participate in the leave request process. Due to length constraints, we limit ourselves to the part of the process in the role of the employee. The scenario is depicted in figure 1 using the Business Process Modeling Notation (BPMN [6]). The activities in the diagram correspond to Web service operations. To describe the semantics of the operations, we extended the BPMN syntax so that we can depict WSMO service capabilities: The inputs that a service consumes and the conditions over these inputs make up the "precondition". The outputs of a service and the relation between input and output make up the "postcondition".

Before the employee files a leave request, he will typically try to get an overview of his time balance and suitable dates for the leave. Duet will collect this information when the leave request application pane is opened. Therefore, Duet will call the following four Web service operations.

– **Read Employee Time Account.** This operation returns the time balance of an employee consisting of paid vacation, overtime, and sick leaves. The operation takes an employee object uniquely representing the employee and a key date, for which the balances are returned, as input.

---

[1] http://www.duet.com

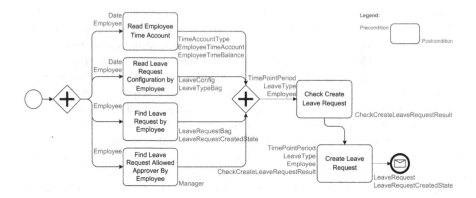

Fig. 1. Leave request scenario

- **Read Leave Request Configuration by Employee.** This operation outputs the leave configuration (allowed leaves such as half or full day) for a specific employee as stored in the ERP system. The operation takes an employee object and a key date as input.
- **Find Leave Request By Employee.** It might be the case that an employee has recently filed other leave requests which are not yet processed. This operation returns an employee's pending leave requests, so that he or she can consider them together with the time balance. The operation takes an employee object as input.
- **Find Leave Request Allowed Approver by Employee.** A leave request is approved by the line manager of the employee filing it. In some cases, a different approver or no approval at all is necessary. This operation returns the employee object corresponding to the allowed approver for the leave request. It takes an employee object as input.

The information retrieved by the four service operation described above is visualized in Duet and the employee can decide on a day or a period browsing his Outlook calendar. This yields the sequential invocation of the two following operations:

- **Check Create Leave Request.** Before a leave request is created in the ERP system, it must be checked for plausibility. This operation takes the same inputs as the operation that creates the leave request, which are an employee object, the leave period and the leave type. If the check is successful, the operation returns a positive result.
- **Create Leave Request.** After the plausibility check has been successful, this operation finally creates the leave request in the ERP system. As a result, a leave request is created.

3   Mixed Initiative Features

In this section, we will describe three mixed initiative features which are characteristic for semi-automated service composition. The leave request business process from the previous section will be constructed step by step supporting and motivating the three features. We will then present the realization of each feature in detail. A more general introduction of the mixed initiative features for semi-automated composition can be found in [7].

3.1 Filter Inappropriate Services

The number of service operations that are available as building blocks for the composition can be extremely high. In the context of SAP, for example, the central repository contains more than 1000 services. This results in a complexity that is hard to oversee. Especially if compositions are to be realized by users from a non-technical background, a modeling tool for service compositions should filter the set of available services. Such filtering can be done based on semantic service descriptions.

Business Scenario. When the leave request is to be created from scratch, the tool will first retrieve all available Web services. The modeler starts out with adding the role "employee" to the composition by selecting this role from a list of all available roles (e.g., "supplier", "customer", "manager"). Our tool then assumes the implicit availability of a variable of the complex type "employee", representing the person who takes part in the business process in this role. The tool is now able to filter the list of available service operations to those that require an employee object as an input. Our experiments have shown that filtering all service operations that are not be invocable in the current step of the composition is too strict. The tool therefore also presents service operations that are nearly invocable in the sense that only one input is missing. Using this technique, we are able to retrieve very reasonable suggestions from SAP's service repository. The operations in this repository are grouped around so-called enterprise services. In our example, the modeler would therefore now expand the "Time and Leave Management" enterprise service and select the first four operations depicted in figure 1. As there are no dependencies between the activities, the user connects the operations using a parallel control flow. This is shown in figure 2.

At this point, the modeler is able to retrieve more service suggestions through the filtering mechanism by clicking on the merge node of the parallel split. Our tool will then present a list of service operations that are invocable or nearly invocable based on the union all postconditions of the services which are in the composition so far. The postconditions (i.e., the output data types) of the operations are also depicted in figure 1. Amongst others, our tool will suggest the operation *Check Create Leave Request* as a nearly invocable service. The modeler adds it to the composition and creates a link between the merge node and the operation.

Realization. At each step of the composition (i.e., each change in the process by the modeler) the state of the composition is translated into a query against our semi-automated service composition engine, which is built on top of a WSML reasoner. In this context, the term "state" refers to the postconditions of all service operations that are currently in the composition. The currently selected role (e.g., "employee") is also added to the state. As already mentioned in the business scenario, our tool suggests both invocable services and nearly invocable services. Therefore, two corresponding methods are provided by our semi-automated composition engine.

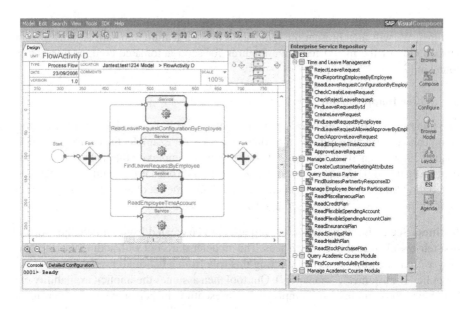

Fig. 2. Screenshot of the modeling tool

The first method returns a list of invocable service operations, alongside their pre- and postconditions, possible roles in which they can be executed, the default role, possible variable bindings for the current state of the composition, a default variable binding and the enterprise service they belong to. Moreover, this list is ordered by relevance for the user in the current context. Listing 1.1 presents our algorithm for finding and weighting invocable services for a given state in pseudo code.

```
1  findInvocableServicesOrdered ( State state, String role)
     register state with reasoner ;
3    retrieve  list  of  registered  operations  from reasoner ;
     for each  registered  operation  do
5      if operation is  invocable  do
         compute match distance  for each  binding ;
7        store  binding  with  lowest  match  distance  as  default  binding ;
         store  all  other  bindings , preconditions  and  postconditions ;
9    unregister  state  with  reasoner ;
     compute  weightings  based  on  lowest  match  distances ;
11   for each  invocable  operation  do
       if NFP  specifying an intended  roles  for  the  operation  exists
13       if  NFP  matches role
           increase  weighting  by 1;
15   order  operations  by  weighting ;
     return  ordered  list  of  operations ;
```

Listing 1.1. Compute ordered list of invocable service operations

The match distance in line 6 of listing 1.1 is computed based on the distance of the data types in the variable bindings and the data types specified in the preconditions of the operations. As an example, we consider an operation that consumes a parameter "employee" as a precondition. Additionally to the "employee" concept there as subconcept of "employee" called "manager". Given a state with an "employee" instance the match distance between a variable binding and the service's precondition is 0. But if we only have a "manager" instance, the distance between the variable binding and the precondition is 1. Because the first binding has a lower match distance than the second, it is the default binding of the operation in the current state. If a precondition requires more than one data type, the match distance is aggregated over all variables in a binding.

The weightings for the operations (line 10 listing 1.1) are based on the match distances: For each operation, we take variable binding with the lowest match distance (i.e., the default binding) into account. The operation corresponding to the binding with the highest match distance gets the lowest weighting, and so forth. To further differentiate the relevance of the discovered services, the role of the current state of the composition is compared to the intended role of each invocable operation. An intended role is the role for which an operation has been designed. For example, the operation *Create Leave Request* is designed for the role "employee", while it is also invocable for composition states with the role "manager". If the role of the current composition state and the intended role of an operation match, the weighting of the operation is increased.

The second method provided by our semi-automated service composition engines discovers service operations that are nearly invocable in the current state of the composition. An operation is nearly invocable, if only one input parameter is missing. Listing 1.2 lists the pseudo code of this method. We traverse the ontology, add each concept to the current composition state one after another, and check for invocable operations in the modified state. Please note that there is no ranking in case the method returns multiple nearly invocable operations. This allows for an optimization in the process of discovering the nearly invocable services: We use the most specific subconcept for each concept in the ontology before we search for invocable services in the modified state. In doing so, we only have to perform this search operation for a subset of the concepts in the ontology, which improves the response time.

3.2 Check Validity

As the human modeler has full control over the modeling, it is possible that he introduces errors. It is therefore necessary to be able to check the semantic validity of the process. As opposed to syntactic validity checking structural correctness criteria like soundness [8], semantic validity bases on semantic descriptions for individual activities to define correctness of processes on a semantical level. However, when semantic descriptions for the activities of process are available, we are able define correctness criteria for processes on the semantics level. Semantic validation should be interleaved with the actual modeling of the composed service: The user should be informed about problems with the composition in an unobtrusive way. Such problems, which can be seen as unresolved issues, arise from activities in the composition which violate one or

```
   findNearlyInvocableServices ( State state)
2    operations = findInvocableServices (state);
     for each concept in the ontology do
4      if concept is not marked as visited
         sc = findMostSpecificConcepts (c);
6        for each concept s in sc
           add s to state;
8            register state with reasoner ;
             nOps = findInvocableServices (state);
10           add nOps − operations to result;
             deregister state with reasoner ;
12           remove s from state;
             mark s as visited ;
14       return list of nearly invocable operations (result);

16   Concept[] findMostSpecificConcepts (Concept c)
     if c has subconcepts
18     sc = new Concept[];
       for each subconcept s of c
20       sc += findMostSpecificConcept (s);
       return sc;
22   else return [c];
```

Listing 1.2. Compute list of nearly invocable service operations

more aspect of a set of desirable properties for well-formed workflows. According to [9], a composition is well-formed if

- one or more activities are contributing to the composition's overall end result,
- the inputs and preconditions of every activity are satisfied,
- every activity is either an end result or produces at least one output or effect that is required by another activity,
- it does not contain redundant activities.

Business Scenario. As the last step, the modeler added the nearly invocable operation *Check Create Leave Request*. The tool highlights operations for which problems are tracked. As the added operation is not invocable, but nearly invocable, one input type is missing. The tool therefore marks the operation with a red border. This can also be seen in figure 2, where two out of four activities are highlighted. By clicking on the *Check Create Leave Request* operation, the user can open a panel showing its input and output types as inferred from the pre- and postconditions. The user sees that all input types of the operation are currently available in the composition, except *TimePointPeriod*, which is also highlighted using red color in this drill-down view. The user can also get an overview of all current problems with the composition by looking at the agenda, depicted in figure 3.

The missing parameter *TimePointPeriod* represents the date or period for which the employee intends to request a leave. As our scenario has been taken from Duet, this

Fig. 3. Agenda summarizing the problems with the composition

data is provided by Microsoft Outlook after a the user selects a date from the calendar. In our example, the modeler therefore creates a human activity (modeling a task such as marking a period in the calendar) that produces a *TimePointPeriod* output. The modeler connects the human activity with the *Check Create Leave Request* operation. The coloring of the operation and the *TimePointPeriod* input type in the parameter view disappear and the issue is removed from the agenda.

Realization. Information about operations with unsatisfied inputs can be retrieved by traversing the graph of the composition state. Listing 1.3 lists the pseudo code for aggregating all available types in the composition state. The available types are compared to the preconditions of each operation in the composition.

```
   findUnsatisfiedInputs (State state, Role role)
2    for each operation in state do
       availableTypes = {};
4      availableTypes += role;
       requiredInputs = preconditions of current operation;
6      links = links connected to incoming plugs of operation;
       for each link in links do
8        recurseLink (link);
       if unsatisfiedInputs = requiredInputs − availableTypes != {}
10       store unsatisfiedInputs with current operation;

12 recurseLink (Link link)
     if link.source == start node
14     return;
     if link.source is a service operation do
16     currentOperation = link.source;
       availableTypes += currentOperation.postconditions;
18     links = links connected to incoming plugs of currentOperation;
       for each link in links do
20       recurseLink (link);
     else return;
```

Listing 1.3. Compute unsatisfied inputs in the service composition

5   Conclusion

In this paper we presented the realization of three mixed initiative features for semi-automated service composition. We validated it in an implementation of a service orchestration tool, as well as case study and a service repository from a large vendor of service oriented business software. *Filter inappropriate services* allows for selecting only invocable services and performs a ranking among them. *Check validity* allows to check for the semantic correctness of a service composition. And, finally, with *suggest partial plans* we used an approach from automated composition to fill in gaps in service compositions. Our approach is currently the only one implementing all three mixed initiative features. The scenario shows that the ability to interleave all three features is very valuable for the modeler. Also, when service compositions are to be created by users without a strong technical background, usability plays a vital role. Our tool therefore does not impose a specific planning strategy on the modeler.

In the future, we plan to further validate the usefulness of our approach with end users. The goal is to show that these three mixed initiative features significantly improve modeling quality and reduce modeling time. In our current implementation we are facing performance issues when computing the list of nearly executable services. We are currently working on a realization strategy incorporating the partitioning of the ontology and distributing the computation. Finally, the area of semantic correctness is, in contrast to the syntactic correctness of service compositions and processes, still an open field: So far, our orchestration tool only covers unsatisfied inputs. Efforts to automatically discover redundant services are currently underway.

References

1. Zeng, L., Benatallah, B., Lei, H., Ngu, A.H.H., Flaxer, D., Chang, H.: Flexible Composition of Enterprise Web Services. Electronic Markets 13 (2003)
2. Pistore, M., Barbon, F., Bertoli, P., Shaparau, D., Traverso, P.: Planning and Monitoring Web Service Composition. In: Bussler, C.J., Fensel, D. (eds.) AIMSA 2004. LNCS (LNAI), vol. 3192, pp. 106–115. Springer, Heidelberg (2004)
3. Sirin, E., Parsia, B., Wu, D., Hendler, J., Nau, D.: HTN Planning for Web Service Composition Using SHOP2. Journal of Web Semantics 1, 377–396 (2004)
4. Meyer, H., Weske, M.: Automated Service Composition using Heuristic Search. In: Dustdar, S., Fiadeiro, J.L., Sheth, A. (eds.) BPM 2006. LNCS, vol. 4102, pp. 81–96. Springer, Heidelberg (2006)
5. Schaffner, J.: Supporting the Modeling of Business Processes Using Semi-Automated Web Service Composition Techniques). Master's thesis, Hasso-Plattner-Institute for IT Systems Engineering, University of Potsdam, Potsdam, Germany (2006)
6. White, S.A.: Business Process Modeling Notation, Working Draft (1.0). Technical report, The Business Process Modeling Initiative (2003)
7. Schaffner, J., Meyer, H.: Mixed Initiative Use Cases For Semi-Automated Service Composition: A Survey. In: IW-SOSE'06. Proceedings of the International Workshop on Service Oriented Software Engineering, located at ICSE 2006, Shanghai, China, May 27–28, 2006, ACM Press, New York (2006)
8. van der Aalst, W.M.: Verification of Workflow Nets. In: Azéma, P., Balbo, G. (eds.) ICATPN 1997. LNCS, vol. 1248, pp. 407–426. Springer, Heidelberg (1997)

3.3 Suggest Partial Plans

Automated planners plan according to an algorithmic planning strategy, such as for example forward- or backward chaining of services. Human planners, in contrast, will not always behave according to this schema when modeling composed service. Users might have a clear idea about some specific activities that they want to have in the process, without a global understanding how the whole will fit together as a process. For example, they start modeling the composed service by adding some operations and chaining them together, and then continue with a non-invocable operation that is intended to be in a later stage of the composition. In such and similar cases, it is desirable for the user to let the editor generate valid service chains that connect two unrelated activities.

Business Scenario. In the last step the modeler resolved a problem with the *Check Create Leave Request* operation. If the user clicks on the operation to refresh the filtered list of available services, the tool will suggest the *Create Leave Request* operation. From the perspective of the user, this is the final operation. However, the modeler might not be familiar with the fact that a specific check operation needs to be invoked in order to create a leave request in the system. He then directly selected the *Create Leave Request* operation after the merge node depicted in figure 2. The modeler also creates the human activity producing the *TimePointPeriod* and links it to the *Create Leave Request* operation. Now, the modeler tries to create a link between the merge node of the parallel flow and *Create Leave Request*. The tool will detect that the set of postconditions up to the merge node does not satisfy the preconditions of *Create Leave Request* (the type *CheckCreateLeaveRequestResult* is missing). The tool instantly queries the semi-automated composition engine which detects that the insertion of the *Check Create Leave Request* operation would satisfy this open information requirement. The user is prompted whether or not the *Check Create Leave Request* should be inserted. The modeler approves this suggestion and the composition is complete.

Realization. The suggestion of partial plans can be mapped to an automated service composition task: given an initial state and a goal state, a composition is created that leads from the initial state to the goal state. If we only want to suggest a partial plan to connect two operations A and B, we can derive the initial state from the postconditions A and its preceding services. The goal state then consists of the unfulfilled preconditions of B. An approach from automated service composition is used to create a partial plan. For this purpose, we are using an extended version of enforced hill-climbing as presented in [4]. The principle of this algorithm will be briefly described in the following.

Enforced hill-climbing is an heuristic forward search algorithm in state space. Guided by a goal distance heuristic, it starts with the initial state and consecutively selects new services and reaches new states through the virtual invocation of selected services until the goal state is reached. Given a state all invocable services are determined. We use *findInvocableServices* mentioned above but without ranking. From these services, states are calculated using virtual invocation: Only the postconditions are applied without actually invoking the service.

For these states, goal distance estimations are calculated using an heuristic. The first state that has a lower goal distance estimation than the current state is selected as the new current state. If this state satisfies the goal state, we have found a valid composition. Otherwise, we continue until we have reached the goal state. In [4] we extended this algorithm to deal with uncertainty and to compose parallel control flows.

4 Related Work

In the following, we give a brief overview of related work in the field of semi-automated composition.

Sirin, Parsia and Hendler [10] present Web Service Composer. Their tool allows creating executable compositions of Web services that are semantically specified with OWL-S. In order to create a composed service, the user follows a backward chaining approach. He begins with selecting a Web service that has an output producing the desired result of the composition from a list of available services. Next, the user interface presents additional lists connected to each OWL input type of the service producing the end result. In contrast to the first composition step, these lists do not contain all available services: They contain only those services that generate an output satisfying the particular input type they are connected to. As a consequence, the plans constructed with the tool are not always optimal. For example, when one service operation delivers two outputs each of which satisfies a different input of a downstream service, this service operation occurs twice in the composed service.

IRS-III [11] includes a tool that supports a user-guided interactive composition approach by recommending component Web services according to the composition context. Their approach uses the Web Services Modeling Ontology (WSMO) as the language to describe the functionality of the Web services. Similar to Web Service Composer, the available services are filtered at each composition step. It is not possible to further shorten the filtered list based on nonfunctional properties. Our approach, in contrast, interprets the intended role of a service in form of a nonfunctional property when the weightings are assigned.

Kim, Spraragen and Gil introduce CAT (Composition Analysis Tool) [9]. At each composition step, CAT provides a list of suggestions about what to do next. These suggestions resolve errors and warnings, which are also displayed. The idea is that consequently applying suggestions will produce a "well-formed" workflow as a result. The authors therefore introduce a set of properties that must be satisfied by all operations in the composition in order for the process to be well-formed. The tool does not provide filtering functionality nor the ability to create partial plans.

PASSAT (Plan-Authoring System based on Sketches, Advice, and Templates) [12] is an interactive tool for constructing plans. Similar to CAT, PASSAT is not directly concerned with the creation of composed services, but its concepts can be mapped into the context of service composition. PASSAT is based on hierarchical task networks (HTN) [13]. In HTN planning, a task network is a set of tasks (or service calls) that have to be carried out as well as constraints on the ordering of these tasks. The HTN based approach imposes top-down plan refinement as the planning strategy the user must adhere to: The user can start by adding tasks to a plan and refine them by applying matching HTN templates. A template consists of a set of subtasks that replace the task being refined, as well as the postconditions of applying individual tasks and the entire template.

9. Kim, J., Spraragen, M., Gil, Y.: An Intelligent Assistant for Interactive Workflow Composition. In: IUI '04. Proceedings of the 9th international conference on Intelligent user interface, pp. 125–131. ACM Press, New York (2004)
10. Sirin, E., Parsia, B., Hendler, J.: Filtering and Selecting Semantic Web Services with Interactive Composition Techniques. IEEE Intelligent Systems 19, 42–49 (2004)
11. Hakimpour, F., Sell, D., Cabral, L., Domingue, J., Motta, E.: Semantic Web Service Composition in IRS-III: The Structured Approach. In: CEC 2005. 7th IEEE International Conference on E-Commerce Technology, München, Germany, pp. 484–487. IEEE Computer Society Press, Los Alamitos (2005)
12. Myers, K.L., et al.: PASSAT: A User-centric Planning Framework. In: Proceedings of the 3rd International NASA Workshop on Planning and Scheduling for Space, Houston, TX, AAAI Press, Stanford, California (2002)
13. Tate, A.: Generating Project Networks. In: Proceedings of the Fifth Joint Conference on Artificial Intelligence, Cambridge, MA, pp. 888–893. Morgan Kaufmann Publishers, San Francisco (1977)

Web Service Composition: An Approach Using Effect-Based Reasoning

Puwei Wang[1,3] and Zhi Jin[1,2]

[1] Institute of Computing Technology, Chinese Academy of Sciences
[2] Academy of Mathematics and System Sciences, Chinese Academy of Sciences
[3] Graduate University of Chinese Academy of Sciences
Beijing 100080, China
wangpw@ict.ac.cn, zhijin@amss.ac.cn

Abstract. This paper proposes an ontology-based approach to compose Web services using the effect-based reasoning. The environment ontology is to provide formal and sharable specifications of environment entities of Web services in a particular domain. For each environment entity, there is a corresponding hierarchical state machine for specifying its dynamic characteristics. Then, this approach proposes to use the effects of a Web service on its environment entities for specifying the Web service's capabilities and designates the effect as the traces of the state transitions the Web service can impose on its environment entities. So, the service composition can be conducted by the effect-based reasoning.

1 Introduction

Web services are self-contained and modular components which are autonomous and loosely-coupled. Web service composition happens when a request can not be satisfied by any elementary Web services. It combines some elementary Web services to create a new and composite Web service so that the composite Web service has the capabilities to satisfy the request. Capability descriptions of Web services are important for enhancing the quality of the composition. Therefore, we need an expressive external manifestation of Web services to describe service capabilities for the composition.

This paper proposes an approach for Web service composition by using effect-based reasoning on the environment entities. The distinct feature is to introduce environments as the objective reference of Web service capability. In fact, environment is a key concern in the requirements modelling and has been recognized as the semantic basis of the meaning of the requirements. In our approach, we view environment of a Web service to be composed of those controllable entities (or called "environment entities") that the Web service can impose effects on. Our motivations are listed as follows: 1) *Environment can exhibit the capabilities of Web services while Web services' behaviors are installed in the environment.* In requirement engineering domain, it has been argued that the meaning of requirements can be depicted by the optative interaction of software system with its environment as well as the causal relationships among these interactions [1].

D. Georgakopoulos et al. (Eds.): ICSOC 2006 Ws, LNCS 4652, pp. 62–73, 2007.

2) *Environment entities are inherent sharable for loosely coupled Web services.* Web services are often developed by different teams, and are described in different conceptual framework without agreement. Based on the optative interaction of Web services with its environment entities, understanding between the Web services are assured by instinct. 3) *Dynamic composition of Web services are depicted based on their stable environment.* Though Web services are autonomous and evolving in their life-cycles for continual users' demands, the environments which exhibit their capabilities are usually stable.

Example 1. An example is embedded in this paper to illustrate our ideas. Assume that there are four services, *ticket-selling service(TSA)*, *ticket-delivery service(TDS)*, *hotel service(HOS)* and *bank service(BAS)* respectively. There are three sharable environment entities for the four services, *ticket*, *hotelroom* and *creditcard*. Given a goal $\mathcal{G}_{travel}$ that needs *budget traveling service* for travelers. This goal can be represented as a set of desired effects on *ticket*, *hotelroom* and *creditcard*. Obviously, any of the four services can not satisfy $\mathcal{G}_{travel}$ by its own. What we expect to do is to obtain a composition of the four services satisfying $\mathcal{G}_{travel}$ conducted by reasoning on *ticket*, *hotelroom* and *creditcard* in terms of satisfiability of the desired effects on these environment entities.

The rest of this paper is structured as follows: Section 2 gives the definition of the environment ontology. Section 3 defines the effect on an environment entity and the effect-based Web service capability profile. Section 4 describes a Web service composition conducted by the effect-based reasoning. Finally, section 5 analyzes related works and draws a conclusion.

2   Environment Ontology

Environment entities are domain-relevant, and then the conceptualization of environment entities, i.e., the environment ontology, can constitute as sharable domain knowledge base for Web services. We extend the general ontology structure by attaching each environment entity a tree-like hierarchical state machine for specifying its domain life-cycle. The environment ontology is defined as follows.

Definition 1. $\mathcal{E}nv\mathcal{O} \overset{\text{def}}{=} \{Ent, \mathcal{X}^c, \mathcal{H}^c, \mathcal{HSM}, inter, res\}$, *in which:*

- *Ent is a finite set of environment entities,*
- $\mathcal{X}^c \subseteq Ent \times Ent$ *is an ingredient relation between the environment entities,* $\forall e_1, e_2 \in Ent, \langle e_1, e_2 \rangle \in \mathcal{X}^c$ *means that e_1 is an ingredient of e_2,*
- $\mathcal{H}^c \subseteq Ent \times Ent$ *is a taxonomic relation between the environment entities.* $\forall e_1, e_2 \in Ent, \langle e_1, e_2 \rangle \in \mathcal{H}^c$ *means that e_1 is a subconcept of e_2,*
- $\mathcal{HSM}$ *is a finite set of tree-like hierarchical state machines (called "THSM"),*
- *inter* $\subseteq \mathcal{HSM} \times \mathcal{HSM}$ *is a message exchange relation between THSMs.* $hsm_1, hsm_2 \in \mathcal{HSM}, \langle hsm_1, hsm_2 \rangle \in inter$ *means that hsm_1 and hsm_2 interact with each other by message exchange,*
- *res* $: Ent \leftrightarrow \mathcal{HSM}$ *is a bijective relation.* $\forall e \in Ent$, *there is one and only $hsm \in \mathcal{HSM}$, such that $hsm=res(e)$.It is say that hsm is the THSM of e.*

For a THSM, its states may be ordinary states or super-states (s_{super}) which can be further subdivided into another basic state machines ($\mathcal{N}_{sub}$). In our approach, each state s' in $\mathcal{N}_{sub}$ is called a *child* of super-state s_{super} (s' *child* s_{super}), and start state λ_0 in $\mathcal{N}_{sub}$ is called *default child* of s_{super}. Hierarchical skeleton is expected to assure that hierarchical state machine has flexibility and different granularity. Tree-like skeleton assures that each basic state machine has one and only one super-state. A THSM (called "domain THSM") in the environment ontology is designed for life-cycle description of an environment entity in a domain. The effects of Web services then can be modeled based on the domain THSMs.

For the four elementary services in above example, their environment is specified as a simplified Budget Traveling Environment Ontology (called "*BTO*").

Table 1. Budget Traveling Environment Ontology

Entity	Meaning
ticket	Taking travelers to their destinations. Its domain THSM is $hsm(ticket)$
hotelroom	Housing travelers. Its domain THSM is $hsm(hotelroom)$
creditcard	Providing a method of payment. Its domain THSM is $hsm(creditcard)$
merchandise	Goods in business. Its domain THSM is $hsm(merchandise)$
itinerary	Route of ticket. Its domain THSM is $hsm(itierary)$

Relation		Meaning
$\langle ticket, merchandise \rangle \in \mathcal{H}^c_{bto}$		Ticket is a merchandise, i.e., domain THSM of ticket inherits domain THSM of merchandise
$\langle itinerary, ticket \rangle \in \mathcal{X}^c_{bto}$		Itinerary is a part of ticket, i.e., domain THSM of itinerary is a part of domain THSM of ticket
$\langle hsm(ticket), hsm(creditcard) \rangle \in inter_{bto}$		Ticket can be paid by credit card
$\langle hsm(hotelroom), hsm(creditcard) \rangle \in inter_{bto}$		Hotel room can be paid by credit card

We develop an application demo for visualizing the representation of *BTO* which is encoded in XML-style. Fig.1 is a screenshot for showing the domain THSMs, $hsm(ticket)$, $hsm(hotelroom)$ and $hsm(creditcard)$, and the message exchange relation between them. They are used to represent life-cycle of environment entities *ticket*, *hotelroom* and *creditcard*. In the *ticket*'s domain THSM, *instantiated*, *available* and *sold* are three super-states, which are subdivided into three basic state machines respectively. Similarly, domain THSMs of environment entities *creditcard* and *hotelroom* are described.

Moreover, there is a message exchange relation between $hsm(ticket)$ and $hsm(creditcard)$, i.e., $\langle hsm(ticket), hsm(creditcard) \rangle \in inter$, because that output from *creditcard*'s state *valid* can trigger the state transition of *ticket* from *ordered* to *sold*, and output from *ticket*'s state *sold* can trigger state transition of *creditcard* from *non-charged* to *charged*.

Obviously, it describes that ticket can be paid by credit card. Similarly, there also is a message exchange relation between $hsm(hotelroom)$ and hsm (*creditcard*) because that hotel room also can be paid by credit card. For simplicity, message exchanges are only denoted as light-gray lines with double arrowheads in Fig.1.

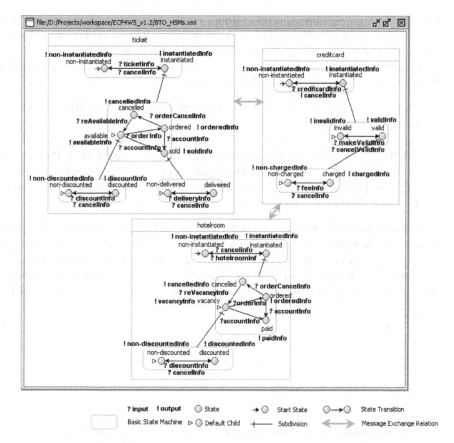

Fig. 1. Screeenshot of domain THSMs of *ticket*, *hotelroom* and *creditcard*

3   Web Service Capability Profile

With the explicit representation of the environment ontology, the capability profile of a Web service can be given. We first define the effect of Web services on
their environment entities. An effect on an environment entity is described as a
triplet which contains an initial state, a target state and a set of middle states
(these middle states will be included in the trace from the initial state to the target state) of this environment entity. Let e be an environment entity. The effect
on e can be formulated as: $effect(e) = e : \langle s_i, \mathcal{S}_m, s_t \rangle, s_i, s_t \in e.State, \mathcal{S}_m \subseteq$
$e.State$, in which s_i is an initial state, s_t is a target state and $\mathcal{S}_m$ is a set of middle
states ($e.State$ is the set of states in e's domain THSM). The traces from s_i to s_t
via $\mathcal{S}_m$ consist of: (1) state transition in a basic state machine, or (2) transition
from a state to its default child, or (3) transition from a state to its super-state.
For example, an effect that a simple ticket-selling service imposes on environment
entity *ticket* can be described as *ticket* : $\langle available, \{ordered\}, sold \rangle$. Based on

the effect, we can acquire the trace from $hsm(ticket)$ (shown in Fig.1) in BTO: $available \rightarrow ordered \rightarrow sold$. This trace actually is the specific life-cycle description while the ticket-selling service imposes the effect on $ticket$.

A capability profile of Web service is given based on effects of the Web service. It is defined as $\{Ent_{sub}, \mathcal{M}s, effs\}$, in which:

- $Ent_{sub} = \{e_1, ..., e_n\}$ is a set of environment entities that Web service can impose effects on;
- $\mathcal{M}s = \{\mathcal{M}(e_1), ..., \mathcal{M}(e_n)\}$. Each $\mathcal{M}(e_i)$ is partitioned into two subsets: $\mathcal{M}^{in}(e_i)$ and $\mathcal{M}^{out}(e_i)$ for denoting inputs and outputs that Web service needs and produces about the environment entity $e_i (i \in [1, n])$;
- $effs = \{effect(e_1), ..., effect(e_n)\}$ is a set of effects (called "effect set") that Web service imposes on $e_1, ..., e_n$.

Capability specification can be generated by adding rich semantics (i.e., state transitions) automatically to the capability profile from environment ontology.

The effect-based capability profile of $ticket$-$selling\ service(TSA)$ then can be given. The effect set of TSA is described as $\{ticket: \langle available, \{ordered, cancelled\}, sold \rangle\}$. The following is the XML-style capability profile of TSA.

```
<capability Id="ticket-selling service,TSA">
  <entity>BTO:ticket</entity>
  <input ent="ticket">orderInfo,orderCancelInfo,accountInfo,reAvailableInfo</input>
  <output ent="ticket">soldInfo</output>
  <effect ent="ticket">
    <initialState>available</initialState>
    <middleSet>ordered,cancelled<middleSet>
    <targetState>sold</targetState>
  </effect>
</capability>
```

This capability profile describes that *a service TSA which provides ticket selling service, where users can put tickets on hold without being charged, and they also have opportunity to cancel the pending tickets.* Similarly, the capability profiles of TDS, HOS and BAS also can be given using the same structure.

The environment ontology is a sharable knowledge base for Web services. By traversing domain THSM of an environment entity, traces from the initial state to the target state via a set of middle states (i.e., go through an effect $e : \langle s_i, \mathcal{S}_m, s_t \rangle$ on the environment entity e) triggered by a series of inputs can be generated. These traces constitute a THSM (called "specific THSM"). Therefore, each specific THSM is corresponding to an effect on an environment entity.

A model $\mathcal{I} = \{\mathcal{K}, inter_k\}$ then is presented, in which $\mathcal{K} = \{k_{e1}, ..., k_{en}\}$ is a set of specific THSMs corresponding to effect set $effs = \{effect(e_1), ..., effect(e_n)\}$, and $inter_k$ contains the set of message exchange relations on $\mathcal{K}$. The model $\mathcal{I}$ is called the *semantic schema* of the effect set $effs$. It is viewed to be a capability specification of Web service. This capability specification is based on a process model and will not be entangled by implementation of Web services. The algorithm for generating the semantic schema of the effect set based on environment ontology is presented in our previous works [2].

Let us look at the effect sets and their semantic schemas of the four elementary services: TSA, TDS, HOS and BAS. They are listed in Table.2.

Table 2. Elementary Effect Sets and Their Semantic Schemas

Ticket-Selling Service (TSA)
$effs_{tsa} = \{ticket:\langle available, \{ordered, cancelled\}, sold\rangle\}$
$\mathcal{I}_{tsa} = \{\{k_{ticket}^{tsa}\}, \phi\}$ Fig.2(a)
Ticket-Delivery Service (TDS)
$effs_{tds} = \{ticket:\langle sold, \phi, delivered\rangle\}$
$\mathcal{I}_{tds} = \{\{k_{ticket}^{tds}\}, \phi\}$ Fig.2(b)
Hotel Service (HOS)
$effs_{hos} = \{hotelroom: \langle vacancy, \{ordered, cancelled\}, paid\rangle\}$
$\mathcal{I}_{hos} = \{\{k_{hotelroom}^{hos}\}, \phi\}$ Fig.2(c)
Bank Service (BAS)
$effs_{bas} = \{creditcard:\langle valid, \phi, chareged\rangle\}$
$\mathcal{I}_{bas} = \{\{k_{creditcard}^{bas}\}, \phi\}$ Fig.2(d)

Fig.2 is the screenshot showing the semantic schemas $\mathcal{I}_{tsa}, \mathcal{I}_{tds}, \mathcal{I}_{hos}, \mathcal{I}_{bas}$ (k_{ticket}^{tsa} is denoted by tsa_ticket, k_{ticket}^{tds} is denoted by tds_ticket, $k_{hotelroom}^{hos}$ is denoted by hos_hotelroom, and $k_{creditcard}^{bas}$ is denoted by bas_creditcard), which are viewed as the capability specifications of the four elementary services.

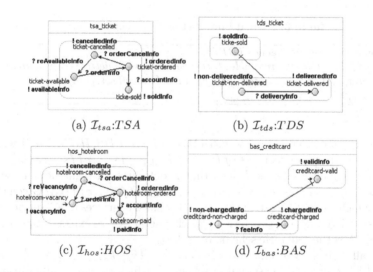

(a) $\mathcal{I}_{tsa}$:TSA (b) $\mathcal{I}_{tds}$:TDS

(c) $\mathcal{I}_{hos}$:HOS (d) $\mathcal{I}_{bas}$:BAS

Fig. 2. Screenshot of semantic schemas of the four elementary services

4   Service Composition by Effect-Based Reasoning

Web service composition is to generate a composite service that consists of a set of elementary services to satisfy a goal. In our approach, Web service composition is conducted by effect-based reasoning.

A goal $\mathcal{G}_{travel}$, which describes a desired service for providing *budget traveling agency (BTA)*, is given as a capability profile in XML style.

```
<goal Id="Budget Traveling Agency,BTA">
  <entity>BTO:ticket,BTO:hotelroom,BTO:creditcard</entity>
  <input ent="ticket">orderInfo,orderCancelInfo,deliveryInfo,reAvailableInfo</input>
  <input ent="hotelroom">orderInfo,orderCancelInfo,reVacancyInfo</input>
  <output ent="ticket">deliveredInfo</output>
  <output ent="hotelroom">paidInfo</output>
  <ourput ent="creditcard">chargedInfo</output>
  <effect ent="ticket">
    <initialState>available</initialState>
    <middleSet>ordered,cancelled<middleSet>
    <targetState>delivered</targetState>
  </effect>
  <effect ent="hotelroom">
    <initialState>vacancy</initialState>
    <middleSet>ordered,cancelled<middleSet>
    <targetState>paid</targetState>
  </effect>
  <effect ent="creditcard">
    <initialState>valid</initialState>
    <targetState>charged</targetState>
  </effect>
</goal>
```

This goal profile describes that *"A service BTA which provides ticket selling and hotel service, where user can order ticket and hotel room, and if there is an emergency,user can cancel the pending ticket or hotel room."* In this goal profile, the effect set is described in Table.3.

Table 3. Desired Effect Set and Its Semantic Schema

Budget Traveling Agency (BTA)

$effs_{bta} = \{ticket: \langle available, \{ordered, cancelled\}, delivered\rangle, creditcard:$
$\langle valid, \phi, chareged\rangle, hotelroom: \langle vacancy, \{cancelled\}, paid\rangle\}$
$\mathcal{I}_{bta} = \{\{k_{ticket}^{bta}, k_{creditcard}^{bta}, k_{hotelroom}^{bta}\}, inter_{bta}\}$

Given the four elementary services $\mathcal{W} = \{TSA, TDS, HOS, BAS\}$ which are described by the four effect sets $effs_{tsa}, effs_{tds}, effs_{hos}, effs_{bas}$, a *composition* of $\mathcal{W}$ is a semantic schema $\mathcal{I}$ such that $\mathcal{I}$ delegates all transitions in semantic schemas $\mathcal{I}_{tsa}, \mathcal{I}_{tds}, \mathcal{I}_{hos}, \mathcal{I}_{bas}$ of $effs_{tsa}, effs_{tds}, effs_{hos}, effs_{bas}$. Given the goal $\mathcal{G}_{travel}$ which can not be satisfied by any elementary services in $\mathcal{W}$, service composition to satisfy the goal $\mathcal{G}_{travel}$ is to check whether there exists composition $\mathcal{I}_{bta}$ of $\mathcal{W}$ which is the semantic schema of $effs_{bta}$.

Formally, given two semantic schemas $\mathcal{I}_1 = \{\{k_{e1}^1, k_{e2}^1\}, \{\langle k_{e1}^1, k_{e2}^1\rangle\}\}$ and $\mathcal{I}_2 = \{\{k_{e1}^2, k_{e2}^2\}, \{\langle k_{e1}^2, k_{e2}^2\rangle\}\}$, semantic schema $\mathcal{I}$ which delegates all transitions in $\mathcal{I}_1$ and $\mathcal{I}_1$ is constructed as $\mathcal{I} = \{\{k_{e1}, k_{e2}\}, \{\langle k_{e1}, k_{e2}\rangle\}\}$, where $k_{e1} = k_{e1}^1 \diamond k_{e1}^2$ and $k_{e2} = k_{e2}^1 \diamond k_{e2}^2$ (k_e^i denotes a specific THSM of an environment entity e and $\diamond$ is a composition operator). Concretely, the task to obtain desired composition $\mathcal{I}$ of $\mathcal{I}_1, \mathcal{I}_2$ can be decomposed to two sub-tasks.

First, we compose specific THSMs in $\mathcal{I}_i (i = 1, 2)$ which are of same environment entity. For example, in the two semantic schemas $\mathcal{I}_{tsa} = \{\{k_{ticket}^{tsa}\}, \phi\}$ (Fig.2(a)), $\mathcal{I}_{tds} = \{\{k_{ticket}^{tds}\}, \phi\}$(Fig.2(b)), k_{ticket}^{tsa} and k_{ticket}^{tds} are of same environment entity *ticket*, we need to check whether there exists target THSM k_{ticket}^{bta}(seeing Table.3) by composing k_{ticket}^{tsa} and k_{ticket}^{tds}.

Second, message exchange relations between these composed specific THSMs are constructed according to sharable domain knowledge, i.e., environment ontology. For example, we suppose that $k_{creditcard}^{bta}$(seeing Table.3) is the composition of $k_{creditcard}^{bas}$ and ϕ (There is not another specific THSM of *creditcard* except for $k_{creditcard}^{bas}$ in elementary semantic schemas). It is described in BTO that a state *valid* in $k_{creditcard}^{bta}$ can trigger a state transition from *ordered* to *sold* in k_{ticket}^{bta}. Therefore, there is a message exchange relation between k_{ticket}^{bta} and $k_{creditcard}^{bta}$.

Back to the example, we present here how to compose the semantic schemas, $\mathcal{I}_{tsa}, \mathcal{I}_{tds}, \mathcal{I}_{hos}$, and $\mathcal{I}_{bas}$, of four elementary services (Ticket-Selling Service(TSA), Ticket-Delivering Service(TDS), Hotel Service (HOS) and Bank Service(BAS), seeing Fig.2) to obtain the desired semantic schema $\mathcal{I}_{bta}$.

First, we present how to check whether there exists target THSM k_{ticket}^{bta} by composing elementary THSMs k_{ticket}^{tsa} and k_{ticket}^{tds}. In [3], D.Berardi has developed a technique for composition of finite state machines in terms of satisfiability of a formula of Deterministic Propositional Dynamic Logic (DPDL). We formulate the problem on *composition existency* of the target THSM k_{ticket}^{bta} based on the Berardi's formula of DPDL: *The DPDL formula Φ_{travel}, built as a conjunction of the following formulas, is satisfiable if and only if there exists the target THSM k_{ticket}^{bta} by composing elementary THSMs k_{ticket}^{tsa} and k_{ticket}^{tds}.*

Concretely, there is a set of atomic propositions $\mathcal{P}_{travel}$ in Φ_{travel}. We have (*i*) one proposition s_j for each state s_j of k_{ticket}^j, $j \in \{bta, tsa, tds\}$, which is true if k_{ticket}^j is in state s_j; (*ii*) propositions $moved_j$, $j \in \{bta, tsa, tds\}$, denoting whether k_{ticket}^j performed a state transition. And the transition from a state to its default child state or a state to its super-state are viewed to be a state transition. Formally, s_d' *child* $s \Leftrightarrow s' = \delta(s, \tau)$, where τ denotes a special input that triggers the transition from state s to its default child s_d'. Moreover, s' *child* $s \Leftrightarrow s = \delta(s', \varsigma)$, where ς denotes another special input that triggers the transition from child state s' to its super-state s. And, α denotes an input $\alpha \in \{\tau, \varsigma\} \cup \Sigma^{in} \cup \Sigma_1^{in} \cup ... \cup \Sigma_n^{in}$, where Σ_i^{in} denotes inputs of each elementary THSM. The master modality $[u]$, which states universal assertions, denotes the closure of inputs. The modality $\langle u \rangle$ states existence assertions. Then, we have the following formulas.

(*i*) *Formulas capturing the target THSM k_{ticket}^{bta}.*

$$[u](ticket\text{-}available_{bta} \rightarrow \neg ticket\text{-}ordered_{bta})$$

This kind of formulas states that k_{ticket}^{bta} can never be simultaneously in the two states $ticket\text{-}available_{bta}$ and $ticket\text{-}ordered_{bta}$.

$$[u](ticket\text{-}available_{bta} \rightarrow \langle orderInfo \rangle true \wedge [orderInfo]ticket\text{-}ordered_{bta})$$
$$[u](ticket\text{-}sold_{bta} \rightarrow \langle \tau \rangle true \wedge [\tau]ticket\text{-}non\text{-}delivered_{bta})$$
$$[u](ticket\text{-}non_{bta}\text{-}delivered \rightarrow \langle \varsigma \rangle true \wedge [\varsigma]ticket\text{-}sold_{bta})$$

This kind of formulas encodes the state transitions that k_{ticket}^{bta} can perform. The first formula asserts that if k_{ticket}^{bta} is in state $ticket\text{-}available_{bta}$ and receives the input $orderInfo$, it necessarily moves to state $ticket\text{-}ordered_{bta}$. The second formula asserts that if k_{ticket}^{bta} is in state $ticket\text{-}sold_{bta}$ and receives the special input

τ, it necessarily moves to its default child $ticket\text{-}non\text{-}delivered_{bta}$. It encodes a transition from state $ticket\text{-}sold_{bta}$ to its default child $ticket\text{-}non\text{-}delivered_{bta}$. Similarly, the third one encodes a transition from state $ticket\text{-}non\text{-}delivered_{bta}$ to its super-state $ticket\text{-}sold_{bta}$.

$$[u](ticket\text{-}available_{bta} \rightarrow [cancelInfo]false)$$
$$[u](ticket\text{-}ordered_{bta} \rightarrow [\tau]false)$$
$$[u](ticket\text{-}ordered_{bta} \rightarrow [\varsigma]false)$$

This kind of formulas encodes the state transitions that are not defined on k_{ticket}^{bta}. The first formula asserts that k_{ticket}^{bta} never move when it is in state $ticket\text{-}available_{bta}$ and receives the input $cancelInfo$. The second formula asserts that $ticket\text{-}ordered_{bta}$ has no children. The third formula asserts that $ticket\text{-}ordered_{bta}$ has no super-state.

(ii) *Formulas capturing elementary THSMs (e.g., k_{ticket}^{tsa}).*

$$[u](ticket\text{-}available_{tsa} \rightarrow \neg ticket\text{-}ordered_{tsa})$$

This kind of formulas asserts that k_{ticket}^{tsa} can never be simultaneously in the two states $ticket\text{-}available_{tsa}$ and $ticket\text{-}ordered_{tsa}$, which has an analogous meaning as that relative to k_{ticket}^{bta}.

$$[u](ticket\text{-}available_{tsa} \rightarrow [orderInfo](moved_{tsa} \wedge ticket\text{-}ordered_{tsa} \vee$$
$$\neg moved_{tsa} \wedge ticket\text{-}available_{tsa}))$$

This kind of formulas asserts that in the composition, either it is k_{ticket}^{tsa} that performs the state transition and therefore it moves to state $ticket\text{-}ordered_{tsa}$, or the state transition is performed by another elementary THSM, hence, k_{ticket}^{tsa} did not move and remained in the current state $ticket\text{-}available_{tsa}$.

$$[u](ticket\text{-}available_{tsa} \rightarrow [deliveryInfo]\neg moved_{tsa})$$

This kind of formulas encodes the situation when a state transition is not defined. The formula asserts that if the THSM k_{ticket}^{tsa} is in state $ticket\text{-}availabel_{tsa}$ and it receives an input $deliveryInfo$, it dose not move.

(iii) *The following formulas must hold for the overall composition.*

$$ticket\text{-}available_{bta} \wedge ticket\text{-}available_{tsa} \wedge ticket\text{-}sold_{tds}$$

It asserts that THSMs k_{ticket}^{bta}, k_{ticket}^{tsa} and k_{ticket}^{tds} start from their start states.

$$[u](\langle orderInfo \rangle true \rightarrow [orderInfo](moved_{tsa} \vee moved_{tds}))$$

This kind of formulas express that at each step at an elementary THSM moves. The formula asserts that if input $orderInfo$ is received, then necessarily a state transition ($moved_{tsa}$ or $moved_{tds}$) is executed by at least an elementary THSM.

Based on standard Tableau Algorithm [3], we construct the target THSM k_{ticket}^{bta} by composing k_{ticket}^{tsa} and k_{ticket}^{tds} when validating the satisfiability of formula Φ_{travel}. Because that there is only and only one $k_{creditcard}^{bas}$ which is a specific THSM of $creditcard$ in the four elementary semantic schemas, $k_{creditcard}^{bta}$ just is $k_{creditcard}^{bas}$. Similarly, $k_{hotelroom}^{bta}$ also just is $k_{hotelroom}^{hos}$.

$$creditcard\text{-}valid_{bta} \uparrow \langle ticket\text{-}ordered_{bta}, \text{accountInfo}, ticket\text{-}sold_{bta} \rangle$$
$$ticket\text{-}sold_{bta} \uparrow \langle creditcard\text{-}non\text{-}charged_{bta}, \text{feeInfo}, creditcard\text{-}chareged_{bta} \rangle$$

Second, above two message exchanges are described in *BTO* about environment entities *ticket* and *creditcard*. Therefore, $\langle k_{ticket}^{bta}, k_{creditcard}^{bta} \rangle \in inter_{bta}$. Similarly, we also can get $\langle k_{hotelroom}^{bta}, k_{creditcard}^{bta} \rangle \in inter_{bta}$

Finally, target Web service (*BTA*, its capability specification is $\mathcal{I}_{bta}$) that satisfies goal $\mathcal{G}_{travel}$ is constructed by composing the semantic schemas of effect sets of elementary services, i.e., $TSA(\mathcal{I}_{tsa})$, $TDS(\mathcal{I}_{tds})$, $HOS(\mathcal{I}_{hos})$ and $BAS(\mathcal{I}_{bas})$. The result $\mathcal{I}_{bta}$ by composing the four elementary services is shown in Fig.3.

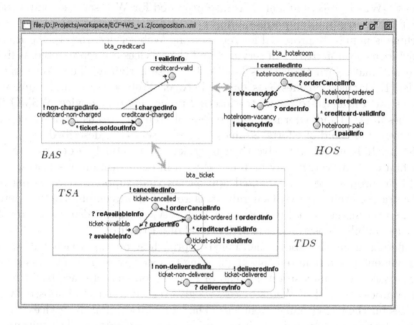

Fig. 3. Composition that satisfies goal $\mathcal{G}_{travel}$ of TSA, TDS, HOS, BAS

Concretely, TSA changes environment entity *ticket* from state *available* to state *sold* via a two middle states {*ordered, cancelled*}. At the same time, BAS changes environment entity *creditcard* from state *valid* to state *charged*. The two processes are synchronous by using two message exchanges. output of *creditcard*'s state *valid* triggers state transition of *ticket* from *ordered* to *sold*, and output of *ticket*'s state *sold* triggers state transition of *creditcard* from *non-charged* to *charged*, i.e., ticket is paid by credit card. Sequentially, TDS changes environment entity *ticket* from state *sold* to state *delivered*. In the same way, HOS changes environment entity *hotelroom* from state *vacancy* to state *paid* by using message exchanges with BAS. The goal $\mathcal{G}_{travel}$ can be satisfied.

5   Related Work and Conclusion

There are some available approaches to Web service composition. For the service composition, service description is an important issue. [4] propose an approach to the automated composition of Web services based on a translation of OWL-S service description [5] to situation calculus. Moreover, [6] has proposed a framework which uses a Hierarchical Task Network planner called SHOP2 to compose Web services. SHOP2 provides algorithms for translating an OWL-S service description to a SHOP2 domain. This kind of efforts assumes that Web service is described as interface-based model. However, it is not enough to describe service capabilities.

The OWL-S process model [7] is also proposed for Web service composition. Other representative composition efforts [8,9,10] use Petri net. Moreover, state machine is popularly proposed for representing Web service. In [11], the *Roman* model focuses on *activities* of services, and the services are represented as finite state automata with transitions labeled by these activities. The Conversation model [12] focuses on messages passed between Web services, and again uses finite state automata to model the internal processing of a service. WSMO [13] specifies internal and external choreography of Web services using abstract state machines. This kind of efforts assumes that Web service is described as its local behavior. It is more expressive than interface-based model to describe service capabilities. However, it may be too tied with implementation of services.

[14,15] propose context-oriented approaches that support coordinating and collaborating Web services. Generally, this kind of efforts emphasize the context information in the actual execution of Web services. They also do not involve service capability description at higher-level of abstraction.

Different from the above mentioned approaches, our approach follows the environment-based requirements engineering to specify requirement and elementary services for composition. Instead of focusing on the interface-based model or the process model of Web services, we give regard to effects imposed by the services on their environment entities. The capabilities of Web services are expressed by the traces of optative interactions of the services with the environment entities. Thus, environment entities play the role of collaborating Web services. The main contributions of this paper include that:

- The structured effects of the sharable environment entities, which are modeled by state machines, make the Web service specifications expressive and understandable with each other;
- The effect based capability profile makes the Web service capability specification more meticulous without exposing the Web service's realization details;
- We present that the problem of Web service composition is characterized to be a combination of effects of elementary services on their environment.

In our future work, a logic formalism will be given to express the constraints on Web services. We also will improve the Description Logic-based system for implementing more effective service composition. Moreover, the environment ontology and capability, goal profiles will be related to current popular semantic description language of Web services, such as OWL-S. We also will focus on how to create and verify the capability and goal profiles.

Acknowledgment

Supported by the National Natural Science Fund for Distinguished Young Scholars of China under Grant No.60625204, the Key Project of National Natural Science Foundation of China under Grant No.60496324, the National 863 High-tech Project of China under Grant No.2006AA01Z155, the National 973 Fundamental Research and Development Program of China under Grant No.2002CB312004, the Knowledge Innovation Program of Chinese Academy of Sciences and MADIS.

References

1. Jin, Z.: Revisiting the Meaning of Requirements. Journal of Computer Science and Technology 22(1), 32–40 (2006)
2. Wang, P., Jin, Z., Liu, L.: An Approach for Specifying Capability of Web Services based on Environment Ontology. In: ICWS 2006, pp. 365–372 (2006)
3. Berardi, D., Calvanese, D., Giacomo, G.D., et al.: Automatic Composition of E-services That Export Their Behavior. In: Orlowska, M.E., Weerawarana, S., Papazoglou, M.M.P., Yang, J. (eds.) ICSOC 2003. LNCS, vol. 2910, Springer, Heidelberg (2003)
4. McIlraith, S., Son, T.C.: Adapting Golog for Composition of Semantic Web Services. In: KR 2002, pp. 482–496 (2002)
5. The OWL Services Coalition: OWL-S: Semantic Markup for Web Services (2004), http://www.daml.org/services/owl-s/1.1/overview/
6. Sirin, E., Parsia, B., Wu, D., Hendler, J., Nau, D.: HTN planning for Web Service composition using SHOP2. Journal of Web Semantics (2004)
7. Pistore, M., et al.: Process-Level Composition of Executable Web Services: On-the-fly Versus Once-for-all Composition. In: Gómez-Pérez, A., Euzenat, J. (eds.) ESWC 2005. LNCS, vol. 3532, pp. 62–77. Springer, Heidelberg (2005)
8. Narayanan, S., McIlraith, S.: Simulation, Verification and Automated Composition of Web Services. In: WWW 2002
9. Hamadi, R., Benatallah, B.: A Petri Net-based Model for Web Service Composition. In: ADC 2003, pp. 191–200 (2003)
10. Yu Tang, et al.: SRN: An Extended Petri-Net-Based Workflow Model for Web Service Composition. In: ICWS 2004
11. Berardi, D., Calvanese, D., Giacomo, G.D., et al.: Automatic Composition of Transition based Semantic Web Services with Messaging. In: VLDB 2005
12. Bultan, T., Fu, X., Hull, R., Su, J.: Conversation Specification: A New Approach to Design and Analysis of E-Service Composition. In: WWW 2003, pp. 403–410 (2003)
13. Fensel, D., et al.: Ontology-based Choreography of WSMO Services. In: WSMO Final Draft, http://www.wsmo.org/TR/d14/v0.4/
14. Maamar, Z., Mostefaoui, S.K., Yahyaoui, H.: Toward an Agent-Based and Context-Oriented Approach for Web Services Composition. In: IEEE Transactions on Knowledge and Data Engineering, May 2005, vol. 17(5), pp. 686–697 (2005)
15. Little, M., et al.: Web Services Context Specification (WS-Context) (April 2007), http://docs.oasis-open.org/ws-caf/ws-context/v1.0/wsctx.html

Analysis of Composite Web Services Using Logging Facilities

Mohsen Rouached and Claude Godart

LORIA-INRIA-UMR 7503
BP 239, F-54506 Vandœuvre-les-Nancy Cedex, France
{mohsen.rouached,claude.godart}@loria.fr

Abstract. In order to fully explore Web service business opportunities while ensuring a correct and reliable modelling and execution, analyzing and tracking Web services interactions will enable them to be well understood and controlled.

This paper advocates a novel technique to log composite Web services and a formal approach, based on an algebraic specification of the discrete event calculus language $\mathcal{DEC}$, to check behavioural properties of composite Web services regarding their execution log. An automated induction-based theorem prover SPIKE is used as verification back-end.

1 Introduction

Creating new services by combining a number of existing ones is becoming an attractive way of developing value added Web services. This pattern is not new but it does pose some new challenges which have yet to be addressed by current technologies and tools for Web service composition.

In order to satisfy current users and to attract new customers, services providers need to pay special attention to the quality of their services. In particular, they need to trace executions of these services in order to ensure explainability in case of failure or auditing, as well as to support decision-making aimed at improving the structure and dynamics of the services. These traces of ongoing and past executions of services provide also the information required to detect services whose executions tend to fail, and to conduct routine or ad-hoc checks involving the executions of a service.

In the research related to Web services, several initiatives have been conducted with the intention to provide logging facilities. Despite all these efforts, the Web service logging activity is a highly complex task. The complexity, in general, comes from the following sources. First, the number of services available over the Web increases dramatically during the recent years, and one can expect to have a huge Web service repository to be searched. Second, Web services can be created and updated on the fly, thus the composition system needs to detect the updating at runtime and the decision should be made based on the up to date information.

To a service composer, it is desirable to be able to verify that the composition is well formed: for example that it does not contain any deadlocks or livelocks which would cause the composition to not terminate under certain conditions; and that the composition uses each Web service *correctly*. It is possible to verify the former using formal

D. Georgakopoulos et al. (Eds.): ICSOC 2006 Ws, LNCS 4652, pp. 74–85, 2007.

notations and model checkers but for the latter it is necessary to precise what is meant by *correctly*. One aspect of using a Web service correctly is invoking the operations in the order in which the provider intended. However, the WSDL description of a Web service does not specify any ordering information for the operations which are exposed by the service. To allow a service composer to verify this aspect of correctness of the composition, we focus in this paper on defining ordering information about services' behaviours regarding the execution log. Indeed, we consider behavioural properties where ordering and timing are relevant and we check whether certain properties hold or not assuming that the information system at hand left a "footprint" in some event log.

The remainder of the paper is structured as follows. Section 2 discusses existing Logging facilities for Web services and introduces our technique to collect composite Web services executions. Section 3 presents an algebraic specification of the $\mathcal{DEC}$ language. An illustrative example is used to illustrate our ideas. In Section 4, an overview of SPIKE is given. The encoding of $\mathcal{DEC}$ in SPIKE is explained in Section 5. Using this encoding, behavioural properties are checked in Section 6. The related work is discussed in section 7. Finally, Section 8 concludes the paper.

2   Web Service Logging

In this section we examine and formalize the logging possibilities in service-oriented architectures.Then, we introduce our technique to log Web services executions and more specifically the composite ones. The levels of logging vary in the richness of the information that is logged and in the additional development effort that is needed when implementing the respective features.

2.1   Web Service Collecting Solutions and Web Log Structure

The first step in the Web service analysis process consists of gathering the relevant Web data, which will be analyzed to provide useful information about the Web Service behaviour. We discuss how these log records could be obtained by using existing tools or specifying additional solutions. Then, we show that the analysis process is tightly related to what of information provided in Web service log and depend strongly on its richness.

Existing logging solutions provide a set of tools to capture web services logs. These solutions remain quite "poor" to analyze advanced web service behaviours. That is why *advanced logging solutions* should propose a set of developed techniques that allows us to record the needed information to analyze more advanced behaviour. This additional information is needed in order to be able to distinguish between Web services composition instances.

2.2   Existing Logging Solutions

There are two main sources of data for Web log collecting, corresponding to the interacting two software systems: data on the Web server side and data on the client side (see Figure 1). The existing techniques are commonly achieved by enabling the respective

Web server's logging facilities. There already exist many investigations and proposals on Web server log and associated analysis techniques. Actually, papers on Web Usage Mining WUM [10] describe the most weel-known means of web log collection. Basically, server logs are either stored in the *Common Log Format* [1] or the more recent *Combined Log Format* [2]. They consist primarily of various types of logs generated by the Web server. Most of the Web servers support as a default option the *Common Log Format*, which is a fairly basic form of Web server logging. The log entry recorded in Apache Tomcat when a request is sent to a Web service *ExampleService* may look as follows:

```
127.0.0.1 - - [15/Mar/2005:19:50:13 +0100] "POST /axis/
services/ExampleService HTTP/1.0" 200 819 "-" "Axis/1.1"
```

The log entry contains the requestor's IP address, a timestamp, the request line, the HTTP code returned by the server, i.e., 200 for OK, the size of the returned resource, and the User-Agent, i.e., Axis/1.1. The empty element, i.e. "-", indicates that no referer-information is available. Such log records allow for tracking of the service consumer, determining which service is called how often (but not which operation of the service), or analyzing service failure rates.

Level	Logged information	Logging facility
(1) Standard HTTP-server logging	consumer'IP,invoked WS,timestamp,HTTP'status code	Web server
(2) Logging of complete HTTP requests and responses	(1)+ SOAP request and response,timestamps	HTTP listener and logger
(3) Logging at Web service container level	invoked WS and operation,SOAP request and response,timestamps	WS container, SOAP handlers
(4) Logging client activity	(3)+ consumer-side activity	WS container,SOAP handlers
(5) Providing for process information	(4)+ workflow information	(4)+ Web services

Fig. 1. Summary of logging features

However, the emerging paradigm of Web services requires richer information in order to fully capture business interactions and customer electronic behaviour in this new Web environment. Since the Web server log is derived from requests resulting from users accessing pages, it is not tailored to capture service composition or orchestration. That is why, we propose in the following a set of advanced logging techniques that allows to record the additional information to analyze more advanced behaviour.

2.3 Advanced Logging Solutions

Identifying Web Service Composition Instance: Successful analysis for advanced architectures in Web services models requires composition (choreography/orchestration) information in the log record. Such information is not available in conventional Web server logs. Therefore, the advanced logging solutions must provide for both a choreography or orchestration identifier and a case identifier in each interaction that is logged.

---

[1] http://httpd.apache.org/docs/logs.html

[2] http://www.w3.org/TR/WD-logfile.html

A known method for debugging, is to insert logging statements into the source code of each service in order to call another service or component, responsible for logging. However, this solution has a main disadvantage: we do not have ownership over third parties code and we cannot guarantee they are willing to change it on someone else behalf. Furthermore, modifying existing applications may be time consuming and error prone.

Since all interactions between Web services happen through the exchange of SOAP message (over HTTP), an other alternative is to use SOAP headers that provides additional information on the message's content concerning **choreography**. Basically, we modify SOAP headers to include and gather the additional needed information capturing **choreography** details. Those data are stored in the special <WSHeaders>. This tag encapsulates headers attributes like: choreographyprotocol, choreographyname, choreographycase and any other tag inserted by the service to record optional information; for example, the <soapenv:choreographyprotocol> tag, may be used to register that the service was called by *WS-CDL* choreography protocol. The SOAP message header may look as shown in Figure 2. Then, we use SOAP intermediaries [2] which are an application located between a client and a service provider side. These intermediaries are capable of both receiving and forwarding SOAP messages. They are located on Web services provider side and they intercept SOAP request messages from either a Web service sender or captures SOAP response messages from either a Web service provider. On Web service client-side, this remote agent can be implemented to intercept those messages and extract the needed information. The implementation of client-side data collection methods requires user cooperation, either in enabling the functionality of the remote agent, or to voluntarily use and process the modified SOAP headers but without changing the Web service implementation itself (the disadvantage of the previous solution).

Concerning **orchestration** log collecting, since the most Web services orchestration are using a WSBPEL engine, which coordinates the various orchestration's web services, interprets and executes the grammar describing the control logic, we can extend this engine with a sniffer that captures orchestration information, i.e., the orchestration-ID and its instance-ID. This solution provides is centralized, but less constrained than the previous one which collects choreography information.

Using these advanced logging facilities, we aim at taking into account Web services' neighbors in the analysis process. The term neighbors refers to other Web services that the examined Web service interacts with. The concerned levels deal with analyzing Web service choreography interface (abstract process) through which it communicates with others web services to accomplish a choreography, or discovering the set of interactions exchanged within the context of a given choreography or composition.

Collecting Web Service Composition Instance: The focus in this section is on collecting and analysing **single** web service composition instance. The issue of identifying several instances has been discussed in the previous section. The exact structure of the web logs or the event collector depends on the web service execution engine that is used. In our experiments, where we have used the engine bpws4j [3] uses log4j[4] to

---

[3] http://alphaworks.ibm.com/tech/bpws4j
[4] http://logging.apache.org/log4j

$$< soapenv : Header >$$
$$< soapenv : choreographyprotocol$$
$$soapenv : mustUnderstand = "0"$$
$$xsi : type = "xsd : string" > WS - CDL$$
$$< /soapenv : choreographyprotocol >$$
$$< soapenv : choreographyname$$
$$soapenv : mustUnderstand = "0"$$
$$xsi : type = "xsd : string" > OTA$$
$$< /soapenv : choreographyname >$$
$$< soapenv : choreographycase$$
$$soapenv : mustUnderstand = "0"$$
$$xsi : type = "xsd : int" > 123$$
$$< /soapenv : choreographycase >$$
$$< /soapenv : Header >$$

Fig. 2. The SOAP message header

generate logging events. Log4j is an OpenSource logging API developed under the Jakarta Apache project. It provides a robust, reliable, fully configurable, easily extendible, and easy to implement framework for logging Java applications for debugging and monitoring purposes. The event collector (which is implemented as a remote log4j server) sets some log4j properties of the bpws4j engine to specify level of event reporting (INFO, DEBUG etc.), and the destination details of the logged events. At runtime bpws4j generates events according to the log4j properties set by the event collector. More details about the implementation can not be presented here due to lack of space but can be found in [11].

3   Analyzing Web Services'Behaviours

In this section, we focus on the process of analyzing Web services'behaviours regarding their execution logs. Indeed, given an event log, we want to verify certain behavioural properties, to provide knowledge about the context of and the reasons for discrepancies between services 'behaviours and related instances.

3.1   Illustrative Example

As an illustrative example, we consider a scenario of a device purchase order shown in Figure 3. This scenario models a 3-party composition, in which a supplier coordinates with its warehouse in order to sell and ship electronic devices. The interaction starts when a *Customer* communicates a purchase order to the *Supplier*. *Supplier* reacts to this request asking the *Warehouse* about the availability of the ordered item. Once received the response, *Supplier* decides to cancel or confirm the order, basing this choice upon Item's availability and *Customer*'s country. In the former case, the execution terminates, whereas in the latter one a concurrent phase is performed: *Customer* sends an order payment, while *Warehouse* handles the item's shipment. When both the payment and the shipment confirmation are received by *Supplier*, it delivers a final receipt to the

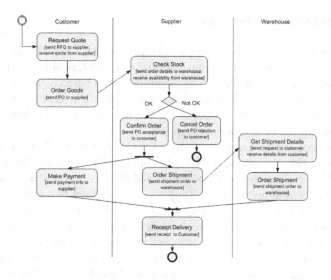

Fig. 3. Device purchase order

Customer. The specification of this scenario is given as follows. The events are represented in the form $msgType(sender, receiver, content_1, ..., content_n)$, where the $msgType$, $sender$, $receiver$ and $content_i$ retain their intuitive meaning.

During the rest of the paper, we focus on a simple execution instance of the previously described example. In this instance, inspired by Disney characters, the criminal *bigTime* (BT) beagle wants to buy a device from the online shop *devOnline* (DO), whose warehouse is *devWare* (DW). Figure 4 contains the log of the scenario from the viewpoint of *devOnline*; note that messages are expressed in an high level way, abstracting from the SOAP exchange format using the technique introduced in Section 2.3. In the

message	sender	receiver	content	t_s	t_e
1.purchase_order	BT	DO	[dev]	1	2
2.isAvailable	DO	DW	[dev]	3	9
3.inform	DW	DO	[dev, 2]	10	11
4.accept_order	DO	BT	[dev]	12	13
5.shipment_order	DO	DW	[dev]	14	15
6.confirm_shipment	DW	DO	[dev]	16	18
7.payment	BT	DO	[dev]	19	20
8.delivery	DO	BT	[dev, r]	21	22

Fig. 4. A fragment of SOAP messages exchanged in the device purchase order

device purchase scenario, we can distinguish several behavioural properties that should be respected. However, due to lack of space, we just mention the following ones. (BP1) specifies that, when *Customer* sends to *Supplier* the purchase order, including the requested *Item* and his/her *Country*, *Supplier* should request Item's availability to *Warehouse*. (BP2) indicates that *Warehouse* should respond within 6 minutes to *Supplier*'s request giving the corresponding quantity Qty. The deadline is a constraint over the variable $Tqty$, that represents the time which the response is sent to.

3.2   Discrete Event Calculus: $\mathcal{DEC}$

Given the fact that we consider behavioural properties where ordering and timing are relevant and we adopt an event driven reasoning, the Event Calculus ($\mathcal{EC}$) [8] seems to be a solid basis to start from. $\mathcal{EC}$ is a temporal formalism based on a first order logic, that can be used to specify the *events* that appear within a system and the effect (or the *fluents*) of these events. It includes an explicit *time structure* that dates the system changes caused by the occurrence of the events.

For our purpose, we have used the discrete Event Calculus ($\mathcal{DEC}$) that is enough expressive to cope with the runtime analysis of composite Web services. $\mathcal{DEC}$ includes the predicates $Happens, Initiates, Terminates$ and $HoldsAt$, as well as some auxiliary predicates defined in terms of these. $Happens(a, t)$ indicates that event (or action) a actually occurs at time-point t. $Initiates(a, f, t)$ (resp. $Terminates(a, f, t)$) means that if event a were to occur at t it would cause fluent f to be *true* (resp. *false*) immediately afterwards. $HoldsAt(f, t)$ indicates that fluent f is true at t. The auxiliary predicate $Clipped(t1, f, t2)$ expresses whether a fluent f was terminated during a time interval $[t1, t2]$. The following four axioms capture the behaviour of fluents once initiated or terminated by an event:

1. $Happens(a, t_1) \wedge (t_1 < t_2) \wedge Terminates(a, f, t_2) \rightarrow Clipped(t_1, f, t_2)$
2. $Happens(a, t_1) \wedge (t_1 < t_2) \wedge Initiates(a, f, t_2) \rightarrow \neg Clipped(t_1, f, t_2)$
3. $Happens(a, t_1) \wedge (t_1 < t_2) \wedge \neg Clipped(t_1, f, t_2) \rightarrow HoldsAt(f, t_2)$
4. $Happens(a, t_1) \wedge (t_1 < t_2) \wedge Clipped(t_1, f, t_2) \rightarrow \neg HoldsAt(f, t_2)$

Thus, the event log fragment depicted in Figure 4 can be easily translated in $\mathcal{DEC}$ formalism as follows:

$L1 : Happens(purchase\_order(BT, DO, dev, country), 2)$
$L2 : Happens(isAvailable(DO, DW, dev), 3)$
$L3 : Happens(inform(DW, DO, dev, 3), 10)$
$L4 : Happens(accept\_order(DO, BT, dev), 12)$
$L5 : Happens(shipment\_order(DO, DW, dev, BT), 13)$
$L6 : Happens(confirm\_shipment(DW, DO, dev), 16)$
$L7 : Happens(payment(BT, DO, dev), 19)$
$L8 : Happens(delivery(DO, BT, dev, rec), 21)$

In the same way, the behavioural properties can be expressed formally. For instance, the properties introduced in Section 3.1 are described in $\mathcal{DEC}$ formalism as follows:

$$(BP1) : Happens(purchase\_order(cu, s, i), T_{po}) \wedge$$
$$Happens(isAvailable(s, w, i), T_{ca}))$$
$$\implies T_{po} < T_{ca}$$

$$(BP2) : Happens(isAvailable(s, w, i), T_{ca}) \wedge$$
$$Happens(inform(w, s, i, Qty), T_{qty}))$$
$$\implies T_{qty} < T_{ca} + 6$$

4 Overview of SPIKE

Theorem provers have been applied to the formal development of software. They are based on logic-based specification languages and they provide support to the proof of correctness properties, expressed as logical formulas. In this work, we use the SPIKE induction prover [14]. SPIKE was chosen for the following reasons: (i) its high automation degree (to help a Web service designer), (ii) its ability on case analysis, (iii) its *refutational completeness* (to find counter-examples), (iv) its incorporation of *decision procedures* (to automatically eliminate arithmetic tautologies produced during the proof attempt[5]) SPIKE proof method is based on cover set induction. Given a theory, SPIKE computes in a first step induction variables where to apply induction and induction terms which basically represent all possibles values that can be taken by the induction variables. Typically for a nonnegative integer variable, the induction terms are 0 and $x + 1$, where x is a variable.

Given a conjecture to be checked, the prover selects induction variables according to the previous computation step, and substitute them in all possible way by induction terms. This operation generates several instances of the conjecture which are then *simplified* by rules, lemmas, and induction hypotheses.

5 Encoding $\mathcal{DEC}$ in SPIKE

In this section, we describe a method for representing $\mathcal{DEC}$ in SPIKE language. In the sequel, we assume that all formulas are universally quantified.

Data. All data information manipulated by the system is ranged over a set of sorts. This data concerns generally the argument types of events and fluents. For instance, the sets of customers, suppliers, items and countries are defined respectively by the sorts $Customer$, $Supplier$, $Item$ and $Country$. The sort $Bool$ represents the boolean values, where $true$ and $false$ are its constant constructors.

Events. We consider that all events of the system are of sort $Event$, where the event symbols are the constructors of this sort. These constructors are free as all event symbols are assumed distincts. For instance, the event symbol $purchase\_order(x, y, z, t)$ is a constructor of $Event$ such that x, y, z and t are variables of sorts $Customer$, $Supplier$, $Item$ and $Country$ respectively. We define also an *idle* event which when occuring it lets the system unchanged. We represent it by the constant constructor $Noact$.

Fluents. The sort $Fluent$ respresents the set of fluents. All fluent symbols of the systems are the constructors of sort $Fluent$, that are also free. The fluent symbol $EqualItem(x, y)$, for example, means that the variables x and y, of sort $Item$, are equal.

Time. We use the sort of natural numbers, Nat, which is reflected by constructors 0 and successor $succ(x)$ (meaning $x + 1$). We have modified the code of SPIKE in order to enable handling of Peano numbers. For example, now we can directly write 17 instead of $s(s(...(0)...))))$ as it was in the previous versions of SPIKE .

---

[5] Like $x + z > y = false \wedge z + x < y = false \implies x + z = y$.

Axioms. We express all predicates used in $\mathcal{DEC}$ as boolean function symbols. The signatures of these function symbols and others additional functions are as follows:

$$
\begin{aligned}
&Happens : Event \times Nat \rightarrow Bool \\
&Initiates : Event \times Fluent \times Nat \rightarrow Bool \\
&Terminates : Event \times Fluent \times Nat \rightarrow Bool \\
&HoldsAt : Fluent \times Nat \times Nat \rightarrow Bool \\
&Clipped : Fluent \times Nat \times Nat \rightarrow Bool \\
&p : Event \times nat \rightarrow EventTime \\
&Cons : EventTime \times List \rightarrow List \\
&member : EventTime \times List \rightarrow bool \\
&Happens : EventTime \rightarrow Bool
\end{aligned}
$$

$HoldsAt$ and $Clipped$ are defined within a time range. For instance, $HoldsAt(f, t_1, n)$ is defined within the range $[t_1, t_1 + n]$. In addition, we define the functions symbols p, $Cons$, and $member$. p is a constructor that associates an event to its occurrence time. $Cons$ is used to group the list of events in the constant $ListEvent$. This provide a certain flexibility in the construction of the log. Then, $member$ is a boolean function that permits to test if an event appears in the log. After defining the p constructor, the signature of the function associated to the predicate $Happens$ is changed from $Happens : Event \times Nat \rightarrow Bool$ to $Happens : EventTime \rightarrow Bool$.

Finally, the four axioms given in Section 3.2 are expressed in conditional equations as follows:

(A1) $event \neq Noact \wedge Happens(p(event, t_1)) = true \wedge Initiates(event, f, t_1) = true \Rightarrow HoldsAt(f, t_1, 0) = true$

(A2) $HoldsAt(f, t_1, t) = true \wedge Clipped(f, t_1 + t, s(0)) = false \Rightarrow HoldsAt(f, t_1, s(t)) = true$

(A3) $event \neq Noact \wedge Happens(p(event, t_1)) = true \wedge Terminates(event, f, t_1) = true \Rightarrow Clipped(f, t_1, s(0)) = true$

(A4) $event \neq Noact \wedge Happens(p(event, t_1 + t + s(0))) = true \wedge Terminates(event, f, t_1 + t + s(0)) = true \Rightarrow Clipped(f, t_1, s(s(t))) = true$

(A5) $Happens(p(Noact, t_1 + t + s(0))) = true \implies Clipped(f, t_1, s(s(t))) = Clipped(f, t_1, t + s(0))$

(A6) $Happens(x) = member(x, ListEvent)$

(A7) $member(x, Nil) = false$

(A8) $x = y \Rightarrow member(x, Cons(y, l)) = true$

(A9) $x \neq y \Rightarrow member(x, Cons(y, l)) = member(x, l)$

Log. Using the function $Cons$ we define the log in equational form:

$$
\begin{aligned}
ListEvent = &\, Cons(p(purchase\_order(BT, DO, dev, country), 2), \\
&Cons(p(isAvailable(DO, DW, dev), 3), \\
&Cons(p(inform(DW, DO, dev, 3), 10), \\
&Cons(p(accept\_order(DO, BT, dev), 12), \\
&Cons(p(shipment\_order(DO, DW, dev, BT), 13), \\
&Cons(p(confirm\_shipment(DW, DO, dev), 16), \\
&Cons(p(payment(BT, DO, dev), 19), \\
&Cons(p(delivery(DO, BT, dev, rec), 21), Nil))))))))
\end{aligned}
$$

Behavioural properties. In the same way, we can express the bahavioural properties in equational form. For instance, the properties $(BP1)$ and $(BP2)$given in Section 3.2, are written as follows:

$$(BP1) : Happens(purchase\_order(x, y, i), t_1) = true \wedge$$
$$Happens(isAvailable(y, w, i), t_2) = true$$
$$\Longrightarrow (t_1 < t_2) = true$$

$$(BP2) : Happens(isAvailable(s, w, i), t_1) = true \wedge$$
$$Happens(inform(w, s, i, q), t_2) = true$$
$$\Longrightarrow (t_2 < t_1 + 6) = true$$

where t_1, t_2, x, y, w, q and i are variables.

Finally, we build an algebraic specification from $\mathcal{DEC}$ specification. Once building this specification, we can check all behavioural properties by means the powerful deductive techniques (rewriting and induction) provided by SPIKE .

6 Checking Behavioural Properties

All the generated axioms can be directly given to the prover SPIKE , which automatically transforms these axioms into conditional rewrite rules. When SPIKE is called, either the behavioural properties proof succeed, or the SPIKE 's proof-trace is used for extracting all scenarios which may lead to potential deviations. There are two possible scenarios. The first scenario is meaningless because conjectures are valid but it comes from a failed proof attempt by SPIKE . Such cases can be overcome by simply introducing new lemmas. The second one concerns cases corresponding to real deviations. The trace of SPIKE gives all necessary informations (events, fluents and timepoints) to understand the inconsistency origin. Consequently, these informations help designer to detect behavioural problems in the composite Web service.

Let consider the example illustrated in this paper. SPIKE has found that $(BP1)$ is true and the reader can be confirm that by analyzing the log. But when submitting $(BP2)$, SPIKE has discovered an error. In the following, we describe how the prover checks the behavioural property $(BP2)$.

Firstly, SPIKE simplifies $(BP2)$ using the axioms (A6) and (A7) introduced in Section 5:

$$p(isAvailable(s, w, i), t_1) \wedge \tag{1}$$
$$p(inform(w, s, i, q), t_2) \tag{2}$$
$$\Longrightarrow (t_2 < t_1 + 6) = true \tag{3}$$

Using the literals $L2$ and $L3$ given by the log (that replace t_1 and t_2 by 3 and 10 respectively), this conjecture becomes $(10 < 3 + 6) = true$ that is always false. Consequently, the prover has detected an anomaly in the log. Below, we present a fragment of the SPIKE trace when checking property $BP2$.

```
Uncaught exception: Failure("fail induction on [ 10973 ] inform (u2, u1, u3, u5)
 <> purchase_order (e1, e2, e3, e4) /\\ inform (u2, u1, u3, u5) <> isAvailable (
e2, e5, e3) /\\ u2 = e5 /\\ u1 = e2 /\\ u3 = e3 /\\ u5 = 3 /\\ u6 = 10 /\\ isAva
ilable (u1, u2, u3) <> purchase_order (e1, e2, e3, e4) /\\ u1 = e2 /\\ u2 = e5 /
\\ u3 = e3 /\\ u4 = 3 => u6 < (u4 + (6)) = true ;")
while proving the following initial conjectures
[ 6584 ] Happens (p (isAvailable (u1, u2, u3), u4)) = true /\ Happens (p (inform
 (u2, u1, u3, u5), u6)) = true => u6 < (u4 + (6)) = true ;
Elapsed time: 0.186 s
We failed
```

7   Related Work

Up to now, few works have been conducted on logging and analyzing Web services usage information. Akkiraju et al. [1] proposed a framework blending logging facilities to private Web service registries. However, no details are provided about the log structure or how to implement it. Irani [6] proposed the use of intermediaries to collect information about authentication, auditing and management of services through the use of logs, but he also does not provide any detail on the log structure. Brittenham et al. [3], from WS-I Test Tools Working Group, proposed an architecture that consists of a message monitor and an analyzer. The monitor is used to log the messages that were sent to and from a Web service, while the analyzer is used to validate that the Web service interactions contained in the message log conform to a WS-I profile. However, WS-I monitor captures in a single log file HTTP data and the whole SOAP message content. These data are captured in their raw format making it difficult to differentiate analytical information from disposable data. Capturing the whole SOAP message brings another problem: huge amount of data, many times larger than traditional HTTP logs.

Formal analysis and verification of Web Services in the aim of detecting anomalies are addressed in several papers. The SPIN model-checker is used for verification [9] by translating Web Services Flow Language (WSFL) descriptions into Promela. [7] uses a process algebra to derive a structural operational semantics of BPEL as a formal basis for verifying properties of the specification. In [4], BPEL processes are translated to Finite State Process (FSP) models and compiled into a Labeled Transition System (LTS) in inferring the correctness of the Web service compositions which are specified using message sequence charts. In [5], finite automata were augmented with (i) XML messages and (ii) XPath expressions as the basis for verifying temporal properties of the conversations of composite Web services.

One common pattern of the above attempts is that they adapt static verification techniques and therefore violations of requirements may not be detectable. This is because Web services that constitute a composition process may not be specified at a level of completeness that would allow the application of static verification, and some of these services may change dynamically at run-time causing unpredictable interactions with other services.

Finally, for a complete overview of using the event calculus in the context of Web services, we refer the reader to our previous work [12,11,13].

8 Conclusions

This paper has outlined a technique to log composite Web services and a methodology, using the logging facilities, to analyze services' behaviours. More specifically, it permits to check whether the observed behaviour of each involved service matches the (un)expected/(un)desirable behaviour. The methodology is also supported by a formal representation of behavioural properties and execution logs considered as the basis for the automatic composition of Web services. The analysis process was supported by a novel specification of the $\mathcal{DEC}$ formalism. As verification back-end we used an automated induction-based theorem prover SPIKE that provide support to the proof of correctness properties, expressed as logical formulas.

References

1. Akkiraju, R., Flaxer, D., Chang, H., Chao, T., Zhang, L., Wu, F., Jeng, J.: A framework for enabling dynamic e-business via web service. In: Proceedings of the OOPSLA, Florida, USA (2001)
2. Baglioni, M., Ferrara, U., Romei, A., Ruggieri, S., Turini, F.: Use soap-based intermediaries to build chains of web service functionality (2002)
3. Brittenham, P., Clune, J., Durand, J., Kleijkers, L., Sankar, K., Seely, S., Stobie, K., Turrell, G.: Ws-i analyzer tool functional specification.
4. Foster, H., Uchitel, S., Magee, J., Kramer, J.: Compatibility verification for web service choreography. In: ICWS'04. Proceedings of the IEEE International Conference on Web Services, Washington, DC, p. 738. IEEE Computer Society Press, Los Alamitos (2004)
5. Fu, X., Bultan, T., Su, J.: Analysis of interacting bpel web services. In: WWW '04. Proceedings of the 13th international conference on World Wide Web, pp. 621–630. ACM Press, New York (2004)
6. Irani, R.: Web services intermediaries adding value to web services (November 2001)
7. Koshina, M., van Breugel, F.: Verification of business processes for web services. Technical report, New York University, SFUCMPT-TR-2003-06 (2003)
8. Kowalski, R., Sergot, M.J.: A logic-based calculus of events. New generation Computing 4(1), 67–95 (1986)
9. Nakajima, S.: Verification of web service flows with model-checking techniques. In: CW, pp. 378–385 (2002)
10. Punin, J., Krishnamoorthy, M., Zaki, M.: Web usage mining: Languages and algorithms. In: Studies in Classification, Data Analysis, and Knowledge Organization, Springer, Heidelberg (2001)
11. Rouached, M., Gaaloul, W., van der Aalst, W.M.P., Bhiri, S., Godart, C.: Web service mining and verification of properties: An approach based on event calculus. In: CoopIS 2006. Proceedings 14th International Conference on Cooperative Information Systems (November 2006)
12. Rouached, M., Perrin, O., Godart, C.: A contract-based approach for monitoring collaborative web services using commitments in the event calculus. In: Ngu, A.H.H., Kitsuregawa, M., Neuhold, E.J., Chung, J.-Y., Sheng, Q.Z. (eds.) WISE 2005. LNCS, vol. 3806, pp. 426–434. Springer, Heidelberg (2005)
13. Rouached, M., Perrin, O., Godart, C.: Towards formal verification of web service composition. In: Dustdar, S., Fiadeiro, J.L., Sheth, A. (eds.) BPM 2006. LNCS, vol. 4102, Springer, Heidelberg (2006)
14. Stratulat, S.: A general framework to build contextual cover set induction provers. Journal of Symbolic Computation 32(4), 403–445 (2001)

QoS Prediction for Composite Web Services with Transactions

Jiangxia Wu and Fangchun Yang

State Key Laboratory of Networking and Switching Technology,
Beijing University of Posts and Telecommunications, 100876 Beijing, China
wujiangxia@gmail.com, fcyang@bupt.edu.cn

Abstract. Prediction of the Quality of Service (QoS) of Composite Web Services (*CWS*) makes it possible to tell whether the CWS meets the non-function requirements, and to choose the CWS with better QoS from those with similar function. QoS prediction is based on the estimation of the execution process of CWS. For the reliability of CWS executions, Web service transaction has been proposed, which will affect the execution process. However, the existing approaches have not considered the effect. Thus they have limited accuracy when predicting the CWS with transactions. The paper proposes an approach for QoS prediction of CWS with transactions. A specification model is defined to specify execution processes of CWS according to the exception handling policies of transactions. Based on the model, an algorithm is proposed. The experiment proves that the algorithm has much lower error rate and better feasibility than the previous approaches when predicting CWS with transactions.

Keywords: Composite Web Service, QoS prediction, Transaction.

1 Introduction and Related Work

Web Service Composition (*WSC*) gives a way to assemble Web services from the view of function requirements. To predict the Quality of Service (*QoS*) of Composite Web Services (*CWS*) makes it possible to tell whether the CWS meet the non-function requirements, and what's more to choose the CWS with better QoS from those with similar function. The existing methods for QoS prediction of CWS include the aggregation function approach [1], the Software Architecture based approach [2], the simulation approach [3] and the Workflow Based Approach (*WBA*) [4, 5, 6, 7]. Among them, the WBA has the best feasibility and accuracy.

The existing approaches are based on the estimation of the execution process of CWS. However, none of them has considered the effect of Web service transaction mechanism on the execution process of CWS. Thus they have limited accuracy when estimating the CWS with transaction mechanism. A fail-aware approach has been proposed in [8], which analyzes the effect of failure recovery on QoS of CWS, also without considering the transaction mechanism. And the difficulty in getting the input parameters leads to the poor feasibility of the method.

D. Georgakopoulos et al. (Eds.): ICSOC 2006 Ws, LNCS 4652, pp. 86–94, 2007.

We analyze the effect of Web service transaction on the execution process of CWS. A specification model of CWS is defined to specify possible execution processes of a transaction according to the exception handling policies of the transaction. On the base of the specification model we propose an algorithm to predict the average value of QoS attributes of CWS with transactions, and the method to estimate the occurrence probability of exceptions as part of the algorithm. The experiment proves the algorithm has much lower error rate and better feasibility than the approach that has not considered the transaction mechanism when predicting the QoS of CWS with transactions.

The rest of the paper is organized as follow: The specification model of CWS is defined in section 2. The algorithm is proposed in section 3. And section 4 discusses the experiment and section 5 concludes the paper.

2   Specification Model of CWS

2.1   Problem Definition

To guarantee the consistency and reliability of the executions of atomic services in WSC, Web service transaction has been proposed. Web service transaction is a set of service invocating operations that follows the Advanced Transaction Models (*ATMs*) [9] which try to relax the rigid demands of ACID attributes because ACID is practical only in tightly coupled systems, and follow the SACReD attributes which are Semantic Atomicity, Consistency, Resiliency and Durability [10]. To ensure the SACReD attributes, a set of exception handling policies will be predefined to coordinate the operations in transactions. When exceptions happen to the transaction, the normal process will be paused and compensation for recovery will be performed according to the exception handling policies that specify what exceptions to handle and how to handle. That is to say, the execution process of CWS with transactions will be affected by the exception handling policies.

An example of CWS with transactions is given in figure 1. The function of the CWS is to order a dress online, including suit and tie. The CWS is composed of four atomic services: OrderReceipt, SuitOrder, TieOrder and OrderResponse. The process is shown in figure 1. As it is nonsensical for only a tie or only a suit, these two things should be gotten at the same time, which means all or nothing. Therefore, SuitOrder and TieOrder make a transaction, and the exception handling policies are defined as that forward recovery through SuitOrderAlter service when SuitOrder failed and backward recovery through SuitOrderCancel service when TieOrder failed. What should be mentioned is that we make the assumption that failure will not happen to SuitOrder and TieOrder at the same time, and exception handling operations will not fail.

The problem is how to predict the execution process of CWS according to the exception handling policies of transactions, and how to compute the QoS of the predicted execution process.

2.2   Model Definition

The aim of the model is to specify the possible execution process of a CWS with transactions.

Definition 2.1 CWS Process (*CWSP*). CWSP specifies the order of atomic service invocations of a CWS when no exception happened, and can be described as a workflow: Tasks of the workflow represent service invocations, and transitions between tasks represent the order of invocation. For example, the CWSP of dress order CWS is showed in figure 1.

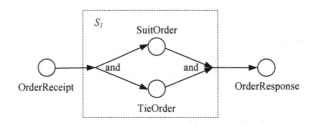

Fig. 1. The CWSP of dress order CWS

Definition 2.2 Scope. Scope is a set of tasks and their transitions which make up of a Web service transaction. Scope can be a part of or the entire CWSP, and there may be more than one scope in a CWSP. Scopes can be nested and obey the rules of transaction nesting [12]. For example, the scope in figure 1 represented by S_1 consists of SuitOrder and TieOrder.

Definition 2.3 Exception Handling Policy Set (*EHPS*). EHPS represents the set of exception handling policies (*ehp*) pre-defined for a transaction, and the EHPS of Scope S_α is described as $EHPS_\alpha = \{ehp_{\alpha 1}, ehp_{\alpha 2}, ..., ehp_{\alpha n}\}$.

$ehp_{\alpha i}$ represents a policy consisting of *exception event* and *exception handling action*, described as $ehp_{\alpha i} = (event_{\alpha i}, action_{\alpha i})$. $event_{\alpha i}$ specifies the activation exception event, and $action_{\alpha i}$ specifies the exception handling operations performed when $event_{\alpha i}$ is true and the order of the operations. $event_{\alpha i}$ can be a simple event which is the failure of a single service invocation or a complex event which is multiple simple events connected by "*AND*". $\forall\ ehp_{\alpha i}, ehp_{\alpha j} \in EHPS_\alpha$, if $i \neq j$, then $event_{\alpha i} \neq event_{\alpha j}$.

For example, the EHPS of Scope S_1 in dress order CWS can be described as $EHPS_1 = \{ehp_{11}, ehp_{12}\}$, and $ehp_{11} = $ (*Failure* (SuitOrder), *Alteration* (SuitOrderAlter), $ehp_{12} = $ (*Failure* (TieOrder), *Compensation* (SuitOrderCancel)).

Definition 2.4 Scope Processes (*SP*). Let $SEPS_\alpha$ be the set of possible execution processes of the scope S_α, and SP of scope S_α described as SP_α is the association of elements in $SEPS_\alpha$ connected by the composition pattern [6] of "*XOR-XOR*", as the actual execution process of the scope must be one of the elements in $SEPS_\alpha$.

There are two types of elements in $SEPS_\alpha$. One is normal process and the other is exception process. The former represents the scope execution process when no exception happened which is same as the scope process specified in CWSP, and is described as $sep_{\alpha 0}$. And the latter specifies the scope execution process when exceptions happened in the scope, and is described as $sep_{\alpha i}$ ($i > 0$).

Now we want to compute all the elements in $SEPS_\alpha$. Normal process $sep_{\alpha0}$ can be specified according to the CWSP. And exception processes can be specified according to the exception handling policies. Let $EHPS_\alpha = \{ehp_{\alpha1}, ehp_{\alpha2},..., ehp_{\alpha n}\}$, in which $ehp_{\alpha i} = (event_{\alpha i}, action_{\alpha i})$. Different exceptions and exception handling actions will lead to different exception processes. And with the assumption that only one exception happened in an execution of scope and the exception handling operation will not fail, the n exception handling policies in $EHPS_\alpha$ will lead to n exception processes. And the n exception processes are described as $sep_{\alpha1}$, $sep_{\alpha2},..., sep_{\alpha n}$. $sep_{\alpha i}$ $(i=1,2\cdots,n)$ includes two parts: Pre exception handling part (*PRE-EH*) and exception handling part (*EH*). PRE-EH of $sep_{\alpha i}$ consists of the tasks and their transitions in the S_α which are in completed, failure or active state when $event_{\alpha i}$ happened between them, and EH of $sep_{\alpha i}$ consists of the tasks and transitions respectively representing the operations and their order specified in $action_{\alpha i}$.

For example, the SEPS of scope S_1 described as $SEPS_1 = \{sep_{10}, sep_{11}, sep_{12}\}$ is showed in figure 2. And the SP of scope S_1 described as SP_1 is showed in figure 3.

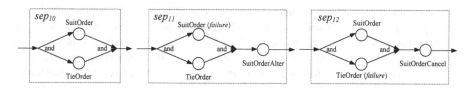

Fig. 2. The SEPS of scope S_1

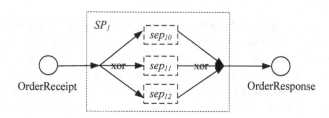

Fig. 3. The SP of scope S_1

3 Prediction Algorithm

Based on the specification model, we define the QoS Prediction Algorithm (*QPA*) to predict the average value of QoS attributes of CWS with transactions which include performance, cost and reputation. The attributes definition has been given in [1].

QPA is composed of three steps, which are (1) to compute the QoS attribute of each scope in the CWSP, and (2) to transform the scopes to the tasks with equal attribute value, and (3) to compute the attribute of the result process got from the transformation.

The QoS of scope S_α is defined as the QoS of SP_α, and is described as SQ_α. SQ_α can be computed through formula (1) according to the Workflow QoS Computation Method ($WQCM$) [5, 7] which gives the way to compute the average value of QoS attributes of workflow by aggregating the attributes value of tasks in the workflow. In formula (1), $q_{\alpha i}$ and $p_{\alpha i}$ ($i = 0, 1, \cdots, n$) respectively represent the attribute value and the occurrence probability of $sep_{\alpha i}$, and $\sum_{i=0} p_{\alpha i} = 1$. For nested scopes, recursive procedure will be used.

$$SQ_\alpha = \sum_{i=0}^{n} (p_i \cdot q_i)$$ (1)

And $p_{\alpha i}$ ($i > 0$) is equal to the occurrence probability of the $event_{\alpha i}$ which can be calculated as following: For the $event_{\alpha i}$ of simple event, $p_{\alpha i}$ is the failure probability of the corresponding atomic service, and for the $event_{\alpha i}$ of complex event, $p_{\alpha i}$ can be computed with the rule of $P(A \cdot B) = PA \cdot PB$. And $p_{\alpha 0} = 1 - \sum_{1}^{n} p_{\alpha i}$.

The failure probability of atomic services, described as p, can be computed through $p = c_1 p' + c_2 p'' + c_3 p'''$, in which $c_1 + c_2 + c_3 = 1$, and p' represents the failure probability given by the service provider on the interface of Web service, and p'' represents the failure probability got from the history statistic of service execution, and p''' represents the failure probability got from the history statistic of service execution in the CWS. Weight c_i reflect the similarity between the item and failure probability. The higher the similarity, the larger the weight. In generally, the third item p''' has the highest similarity. When one of the items can not be gotten, the item weight can be set as zero.

In order to get $q_{\alpha i}$ through WQCM we must get the attribute value of tasks in SP_α. The way to get the attribute of normal service invocation task is given in [5]. As the task with exception is concerned, because the state of the exception task can not be determined we take the normal attribute value as that of task with exception. And as the task of exception handling operation is concerned, because the task is to invoke the Web service with forward or backward recovery function, we can use the way in [5] to get the its attribute value.

Scope transformation is to convert a scope to the task with equal QoS to the scope. And those transitions terminating on tasks inside the scope, and initiating from tasks outside the scope, should be transformed to terminate on the substitute task. And those initiating from tasks inside the scope, and terminating on tasks outside the scope, should be transformed to initiate from the substitute task. And the attribute of processes resulting from transformation can be computed through WQCM method.

For example, the performance attribute of the dress order CWS can be predicted as following. Performance attribute is the time interval between sending the request message and receiving the response message [1].

The performance and failure probability of each task in SP_1 have been gotten through the history statistic, and are showed in table 1.

Table 1. Performance and failure probability of tasks in SP_1

	Performance(s)	FailureProbability(%)
OrderReceipt	3.9	-
SuitOrder	7.7	21.2
TieOrder	5.4	15.1
OrderResponse	2.8	-
SuitOrderAlter	9.1	-
SuitOrderCancel	9.7	-

With the data on tasks, we can get $q_{\alpha i}$ and $p_{\alpha i}$ for the elements in $SEPS_1=\{sep_{10},$ $sep_{11}, sep_{12}\}$, which are showed in table 2. According to formula (1), the performance of the scope S_1 is 11.1.

Table 2. $p_{\alpha i}$ and $q_{\alpha i}$ for $SEPS_1$

	sep_{10}	sep_{11}	sep_{12}
$p_{\alpha i}$ (s)	7.7	16.8	17.4
$q_{\alpha i}$ (%)	63.7	21.2	15.1

The result process of scope transformation is showed in figure 4. With WQCM, we can get the prediction result for dress order CWS as 17.8.

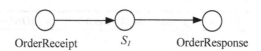

OrderReceipt S_1 OrderResponse

Fig. 4. The result of scope transformation

4 Experiment

To prove the feasibility and accuracy of QPA, we implement the dress order CWS with JOpera [13,14], which offers the visual interface for design and implementation of WSC. The reason to choose JOpera is that JOpera supports exception handling mechanism and offer the log of performance of atomic services and composite service, and has good stability.

The performance log of 15 execution instances of dress order CWS as well as the average are shown in table 3 and table 4. We can see the error between the estimation and actual value of performance and failure probability of tasks. *Failure* (SuitOrder) happened in instance 4, 6, 10 and 15 with the occurrence probability of 26.7%. And *Failure* (TieOrder) happened in instance 9 and 11 with the occurrence probability of 13.3%.

Table 3. The first part of performance log and average of dress order CWS

Instance	CWS	OrderReceipt	SuitOrder	TieOrder
1	15.195	5.538	7.324	6.166
2	16.507	4.466	9.868	6.606
3	16.536	2.301	9.062	3.562
4	26.673	3.315	3.322	4.024
5	15.917	5.478	6.424	8.165
6	31.49	3.294	13.002	4.124
7	12.331	2.674	7.524	5.524
8	18.785	3.416	9.266	7.246
9	25.242	5.478	5.264	11.062
10	20.641	3.417	12.932	5.566
11	25.309	3.717	7.124	10.365
12	17.315	6.231	8.86	4.242
13	13.263	4.598	6.335	6.531
14	14.955	5.768	6.964	5.326
15	28.779	4.478	11.96	5.164
Avg	19.9	4.3	8.3	6.2

Table 4. The second part of performance log and average of dress order CWS

Instance	OrderResponse	SuitOrderAlter	SuitOrderCancel
1	2.333	-	-
2	2.173	--	-
3	5.173	-	-
4	2.273	8.153	-
5	2.274	-	-
6	5.221	8.283	-
7	2.133	-	-
8	6.103	-	-
9	2.213	-	6.489
10	3.375	9.973	-
11	4.213	-	7.014
12	2.224	-	-
13	2.134	-	-
14	2.223	-	-
15	2.303	10.038	-
Avg	3.1	9.1	6.8

Table 5 shows the actual value of the performance of dress order CWS, the prediction result of QPA and *WBA*, and the error rate η .The error rate can be computed through $\eta = \dfrac{|V_e - V_a|}{V_a}$, in which V_e and V_a respectively represent the estimation value and actual value.

Table 5. Comparison of Prediction results

	Actual	*QPA*	*WBA*
Performance (s)	19.9	17.8	14.4
η (%)	-	10.6	28.2

The result in table 5 shows that when predicting the QoS of CWS with transactions, QPA has much lower error rate than WBA which has no special handling of the transaction mechanism. Meanwhile the experiment proves the feasibility and validity of QPA.

5 Conclusion

Prediction of the Quality of Service (*QoS*) of Composite Web Services (*CWS*) makes it possible to tell whether the CWS meet the non-function requirements, and what's more to choose the CWS with better QoS from those with similar function. QoS prediction is based on the estimation of the execution process of CWS. To predict the QoS of CWS with transactions, we analyze the Web service transaction mechanism and its effect on the execution process of CWS. A specification model is defined to specify possible execution processes of a transaction according to the exception handling policies pre-defined for the transaction. On the base of the specification model, we proposed the QPA algorithm to predict the average value of QoS attributes of CWS with transactions. The experiment proves that QPA has much lower error rate than the approach that has not considered the transaction mechanism when predicting the CWS with transactions. Meanwhile the experiment proves the feasibility and validity of QPA.

Acknowledgment. We thank the National Basic Research Priorities Programme (Grant No. 2003CB314806) for funding the project.

References

1. Zeng, L., Benatallah, B., Ngu, A.H.H., et al.: QoS-Aware Middleware for Web Services Composition. Software Engineering, IEEE Transactions on 30(5), 311–327 (2004)
2. Grassi, V.: Architecture-based Reliability Prediction for Service-oriented Computing. In: de Lemos, R., Gacek, C., Romanovsky, A. (eds.) Architecting Dependable Systems III. LNCS, vol. 3549, Springer, Heidelberg (2005)

3. Chadrasekaran, S., Miller, J.A., Silver, G.S., et al.: Composition, performance analysis and simulation of web services. In: Electronic Markets: The International Journal of Electronic Commerce and Business Media (2003)
4. Cardoso, J.: Quality of Service and Semantic Composition of Workflows. PhD thesis, Department of Computer Science, University of Georgia, Athens, GA (USA) (2002)
5. Cardoso, J., Sheth, A., Miller, J.A., et al.: Quality of service for workflows and web service processes. Journal of Web Semantics (2004)
6. Jaeger, M.C., Rojec-Goldmann, G., Muhl, G.: QoS aggregation for service composition using workflow patterns. In: EDOC 2004. Proceedings of the 8th International Enterprise Distributed Object Computing Conference, Monterey, California, pp. 149–159. IEEE Computer Society Press, Los Alamitos (2004)
7. Jaeger, M.C., Rojec-Goldmann, G., Muhl, G.: QoS aggregation in Web service compositions. In: EEE 2005. Proceedings of the IEEE Int. Conf. on e-Technology, e-Commerce and e-Service, pp. 181–185. IEEE Computer Society Press, Los Alamitos (2005)
8. Lakhal, N.B., Kobayashi, T., Yokota, H.: A Failure-Aware Model for Estimating and Analyzing the Efficiency of Web Services Compositions. In: PRDC 2005. Proceedings of 11th IEEE International Symposium on Pacific Rim Dependable Computing, IEEE Computer Society Press, Los Alamitos (2005)
9. Gray, J., Reuter, A.: Transaction Processing: Concepts and Techniques, 9th edn. Morgan Kaufmann Publishers, San Francisco, California (2002)
10. Younas, M., Eaglestone, B., Holton, R.: A Formal Treatment of a SACReD Protocol for Multidatabase Web Transactions. In: Ibrahim, M., Küng, J., Revell, N. (eds.) DEXA 2000. LNCS, vol. 1873, Springer, Heidelberg (2000)
11. Zeng, L., Lei, H., Jeng, J., et al.: Policy-driven exception-management for composite web services. In: CEC 2005. the Proceedings of the 7th IEEE Int. Conf. on E-commerce Technology, pp. 355–363. IEEE Computer Society Press, Los Alamitos (2005)
12. Papazoglou, M.P.: Web services and business transactions. In: the Proceedings of World Wide Web, pp. 49–91. Kluwer Academic Publisher, Netherlands (2003)
13. Pautasso, C., Heinis, T., Alonso, G.: Autonomic execution of service compositions. In: ICWS 2005. the Proceedings of 3rd IEEE Int. Conf. on Web Services, Orlando (2005)
14. Pautasso, C.: A Flexible System for Visual Service Composition. PhD thesis, Eidgenössisch Technische Hochschule (ETH) Zürich (2004)

Service Aggregation Using Relational Operations on Interface Parameters

George Feuerlicht

Faculty of Information Technology,
University of Technology, Sydney,
P.O. Box 123 Broadway, Sydney, NSW 2007, Australia
`jiri@it.uts.edu.au`

Abstract. Many practitioners recommend the use of coarse-grained services that minimize the number of messages and avoid the need to maintain state information between invocations. However, when considered from a software engineering perspective, coarse-grained services suffer from a number of significant drawbacks, including limited reuse and difficult composability. An important challenge for the developers of service-oriented applications is to determine appropriate level of service granularity to ensure that services are reusable and at the same time have good performance characteristics. Decisions about service granularity need to be taken in the context of a methodological framework rather than using ad hoc heuristics. In this paper we describe a method for service aggregation that uses relational operations over interface parameters to assemble services from low granularity atomic service operations. We illustrate the impact of service aggregation on cohesion and coupling using examples and discuss service granularity in the context of application requirements.

Keywords: service design, service aggregation, relational operations.

1 Introduction

Many researchers regard SOA (Service Oriented Architecture) as a message-based paradigm and view service-oriented applications as orchestrations of message exchanges that facilitate service interactions [1]. A frequently used argument in favor of message-orientation is that coarse-grained services (i.e. services with aggregated message payloads) avoid the need to maintain state information between service invocations, simplifying recovery in the event of failure. Furthermore, it is argued that coarse-grained services achieve performance advantages by reducing the number of network interactions required to implement a given business function. Asynchronous message-oriented patterns that characterize SOA alleviate many of the issues associated with synchronous, RPC-based protocols and provide an alternative approach for the implementation of failure-resilient and highly scalable distributed applications. However, when considered from a software engineering perspective, coarse-grained services suffer from a number of significant drawbacks, including limited reuse and poor composability [2].

D. Georgakopoulos et al. (Eds.): ICSOC 2006 Ws, LNCS 4652, pp. 95–103, 2007.
© Springer-Verlag Berlin Heidelberg 2007

A key determinant of service reuse is service granularity, i.e. the scope of functionality that individual services implement. There is an inverse relationship between service granularity and service reusability; as the scope of functionality implemented by a given service increases, the potential for reuse diminishes. Coarse-grained services are associated with complex message structures that often contain embedded business rules, context information, and instructions for processing of the message. This is evident in various industry standard message specifications, for example, the OTA specification (Open Travel Alliance, www.opentravel.org/) that forms the basis for the implementation of Web Services for the travel industry. Using this specification airline flight booking is implemented with the message pair OTA_AirBookRQ and OTA_AirBookRS. The flight booking request document OTA_AirBookRQ is a complex document that contains a large number of data elements (many optional) and includes flight booking, itinerary, and traveler and payment details. Decomposing the flight booking request into separate, lower-granularity operations such as flight enquiry, flight booking, and payment significantly increases potential for reuse (e.g. payment operation can be reused for car rental, or a hotel room booking). At the same time lower-granularity operations facilitate a more conversational interaction between the travel agent and the airline that more closely corresponds to the requirements of the travel booking business process. Also importantly, service granularity impacts on the ability to evolve service-oriented applications. Once externalized, the service interface must be maintained for the duration of the service lifetime to avoid invalidating existing applications that use the service. Coarse-grained services that externalize complex data structures exhibit high levels of data coupling and are difficult to evolve without producing undesirable side-effects.

The main challenge for the developers of service-oriented applications is to determine appropriate level of service aggregation to ensure that services are reusable, exhibit a high degree of mutual independence, and at the same time have good performance characteristics. Decisions about service granularity play a key role in the design of services, and need to be considered in the context of a methodological framework. In previous publications we have described a methodological framework for the design of services that uses top-down decomposition based on the data properties of interface parameters to maximize cohesion and minimize coupling of service operations [2], [3], [4]. In this paper we focus on the problem of service aggregation and extend the original design framework to include bottom-up service aggregation that uses relational operations to combine normalized service interfaces into composite service operations. We analyze the impact of service aggregation on cohesion and coupling and discuss service granularity in the context of application requirements.

In the following section (sections 2) we briefly summarize our method for service design and describe how complex business functions can be decomposed into elementary service operations with normalized interfaces. Section 3 illustrates the method using a Flight Enquiry example loosely based on the OTA specification. We then consider the problem of service granularity and describe a technique for service aggregation that uses relational operations over interface parameters to assemble higher-level services from atomic service operations (section 4). In the concluding section 5 we briefly review related literature, and discuss the benefits of a data engineering approach to service design identifying potential for further work.

2   Service Design Method

The design method consists of two main design stages. The first stage involves top-down decomposition with the objective of identifying elementary, reusable service operations. We provide a brief overview of our approach to service decomposition in this section; full description of the method is available in earlier publications [2], [3]. The second design stage is the focus of this paper and involves service aggregation with the aim of optimizing service granularity with respect to the requirements of a particular message interchange scenario, e.g. airline travel booking dialogue. The level of service aggregation can be also fine-tuned to reflect performance, state management and other related considerations; such considerations are outside the scope of this paper.

For the purpose of this analysis we adopt the Web Services model of services where service interfaces (i.e. the signature of services) consist of port types, operations, and message types. In general, service interface can consist of a number of operations that implement the service, but it is possible for a service interface to support only a single *ProcessMessage* operation [1]; this makes the design method applicable to both RPC and message-oriented approaches. We make no *a priory* assumptions about the implementation style (i.e. binding style, RPC or document) and interaction model (i.e. synchronous or asynchronous) as we regard such decisions as being orthogonal to the task of designing service interfaces. We do not consider non-functional service requirements and focus entirely on data properties of service interfaces, i.e. the properties of inbound and outbound messages that implement data flows between services and determine the level of service coupling.

To support the requirements for service reuse and evolution, services must be designed to maximize cohesion and minimize coupling of service operations [4]. Maximizing cohesion requires that a module (i.e. service operation) performs a single, atomic function. Importantly, a high level of service cohesion leads to orthogonality of services as functional overlap is minimized, or eliminated altogether. The requirement for minimization of coupling dictates that service interfaces consist of individual data parameters rather than more complex data structures such as classes or object references [5]. In order to avoid undesirable interdependencies, services cannot share higher level abstractions (e.g. classes) and use inheritance as the underlying reuse mechanism. Consequently, the reuse mechanism is limited to service aggregation, i.e. the assembly of composite services from elementary (atomic) services. Service assembly is a recursive process that continues until the appropriate level of service granularity that corresponds to a specific business requirement is reached. Furthermore, using individual data parameters rather than complex data structures as inbound and outbound messages in service interfaces enables the application of data engineering principles to further minimize coupling between services.

During the first design stage complex business functions are progressively decomposed into elementary functions and then mapped to corresponding candidate service operations. This approach is consistent with maximizing cohesion as elementary business functions typically accomplish a single conceptual task and exhibit high levels of cohesion. The decomposition of a high-level business function, e.g. airline flight booking business function, can be achieved by modeling the interaction between a travel agent and an airline using a Sequence Diagram [4]. Given the initial set of candidate service operations, further decomposition to maximize cohesion and minimize coupling can be achieved by applying data normalization to the interface data parameters [6], [7].

3 Flight Enquiry Example

We now illustrate our service design framework using an example of the Flight Enquiry business process based on the OTA airline availability request/response messages: OTA_Air_AvailRQ and OTA_Air_AvailRS. For the purpose of this example we make a number of simplifying assumptions and use a subset of the OTA message data elements to populate the service interfaces. Using the service decomposition approach described in section 2 and assuming functional dependencies FD1-FD5 between data parameters of the relevant service interfaces, the corresponding set of operations with normalized interfaces is shown in Table 1.

FD1: OriginLocation, DestinationLocation, DepartureDate → FlightNumber
FD2: FlightNumber → DepartureAirport, DepartureTime, ArrivalAirport, ArrivalTime
FD3: FlightNumber, DepartureDate → ArrivalDate
FD4: FlightNumber, DepartureDate, CabinType → Quantity
FD5: FlightNumber, DepartureDate, CabinType → BasicFare, BasicFareCode

Table 1. Normalized interfaces for the Flight Enquiry Service

Business Function	Operation	Input Parameters	Output Parameters
Requests for available flights for a pair of origin and destination cities on a given departure date.	FlightEnquiry	OriginLocation, DestinationLocation, DepartureDate	FlightNumber
Request for flight schedule information for a given flight number.	ScheduleEnquiry	FlightNumber	DepartureAirport DepartureTime, ArrivalAirport, ArrivalTime
Request for arrival information for a given flight.	ArrivalEnquiry	FlightNumber, DepartureDate	ArrivalDate
Request for seat availability information for a given flight and cabin type.	SeatEnquiry	FlightNumber, DepartureDate, CabinType	Quantity
Request for pricing information for a given flight and cabin type.	PriceEnquiry	FlightNumber, DepartureDate, CabinType	FareBasisCode, BaseFare

We can now implement the Flight Enquiry business process as a dialogue between a travel agent and an airline as illustrated in Figure 1. It is not our intension to fully model the workflow of the Flight Enquiry process as our focus is on data properties of interface parameters and on aggregation of service operations based on data parameters. We simplify the dialogue by excluding alternative execution paths, for example the termination of the booking process due to unavailability of seats on a particular flight.

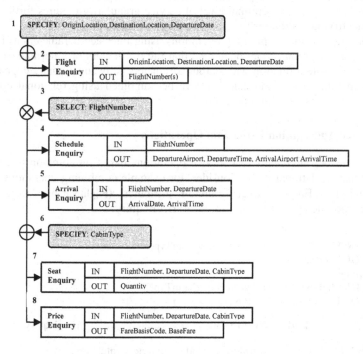

Fig. 1. Implementation of the Flight Enquiry process using elementary service operations

The dialogue proceeds as follows: The travel agent specifies input values for OriginLocation, DestinationLocation, and DepartureDate parameters (1). Following the execution of the FlightEnquiry operation (2), the travel agent selects a suitable flight (i.e. FlightNumber) (3). The travel agent then executes the operations ScheduleEnquiry (4) and ArrivalEnquiry (5) and supplies the value for CabinType, e.g. Economy (6). Finally, the travel agent executes the operations SeatEnquiry (7) and PriceEnquiry (8) to obtain the availability and price information, respectively.

4 Service Aggregation Using Relational Operations

As is evident from the above discussion, using fully normalized service interfaces results in fine-granularity operations with corresponding increase in the number of runtime calls and the complexity of the interaction dialogue. While the resulting interfaces produce a set of elementary and highly reusable services, they do not represent a practical solution. As an alternative the service designer may consider a coarse-granularity solution, supplying all user inputs (i.e. OriginLocation,

DestinationLocation, DepartureDate, CabinType) at the beginning of the dialogue followed by the execution a single composite FlightEnquiry operation. As noted earlier (section 1) this leads to poor reuse and does not correspond to the inherently conversational dialogue that characterizes the flight enquiry business process. These fine-granularity and coarse-granularity alternatives represent two extreme design solutions. Finding a more optimal level of service granularity requires further examination, identifying operations that are suitable candidates for aggregations.

Let us now consider combining operations using interface parameters as the basis for service aggregation. It can be argued that the parameters of a normalized service interface constitute a relation with output parameters fully functionally dependent on the input parameter set, and can therefore be combined using relational operations (i.e. relational joins and union operations).

4.1 Service Aggregation Using Join Operations

We first consider aggregation of service operations based on common interface parameters using relational joins. Consider, for example combining operations SeatEnquiry and PriceEnquiry over common attributes (FlightNumber, DepartureDate, CabinType) producing a new operation SeatPriceEnquiry:

SeatEnquiry
(**IN**: FlightNumber,DepartureDate,CabinType,
        OUT: Quantity   )
PriceEnquiry
(**IN**: FlightNumber,DepartureDate,CabinType,
        OUT: FareBasisCode, BaseFare   )

SeatPriceEnquiry = SeatEnquiry **NJN** $_{(FlightNumber, DepartureDate, CabinType)}$ PriceEnquiry

where **NJN** denotes a natural join, producing a new interface:

SeatPriceEnquiry
(**IN**: FlightNumber, DepartureDate, CabinType,
        OUT: Quantity, FareBasisCode, BaseFare   )

This solution leads to relative loss of cohesion as the resulting operation no longer implements a single atomic task, and in situations where it is used to perform a partial enquiry (e.g. seat availability enquiry only) the operation returns values that are not used by the application. The tradeoff can be justified in this instance on the basis that both operations are frequently performed together, and that the benefits of reduced number of operations and runtime procedure calls outweights the loss of cohesion. Similar considerations apply to combining operations ScheduleEnquiry and ArrivalEnquiry into a new operation TimeTable:

ScheduleEnquiry
(**IN**: FlightNumber,
        OUT: DepartureAirport, DepartureTime, ArrivalAirport, ArrivalTime   )

ArrivalEnquiry
(**IN**: FlightNumber, DepartureDate,
        OUT:ArrivalDate)

The interface for the combined operation TimeTable can then be derived by joining the two interfaces based on the input parameter FlightNumber:

TimeTable = ScheduleEnquiry $\mathbf{NJN}_{(FlightNumber)}$ArrivalEnquiry

TimeTable
(**IN**: FlightNumber, DepartureDate,
     OUT:DepartureAirport, DepartureTime, ArrivalAirport, ArrivalDate, ArrivalTime)

The aggregation of the ScheduleEnquiry and ArrivalEnquiry into a single operation TimeTable results in loss of cohesion, as the TimeTable operation is no longer strictly atomic; however, this can be justified on the basis that the TimeTable query closely corresponds to the requirements of the flight booking business process.

The resulting Flight Enquiry dialogue that uses the aggregated service operations is illustrated in Figure 2, and represent a solution that closely correspond to the conversational requirements of the flight booking business process. Further aggregation could now be considered, for example combining FlightEnquiry and TimeTable operations using the combination of FlightNumber, DepartureDate parameters, reducing the number of runtime calls with a corresponding loss of functional cohesion. Continuing the process of progressive aggregation to include SeatPriceEnquiry would result in a single, coarse granularity Flight Enquiry operation.

4.2 Service Aggregation Using Union Operations

Now consider a common requirement for combining flight availability information from multiple airlines, for example by executing the Flight Enquiry operation for two airlines: for KLM and BA:

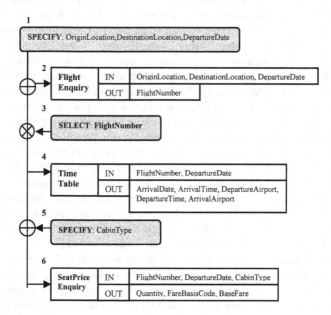

Fig. 2. Implementation of Flight Enquiry business process with aggregated service operations

FlightEnquiry
(**IN**: OriginLocation, DestinationLocation, DepartureDate,
        OUT: FlightNumber   )

This time the resulting interface is obtained using the union operation **UN**:

FlightEnquiry = KLM_FlightEnquiry **UN** BA_ FlightEnquiry

The approach for aggregating service operations based on data properties of inter-face parameters described in this paper provides a framework for making decisions about the level of service granularity while considering the various design tradeoffs. The particular circumstances of a given application scenario would determine the level of service aggregation adopted by the designer. For example, an implementation in the context of fast and reliable local area network may use a fine-granularity solu-tion with minimal aggregation of service operations.

5   Related Work and Conclusions

Most practitioners recommend the use of coarse-grained, message-oriented Web Ser-vices that minimize the number of messages and avoid the need to maintain state information between invocations. While it is evident that using fine-granularity ser-vice operations based on existing components leads to suboptimal design, excessive use of coarse-grained, document-centric services has its own limitations; in particular it results in poor reuse and undesirable interdependencies between services. It is there-fore important that decisions about the level of service aggregation are made in the context of methodological framework, rather than based on ad hoc heuristics.

The study of service granularity is closely related to the work on services aggrega-tion and composition. Service composition is an active research area with many di-verse approaches being currently investigated. Industry based research views Web Services as abstract standardized interfaces to business processes and focuses on describing and implementing service composition using workflow specification lan-guages such as BPEL. The Semantic Web research community takes a different ap-proach and draws on AI planning research and run-time reasoning techniques based on ontological definitions of service semantics. A comprehensive review and com-parison of the two approaches to service composition is provided in [8] and [9], with the conclusion that the Web Services composability problem remains essentially un-solved. In addition to BPEL, other standardization efforts include Web Services Cho-reography Interface (WSCI) and the Business Process Management Language (BPML) each taking a different approach to orchestration and choreography [10]. However, BPEL is today established as the industry standard language for the imple-mentation of loosely coupled asynchronous business-to-business Web Services appli-cations that share common XML data types and documents [11].

The approach described in this paper complements existing literature on the topic of design of services, proposing a methodological framework for making decisions about the level of service aggregation given specific application requirements and business process scenarios. We argue that both service aggregation and composition can be viewed as design-time activities that combine service operations based on data properties of interface parameters. Further research is needed to understand how service aggregation based on interface parameters can be used to achieve optimal service granularity given a set of application requirements. Another area of research interest concerns the application of this methodology in the more general context of services composition.

References

[1] Webber, J., Parastatidis, S.: Realising Service Oriented Architectures Using Web Services to be published in 2006 in Service Oriented Computing. MIT Press, Cambridge (2006)

[2] Feuerlicht, G.: Design of Service Interfaces for e-Business Applications using Data Normalization Techniques. In: Journal of Information Systems and e-Business Management, pp. 1–14. Springer, Heidelberg, ISS:1617-98 (2005)

[3] Feuerlicht, G.: Application of Data Engineering Techniques to Design of Messages Structures for Web Services. In: WDSOA'05. Proceedings of the First International Workshop on Design of Service-Oriented Applications, Amsterdam, The Netherlands, December 12, 2005, IBM Research Report RC23819 (W0512-29) (2005)

[4] Stevens, W.P., Myers, G.J., Constantine, L.L.: Structured Design. IBM Systems Journal 38(S2&3) (1999)

[5] Myers, G.J.: Composite Structured Design, Van Nostrand Reinhold, 175 (1978) ISBN 0-442-80584-5

[6] Codd, E.F.: Normalized Data Structure: A Brief Tutorial. In: Proceedings of 1971 ACM-SIGFIDET Workshop on Data Description, Access and Control, San Diego, California, November 11-12, 1971, pp. 1–17. ACM Press, New York (1971)

[7] Date, C.J., Fagin, R.: Simple Conditions for Guaranteeing Higher Normal Forms in Relational Databases. ACM Transactions on Database Systems (TODS) 17(3), 465–476 (1992)

[8] Srivastava, B., Koehler, J.: Web Service Composition - Current Solutions and Open Problems. In: ICAPS (2003)

[9] Milanovic, N., Malek, M.: Current Solutions for Web Service Composition. IEEE Internet Computing 8(6), 51–59 (2004), http://dx.doi.org/10.1109/MIC.2004.58

[10] Peltz, C.: Web Services Orchestration and Choreography. Computer 36(10), 46–52 (2003)

[11] Pasley, J.: How BPEL and SOA Are Changing Web Services Development. IEEE Internet Computing 9(3), 60–67 (2005)

A BPEL Based Implementation of Online Auctions

Morad Benyoucef[1] and Ronald Pringadi[2]

[1] School of Management
[2] School of Information Technology and Engineering
University of Ottawa, 136 Jean-Jacques Lussier St. Ottawa, Ontario K1N 6N5, Canada
{benyoucef@management.uottawa.ca, pringadi@site.uottawa.ca}

Abstract. Service oriented architectures have been adopted by many organizations in order to increase business automation, integrate enterprise systems, and reach more business partners and customers. Among the business processes that can greatly harness the advantages of web services are online auctions. This paper proposes a new approach for modeling online auctions and provides guidelines on how to use web service orchestration to model them. Our research involves the design of an auction server and its clients for manual as well as automated agent-based bidding. We propose a framework for a server that is generic enough to host various types of auctions and extensible enough for future component additions. We report on an implementation of our framework based on the BPEL web service orchestration language.

Keywords: online auction, process modeling, web service orchestration, BPEL.

1 Introduction

Negotiation, as defined in [1], is an iterative communication and decision making process between two or more parties which can be represented by two or more agents who cannot achieve their objectives through unilateral actions and who search for consensus. Negotiation can be very intensive, time consuming, and costly; therefore, there is a need to automate it [2]. Any negotiation conducted using computers or other electronic devices is referred to as electronic negotiation (*e-negotiation*). Because of the strong domination of auctions in the field of negotiations, some might think that e-negotiations primarily consist of online auctions [4]. This is obviously not true. Although this paper concentrates on online auctions, we believe that other negotiation protocols (i.e., scenarios or styles) can and should be conducted electronically.

Current research on e-negotiation systems (ENS) mostly focuses on negotiating software agents, negotiation strategies, and negotiation automation. Few initiatives addressed the problems of designing a platform that enables these interactions. After a thorough review of the literature on e-negotiation frameworks for servers and clients [5] we learned that although these frameworks have several design qualities, most do not foster reusability and extensibility. Furthermore, most frameworks fail to address the following requirements: the design should support various negotiation protocols [6], it has to offer high flexibility [7], and it must foster easy development and deployment [8]. Moreover, we believe that it must facilitate the interactions of negotiators, enable the participation of human as well as software agents, and permit the

D. Georgakopoulos et al. (Eds.): ICSOC 2006 Ws, LNCS 4652, pp. 104–115, 2007.
© Springer-Verlag Berlin Heidelberg 2007

seamless integration of the e-negotiation platform with different applications inside the organization and across partner organizations.

Designing an e-negotiation platform which addresses all the requirements mentioned above is obviously not an easy task, especially knowing that it will involve business-to-business (B2B) and application-to-application (A2A) integration. According to Basu and Kumar (2002) [9], marketplace-based architecture is a good solution for managing inter-organizational processes such as negotiation. A marketplace-based architecture connects companies more efficiently than a point-to-point connection between every buyer and every supplier. Other design challenges include formalizing the shared protocol [10], extracting the business logic from the server process, which is needed by the clients to properly interact with the server [8], and validating the rules of negotiation to ensure a fair and correct process.

Many companies have recently expanded their presence online. Internet based business enables them to reach more potential customers and suppliers, provide around the clock service, and reduce operational costs. This move has shifted the trend of object-oriented design into a service oriented design, where software modules are converted into web services and published over the Internet to be used as-is or to be integrated with other applications. Because web services are XML based protocols, they have the advantage of providing a platform-independent service which facilitates B2B and A2A integration.

The contributions of this paper are threefold. First, we work within a new vision for designing e-negotiation systems (servers and clients) using a service oriented approach. We propose a design framework for auction servers and clients to be used for manual as well as automated agent-based bidding. The framework is generic enough to host various types of auctions and extensible enough for future component additions. The framework is centered on modeling auctions as web service orchestrations. We deploy a common interface for human participants to interact directly with the server, and for software agents to be configured and controlled by their owner. Second, we report on an implementation of our framework based on the BPEL web service orchestration language. Third, we focus on the task of modeling auction processes as web service orchestrations. Although in this paper we only report on the English auction, we modeled and enacted several auction processes such as the Dutch and sealed-bid auctions as well as negotiation processes such as the two-party negotiation. We provide modeling guidelines and identify common components in the models that can constitute a repository to be used when modeling negotiation protocols.

The rest of the paper is organized as follows. Section 2 discusses auctions as a fundamental form of negotiation. Section 3 introduces general design considerations for e-negotiation systems. Section 4 reports on the architecture and implementation of our online auction framework. Section 5 is dedicated to modeling auction processes. We discuss our modeling approach in Section 6, describe related work in Section 7, and wrap up the paper with a conclusion in Section 8.

2   Auctions as a Form of Negotiation

Auctions are a form of negotiation [4]. Negotiation itself is divided into business and non-business negotiation. Business negotiation includes auctions, two-party negotiation (i.e., bargaining), business procurement, brokerages, exchanges, and cartels [3], while non-business negotiation includes dispute resolution and voting.

There are various types of auctions, and at least five key elements can be extracted from them [9]: (1) a deal which can be in various states such as "negotiable offer" or "final offer"; (2) participants such as buyers, sellers, and auctioneers; (3) messages sent by participants to modify the deal such as "new bid"; (4) process flow describing how the state of the deal changes as a result of the messages sent by participants; and (5) messages sent to participants as the deal changes.

Auction scenarios (also called protocols) specify the rules of the negotiation [11], and different scenarios serve different purposes. Some of the most common scenarios are the English auction, Vickrey auction, sealed bid auction, and Dutch auction. The English auction is perhaps the most widely used scenario. Its popularity has grown mainly as a result of its adoption by eBay (www.eBay.com). There were at least 75.4 million active users in the first quarter of 2006 either buying or selling items using eBay's English auction protocol [12]. The English auction is a process where a seller tries to sell an item and potential buyers bid on the item. The bid increases over time. At the end of the process, which can be triggered by a timeout or when no bids have been received for a period of time, the highest bidder wins the item. A starting bid can be set to ensure that bids are close to the item's estimated value. A reserve price can be set to protect the seller from selling below a certain price. A variation of the English auction is the Vickrey auction. Here, the winning bidder pays the second highest bid, which encourages potential buyers to outbid one another. Sealed bid auctions are held when, among other situations, it is impractical for bidders to prepare bids instantaneously or the bid confidentiality is important. In single round sealed bid auctions, all bidders submit their bids by a deadline; the bids are then evaluated at this deadline. In multi-round sealed bid auctions, there is a deadline for each round of bids. At that deadline, either the auction is closed or a fresh round of bids is started with a new deadline. The Dutch auction is a mechanism where the seller starts the process by setting the price of an item. As the auction progresses, the seller lowers the price gradually until a buyer bids on the item. If there is only one unique item, the auction ends immediately with the bid. Otherwise, the auction continues, and the seller keeps lowering the price and buyers making bids until the last item is sold.

3 General Design Considerations

There are two basic components of e-negotiations: protocols and strategies [13]. Protocols define the rules of interaction between negotiation agents (participants) and the sequences of allowed offers. In general, agents must agree on the protocol before negotiation begins. Strategies are action plans for the negotiation agents to follow in evaluating offers and formulating counteroffers. Usually there are several strategies for a particular protocol, and each one may produce a different outcome.

E-negotiations are further divided into unsupported, supported, and automated [1] processes. In unsupported e-negotiations, the participants control and manage all tasks without support or advice from a system. Supported e-negotiations involve the help of a system for decision making. Automated e-negotiations involve software agents that make decisions based on negotiation strategies and tactics provided by their owner.

Finally, at the system level, e-negotiations are divided into Negotiation Support Systems (NSS), Negotiation Software Agents (NSA), and e-negotiation servers. NSS are software tools that support negotiation activities such as eliciting preferences, evaluating and comparing offers based on the elicited preferences, and recommending strategies. NSS's main functions are to assist users with information gathering, problem structuring and generating alternatives for decision-making activities. NSA are AI (artificial intelligence) enabled software entities which communicate with other entities and make decisions on behalf of their owner [7]. NSA's main concerns are about software agents' strategies and performance [14]. E-negotiation servers are software systems that implement a negotiation protocol and provide a platform for participants to interact. In the literature, negotiation servers are also referred to as negotiation media, platforms, or negotiation-enabled e-marketplaces.

4   Architecture and Implementation

Web service orchestration is a way of composing and coordinating web services to obtain higher-level business processes. It describes how web services interact with each other at the message level and tracks the sequence of messages including the business logic and execution order of the interactions [15].

There are standards available to orchestrate web services such as BPEL (Business Process Execution Language) [16]. BPEL is designed to address the orchestration complexity, thereby reducing time-to-market and costs and increasing the overall efficiency and accuracy of business processes. It stands as a layer on top of WSDL. While WSDL describes the messages' data types, port types, allowed operations, and partner roles, BPEL describes partner bindings, incoming and outgoing variables, and operation logic sequences. BPEL supports common repetition (while-loop), selection (if-then-else, select-case), error handling (try-catch), parallel processing, and Java embedding. As a widely adopted orchestration language providing the necessary business logic to compose complete running processes, we decided to use BPEL to model and enact online auction processes.

4.1   Server Design

The e-negotiation server is where the online auction process is created and executed. It can be deployed either by one of the participants or by a third party provider (i.e., facilitator). We believe a third party deployment is better because it provides for a common ontology and interfaces to be shared by participants as well as transparent, optimal and efficient processes. The server's conceptual architecture is shown in Fig. 1.

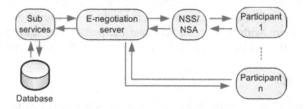

Fig. 1. Conceptual architecture of the e-negotiation server

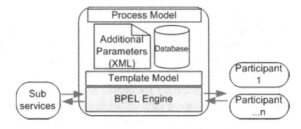

Fig. 2. Internal design of the e-negotiation server

Table 1. XML configuration files

File Name	Listing

English.xml	```<Auction scenario="EnglishAuction">```
	``` <bidVisibility>TRUE</bidVisibility>```
	``` <idleTime>5</idleTime>```
	``` <deadline>15</deadline>```
	``` <highestBidderVisibiity>```
	``` PUBLIC</highestBidderVisibility>```
	``` <useReservePrice>TRUE</useReservePrice>```
	```<Auction>```

Dutch.xml	```<Auction scenario="DutchAuction">```
	``` <quantityVisibility>FALSE</quantityVisibility >```
	``` <deadline>20</deadline>```
	``` <multipleItem>TRUE<multipleItem>```
	```</Auction>```

As suggested in [3], there are several tasks common to all auction scenarios. These are implemented as the following services (sub services in Fig. 1): registration and authentication; posting; bidding; information retrieval, history log, and gateway services which coordinate all the services. Participants have the option to interact with the server directly or through an NSS or NSA. We designed the e-negotiation server and the participants (sellers and buyers) as web services. To orchestrate these web services we use the BPEL Process Manager. We visually model the auction using JDeveloper [17]. The resulting model is compiled and deployed on the BPEL engine (see Fig. 2). To avoid an eventual recompilation and redeployment of the model after a minor change, we transfer additional parameters (bid visibility, idle time, auction deadline, etc.) out of the business logic of the auction process and into an external XML file. The template model in Fig. 2 is a collection of classes which bind together the BPEL process model, the XML configuration file, and the database. This is achieved using the java embedding component. The auction model is implemented in the BPEL process flow, which will be discussed in Section 5. The XML configuration files for the English and Dutch auctions are shown in Table 1. The BPEL engine is the core component of the e-negotiation server where the execution of communication level operations with the sub services and the participants takes place. The participants access all services offered by the server through the BPEL engine.

4.2 Client Design

We consider two types of participants: one who uses the provided interface (*manual negotiation client*), and one who builds an interface and connects it to the e-negotiation server for automation purposes and for employing AI techniques such as learning and using negotiation strategies (*automated negotiation client*). Both clients have the same access point which is the BPEL engine's web service port.

Automated negotiation clients can communicate with the server and join the negotiation process by accessing the BPEL engine and using the WSDL file. They can call the services offered by the server using its operation name and passing the necessary variables. The gateway service will ensure that all clients have valid identification and proper access through every phase of the negotiation process.

The web service discovery does not need to be done through UDDI; instead, it can be done through a web page that gives the location of the WSDL file and explains how to utilize the web service. The automated negotiation clients can process the information they get from the e-negotiation server and pass it to their NSS or NSA using a SOAP message tunneling mechanism.

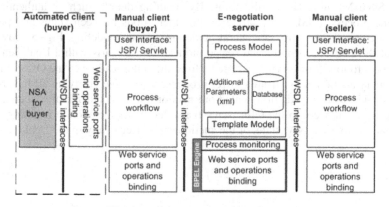

Fig. 3. Manual and automated clients

Fig. 3 shows the manual and automated clients. Every interaction between the e-negotiation server and the clients is executed through web service ports and operations. Similar to the manual client, the automated client also connects to the server using the same web service ports and operations interface; however, the automated client passes the information from the server to the NSA. The NSA is implemented as an independent component offering various strategy-oriented web services. This approach increases the reusability of the NSA. The server's process model in Fig. 3 is the BPEL process mentioned earlier. The java embedding components in the BPEL process access specific negotiation attributes (XML file) and use the database.

To simplify the connection between the BPEL engine and the clients, we use the *Façade* design pattern to get and set variables in the BPEL engine, and to invoke or receive other web services (see Fig. 4). We also use the *Model-View-Controller design pattern*. The *model* holds the logic of the process such as handling incoming or outgoing messages, adding AI capabilities to the system, forwarding information further to a customized NSA, and giving instructions to the Façade object. The *view* is where the display is generated based on the current negotiation phases and variables. The *controller* is an HTML form where the user provides input (see Fig. 4).

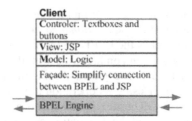

Fig. 4. Client's user interface

5 Modeling

Kumar and Feldman [3] proposed templates for modeling auction processes using Finite State Machine (FSM) diagrams. By omitting details such as authentication from the process, FSMs concentrate on the interactions between states and participants. We use these FSMs as general guidelines in our modeling. Fig. 5 shows the FSM of the English open cry and sealed bid auctions. It starts with a Deal Template (DT) state, followed by an `OfferToSell` from the seller leading to the Offer state. In an open cry auction, a bid from a buyer produces a message notifying all buyers that the best bid has changed; in a sealed-bid auction the best bid remains secret. Two other events can occur in the Offer state: the seller closes the auction resulting in the Negotiation Aborted (NA) state, or the auction ends successfully in the Deal (D) state.

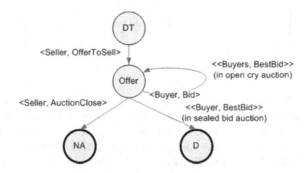

Fig. 5. FSM for the English open cry and sealed bid auctions [3]

Due to the detailed nature of auction processes and the large sizes of the models we developed, showing them in their original form (i.e., screenshots) would sacrifice their details and sharpness. Thus we use an activity diagram notation that provides the same functionalities as BPEL but which is more readable.

Fig. 6 presents the BPEL process description of the English auction. In the diagram, we use the `scope-and-expand` method. A `scope` is a collection of activities represented by a plus sign "(+)" that can be *expanded* into a subsequent activity diagram. We assume that all participants have completed the registration process before the start of the auction. The registration process does not appear in the diagram.

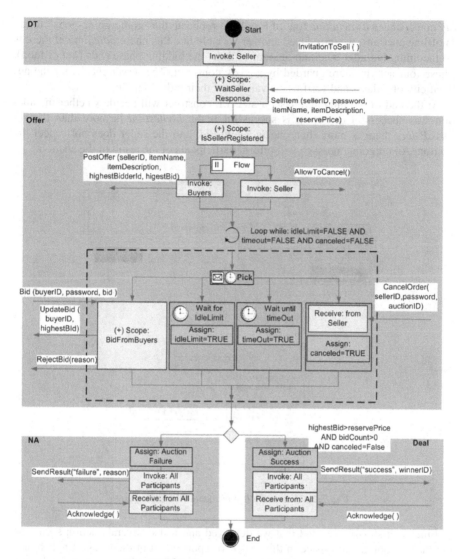

Fig. 6. BPEL diagram for the English auction

The "Scope: WaitSellerResponse" is a collection of activities that wait for a response from a seller for a certain amount of time, ensuring that he/she has enough time to respond. The expansion of this scope is shown in Fig. 7-a. After receiving an *item to sell* message from the seller, the server will check whether the seller is registered or not. If the seller is not registered, the process does not proceed (Fig. 7-b). Otherwise, the server executes a parallel flow to initiate the bidding phase by invoking the seller so he/she can cancel the auction if he/she wishes to do so, and by posting the item so that buyers can start bidding on it. The bidding phase is a loop mechanism. In the English auction FSM (Fig. 5), the activities that can happen during the bidding phase are: *buyer bids* (back to loop); *seller cancels* (out of loop); and *auction reaches its deadline* (out of loop). To replicate the "going-going-gone" found in offline auctions, we introduced another variable into this phase: *idle time*. If there is no incoming bid after a certain amount of time, the bidding phase ends (out of loop). These four activities are guarded by a `pick` construct. The server checks for the authenticity of bidders and verifies the validity of their bids (Fig. 7-c).

At the end of the bidding phase, a `switch` construct will decide whether the auction was successful or not. It is successful if the *highestBid* is more than the *reservePrice;* there is more than one *incomingBid*; and the seller does not cancel the auction. An outgoing message will inform participants of the result of the auction.

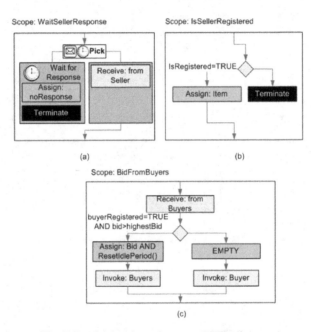

Fig. 7. English auction subsequent BPEL diagrams

Finally, it should be noted that we deployed and tested several auction scenarios, but there is not enough space in this paper to report on all of them. The English auction gives a good idea on the expressive power of BPEL and web service orchestration languages in general for modeling and enacting auction scenarios.

6 Discussion

The formalisms used to describe auction processes usually capture their most common components. In real-life situations the complexity of the auction process may vary, but the basic concepts remain the same. BPEL process flow complexity increases as we deal with sub processes such as authentication, validation of input, and additional negotiation parameters (bid visibility, item quantity, etc.).

By looking at the process diagrams of various auctions, we identified the following similarities which may constitute a basis for a repository of reusable templates.

(1) The Deal Template (DT) state (Fig. 6) consists of specific negotiation rules which are agreed upon before the process starts. Since BPEL stands on top of WSDL, it is easy to manage the message interactions. Every incoming or outgoing message format has to conform to the WSDL description. In all our BPEL process diagrams, the DT is always marked with a void invitation or initiation from the server; the seller has to reply with an offer.

(2) The Offer state (Fig. 6) might vary slightly between different auction protocols. However, there are unique sequences present in all our BPEL process diagrams. The sequences are: `receive` which gets the offer from the seller; `flow` which `invokes` participants and allows them to reply by sending a message to the server; and `pick` which determines what events arrive first. Before the `pick` construct there is a `while` which creates a repetitive cycle for the bidding phase.

(3) Mechanisms in `scope-and-expand` activities (Fig. 7) can act as reusable components for different auction protocols. At the moment, BPEL does not support any process modularization or component reusability; therefore, there are no BPEL fragments that can be invoked from within the same or from different BPEL processes [18]. But IBM and SAP are working on a sub-process extension for BPEL (BPEL-SPE) [19]. In the meantime, there are several possible solutions that we can adopt to address this problem. First, we can implement the reusable components as independent web services. For example, the main process calls a reusable web service such as "IsSellerRegistered", and the web service answers with TRUE or FALSE. However, due to the nature of web services, this approach exposes the sub-components of the system, thus raising a security concern. One solution could be to filter the caller's IP address as a precaution. Second, we can implement the reusable components as java classes. In the BPEL process flow diagram, we can define a `java embedding` component which will replace the `scope-and-expand`. But since this approach would defeat the purpose of visual modeling which we seek in our framework; we prefer the first approach. Additionally, unlike BPEL-SPE, the two approaches do not have a synchronous connection between the main process and the sub processes. For example, if the sub processes are terminated abruptly, the main process cannot be informed; therefore, it may stall or produce errors.

7 Related Work

Kim and Segev (2005) proposed an attribute-based negotiation process composer [7], which is a system that enables the negotiation designer to generate a set of BPEL constructs. These constructs are useful in creating a new e-negotiation marketplace and orchestrating its interactions in a web service environment. The system's main function is to customize, generate, and validate a series of constructs for BPEL processes. There is no user interface, such as dynamic web pages that can access the web service for the participant. After the generation of the BPEL constructs, they still need to be complied and deployed on the BPEL engine. This can become time consuming when slight modifications are introduced. In our framework, we prefer to model the auction scenarios and store the attributes in an external XML configuration file; this way we avoid re-compilation and re-deployment after minor changes.

Rolli and Eberhart (2005) proposed a model to describe and run Internet-based auctions [20]. The model presents three layers: auction data, auction mechanism, and auction participants. The authors implemented a prototype using Collaxa's BPEL4WS modeling editor. This editor is now part of Oracle BPEL PM [21]. The produced models are compiled using BPEL2Java [22] then executed within a Java environment. BPEL was used for modeling the general negotiation activities, and the modeling was completed with Java code, which is not convenient for the negotiation designer. Interactions between the platform and the participants are carried out using Java-RMI [23]. Our approach is more user-friendly and takes advantage of the modeling paradigm.

8 Conclusion

This paper presented a service oriented online auction framework that is generic enough to support various auction protocols. To create an online auction, designers visually model the process using a web service orchestration language such as BPEL, possibly reusing existing components. The approach reduces the need for designers to understand programming concepts (at least for the high level design), allowing them to focus on the business view. Our framework promotes loose coupling and reusability. It is easy to extend the system with additional components such as an NSA and still use the same ports and interfaces. With standard open interfaces such as web services, every service is platform independent. To our knowledge, this research is the first to thoroughly test the use of web service orchestration for hosting online auctions.

There are limitations inherent to web service orchestration languages. Unlike other programming languages, BPEL is still growing. The real purpose of BPEL is to model and orchestrate web services; therefore its expressiveness is not as effective as a real programming language. For instance, there is only one starting point and one exit point in a BPEL process, which makes for one monolithic process. Furthermore, although BPEL provides java embedding, its Java Runtime Environment (JRE) still lacks compatibility with existing java implementations. We did not address or implement any form of security, this issue being beyond the objectives of this paper.

This research opened new opportunities for studying the behavior of software agents when provided with bidding strategies. We are using an implementation of our auction framework to conduct bidding tournaments between software agents. The separation of the auction description (the model) from the server is enabling us to be more efficient in deploying and studying new auction scenarios.

References

1. Bichler, M., Kersten, G., Strecker, S.: Towards a Structured Design of Electronic Negotiations. Group Decision and Negotiation 12, 311–335 (2003)
2. Hurwitz.com, Negotiated Trade: the Next Frontier for B2B e-commerce. Tech Report (2000)

3. Kumar, M., Feldman, S.I.: Business negotiations on the Internet. IBM Research Division - T.J. Watson Research Center (1998)
4. Kersten, G.E.: E-negotiation systems: Interaction of people and technologies to resolve conflicts. In: UNESCAP. Third Annual Forum on Online Dispute Resolution, Melbourne, Australia, July 5-6, 2004, pp. 5–6 (2004)
5. Pringadi, R., Benyoucef, M.: Web Service Orchestration of E-negotiation Interactions. Working Paper #wp06-28, School of Management, University of Ottawa (2006)
6. Benyoucef, M., et al.: Towards a Generic E-Negotiation Platform. In: Kropf, P.G., Babin, G., Plaice, J., Unger, H. (eds.) DCW 2000. LNCS, vol. 1830, pp. 95–109. Springer, Heidelberg (2000)
7. Kim, J.B., Segev, A.: A Web Services-enabled Marketplace Architecture for Negotiation Process Management. Decision Support Systems 40, 71–87 (2005)
8. Mathieu, P., Verrons, M.-H.: ANTS: an API for creating negotiation applications. In: 10th ISPE International conference on concurrent engineering: research and application, Madeira Island - Portugal (July 26-30, 2003)
9. Basu, A., Kumar, A.: Research commentary: workflow management issues in e-business. Information Systems Research 13, 1–14 (2002)
10. Bartolini, C., Preist, C., Jennings, N.R.: A Generic Software Framework for Automated Negotiation. Trusted E-Services Laboratory - HP Laboratories Bristol (2002)
11. Weinhardt, C., Gomber, P.: Agent-Mediated Off-Exchange Trading. In: Proceedings of the 32nd Hawaii Conf. on System Sciences, Maui, Hawaii, January 5-8, 1999, pp. 6–9 (1999)
12. eBay.com. eBay Announces First Quarter, Financial Results - 19 April. 2006 [cited August 2006] (2006), Available from http://investor.ebay.com/releases.cfm?FYear=2006
13. Lomuscio, A.R., Wooldridge, M., Jennings, N.R.: A Classification Scheme for Negotiation in Electronic Commerce. Group Decision and Negotiation 12(12), 31–56 (2003)
14. Rust, J., Miller, J., Palmer, R.: Behavior of trading automata in a computerized double auction market. In: The Double Auction Market: Institutions, Theories, and Evidence, pp. 153–196. Addison Wesley, Reading (1993)
15. Peltz, C.: Web Services Orchestration. Hewlett-Packard Company (2003)
16. IBM, et al.: Business Process Execution Language for Web Services version 1.1, [cited August 2005] (2002), Available from www.ibm.com/developerworks/library/ws-bpel
17. Oracle.com. Oracle JDeveloper 10^g. [cited 2006] (2005), Available from: www.oracle.com/technology/products/jdev/index.html
18. Trickovic, I.: Modularization and reuse in WS-BPEL. SAP Developer Network - SDN Community Contribution Whitepaper (October 2005)
19. Kloppmann, M., et al.: WS-BPEL Extension for Sub-processes - BPEL-SPE. SAP Developer Network Whitepaper (September 2005)
20. Rolli, D., Eberhart, A.: An Auction Reference Model for Describing and Running Auctions. Wirtschaftsinformatik, pp. 289–308 (2005)
21. Boulton, C.: Oracle Goes SOA with Collaxa Buy 2004 [cited 2005 August 15] (2004) Available from: http://www.internetnews.com/bus-news/article.php/3374851
22. eclipse.org. BPEL to Java (B2J) Subproject. [cited 24 August 2006] Available from: http://www.eclipse.org/stp/b2j/
23. sun.com. Java Remote Method Invocation (Java RMI). [cited 24 August 2006] (2006), Available from http://java.sun.com/products/jdk/rmi/

Dynamic Binding for BPEL Processes –
A Lightweight Approach to Integrate Semantics
into Web Services

Ulrich Küster and Birgitta König-Ries

Institute of Computer Science, Friedrich-Schiller-Universität Jena
D-07743 Jena, Germany
ukuester,koenig@informatik.uni-jena.de

Abstract. The area of service oriented computing stretches between two extremes: On the one hand industry has pushed a whole stack of WS-* standards and tools to support the integration of distributed services into business applications. These standards are used in production environments and are applied successfully, e.g. in the area of enterprise application integration. However, the expensive and labor intensive task of putting together services and maintaining and administering the composed applications has to be done manually. In contrast, academia is busily working on numerous efforts leveraging ontology based semantics and various AI planning techniques to automate these tasks. Yet, up to now the developed technologies have rarely if ever been applied in industry. In our opinion, this has two main reasons: there is high cost involved in creating the necessary comprehensive ontologies and businesses are reluctant to trust semantic technologies. In this paper we bring together the extremes in order to combine their strengths. We show how to flexibly integrate advanced semantic service discovery, composition and invocation technology into manually created standard BPEL processes. Our approach leaves it to the discretion of the developer to flexibly choose an appropriate degree of automation for the process at hand and thus offers him complete control over the usage of semantic technology.

1 Introduction

In recent years, service orientation has evolved as a new paradigm for distributed computing. A whole stack of Web service standards and technologies has been created [1,2] that forms the maybe most promising implementation of this paradigm. These standards are widely used in production environments and are applied successfully, e.g. in the area of enterprise application integration. Even though web service technology has thus proven to be an effective way of creating widely distributed and loosely coupled systems, the tasks of gluing together the component services and maintaining the composition is still labor intensive and expensive work. Furthermore, the potential of the web service technology cannot be used to full capacity, if service compositions have to be created manually and component services are bound statically in those compositions. To leverage

D. Georgakopoulos et al. (Eds.): ICSOC 2006 Ws, LNCS 4652, pp. 116–127, 2007.

the potential availability of thousands of services, automated composition and dynamic discovery and binding are needed.

Academia has thus been working busily on numerous efforts providing ontology based semantic descriptions for services. Based on these descriptions, frameworks are designed to support dynamic service discovery and binding. Various AI planning techniques are applied to (semi-)automatically synthesize service compositions from available component services. Together, these techniques will allow to synthesize an application at runtime from the currently most applicable services in a fully automated fashion. This enables low-effort development of robust, dynamically adaptable applications.

However, up to now, the developed semantic based technologies have rarely – if ever – been applied on a large scale in industry. In our opinion, there are two main reasons for this lack of adaptation: First, a prerequisite to using semantic technology is the existence of comprehensive domain ontologies. For most applications, these ontologies do not yet exist. The prospect of having to create them from scratch is rather daunting. The entrance cost for using semantic technology may thus seem forbiddingly high. Second, maybe as a consequence of the AI hype and comparable failure in the past, semantic technologies are regarded with a certain degree of scepticism by many potential users. A widespread –albeit unfounded – lack of trust into the reliability and correctness of these technologies hinders their acceptance.

In this paper, we present an approach to bridge the gap between web service technology used in practice and the promising semantic techniques. This approach enables the gradual integration of semantics-based techniques into existing web service applications. Standard based, well proven web service technology offers stability and control while advanced semantic technology supports dynamic change, adaptability and the potential to take advantage of large numbers of competing service providers. We show how to integrate fully automated service discovery, composition and invocation technology into pre-existing, manually created standard BPEL processes. This leaves it to the discretion of the developer to flexibly choose any appropriate degree of automation within a given process. For instance, a developer may decide to compose modeling intensive tasks or tasks with high security constraints manually, while at the same time using semantic technology for tasks that are highly dynamic or not as expensive to model semantically. We believe that only within such a combination semantic technologies have a chance to overcome the current gap between academia and industry.

Throughout the remainder of the paper, we use the order management system of COS-tec, an imaginary computer online store, as our running example. This order management is currently implemented by a BPEL process. Figure 1 depicts a small cutout of the entire process. Process steps include receiving the order from the customer, checking for item availability and calling a shipment service. In the current BPEL-process, the latter is realized – as is typical for such processes – by a static binding to an external shipment provider. This static binding has a number of disadvantages: If the chosen provider becomes temporarily or permanently unavailable, a new provider has to be searched for and the process has to be manually adapted. Also, the chosen provider may not be the cheapest for all types of packages. There might be considerable potential for cost reduction, by choosing the cheapest provider for each individual package. In the current process, this is not done, since the cost for manually comparing prices and manually binding to the appropriate provider in each case may very well outweigh the reduction in shipment cost. Here, semantic technology offers a solution: In our approach, the BPEL process is adapted to calling a semantics-based middleware instead of the shipment provider. This middleware uses a semantic description of the desired shipment to dynamically find and bind the most appropriate shipment provider. This offers both robustness and cost effectiveness. In the remainder of this paper, we will show that using our approach, the effort involved in adapting the BPEL process and thus the cost of leveraging the advantages of semantic technology is very moderate. The rest of

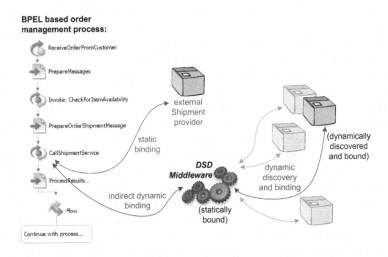

Fig. 1. Dynamic shipment provider discovery and binding for COS-tec's order management BPEL process

this paper is organized as follows: In Section 2 we introduce DSD, the semantic service description language used and the middleware built to support it. In Section 3 we show how to integrate DSD service requests into BPEL processes and how the DSD-Middleware is leveraged to execute these requests when the process runs. In Sections 4 and 5 we evaluate our approach and compare it to the related work and finally in Section 6 we summarize and conclude.

2   DIANE Service Descriptions

At the core of all approaches to semantic web services are *ontology-based languages* that enable the description of service offers and requests and *algorithms* that allow to compare offers and requests in order to find (and bind) the most appropriate service provider for a given offer. The approaches differ in the languages used, the constructs they allow for service descriptions, the information from the descriptions that is taken into account when comparing offers and requests and the degree to which they allow for automatic configuration and binding. This paper uses our *DIANE Service Description, DSD* [3]. DSD is particularly suitable for the task at hand because of its superior matchmaking capabilities that combine expressiveness with efficient matchmaking and the ability of full automation up to the actual invocation of a discovered service. However, the approach presented could be implemented based on other languages that meet the requirements identified in the evaluation section, too.

In addition to the elements usually found in ontology-based languages, i.e. concepts, their attributes and instances, DSD comprises the following elements geared specifically at capturing the specifics of service descriptions:

- *operational elements:* Services change the state of the real-world (or the information space). Operational elements allow to express this world-altering capacity. In the example shown in Figure 2, you'll find the operand *effect*, describing that we are looking for a service that changes the state of the world in such a way, that something is shipped.
- *aggregating elements:* A service is typically able to offer not one specific effect, but a set of similar effects. A shipment service for instance will be able to offer transport of different kinds of goods from one arbitrary destination to another. That means, services offer to provide one out of a set of effects. Requestors on the other hand, typically are not looking for one specific service, but for any element of the set of services that can provide the desired effect. *Sets* are depicted in DSD with a small diagonal line in the upper left corner of a concept.
- *selecting elements:* While a service will offer different effects, the provider will typically allow the requestor to configure the service to choose which of these effects should be provided in a specific instance. In DSD, *variables* are used to for this task. In our example, the requestor will specify the exact weight, dimension and delivery address upon invocation.
- *rating elements:* This type of element is used in service requests only. Requestors will typically be willing to invoke services with slightly differing effects. In our example, the requestor is willing to pay any price below 500 USD but would prefer lower prices over higher ones. These preferences can be expressed by rating elements. Rating elements are a key feature of DSD. They allow the requestor to prescribe the desired effect and also acceptable deviations very precisely, thus maximising the likelihood of finding the most appropriate service.

Let us summarize the service request template depicted in Figure 2: COS-Tec is looking for a service that results in something being shipped from their address to an address that will be specified upon request execution. Weight and dimensions of the good to be shipped will also be filled into the request template as input variables. As an output, COS-Tec expects the price in USD. This price should be at most 500 USD. Available service offers will be described in a similar fashion. During service discovery, the DSD matcher will compare available offers with the request. For this comparison the request tree is traversed and for each set the matcher determines whether the set in the offer is a subset of the set in the request, thereby ensuring that the effect provided by the service is one that the requestor really wanted. This comparison can be done quite efficiently and results in very precise matching results. This is one of the strengths of DSD compared with other matchmaking algorithms: Typically, they either take not all the information avaiable in the offer into account or they are not efficient (most of the time not even decidable).

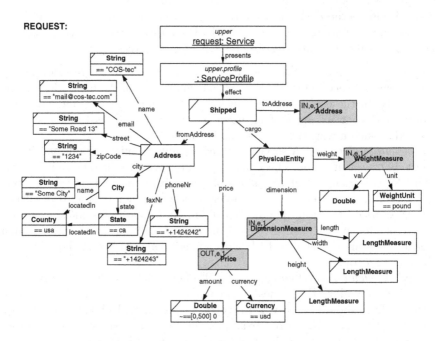

Fig. 2. Example request for a shipment service (some details have been omitted)

3   Integrating DSD into BPEL Processes

The basic idea how to integrate the DSD-Middleware into a BPEL process is to make it available through a web service interface. The BPEL process can then send service requests to that interface, thereby invoking the DSD-Middleware which will locate available offers, find the best suitable one and call the corresponding service provider with appropriately configured parameters. This architecture is shown in Figure 3. The major difficulty involved in this approach is to provide easy to handle yet powerful and expressive mapping mechanisms to translate the XML-based legacy data representation of the BPEL process into ontology based semantic request descriptions understood by

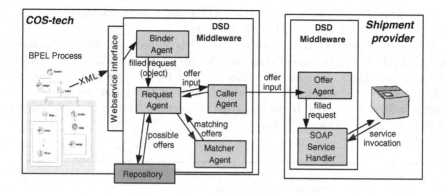

Fig. 3. Overview of implemented architecture

the DSD-Middleware. In the following we will first explain this mechanism and then give some more detail about how the DSD-Middleware works.

3.1 Mapping from Legacy Data to Semantic Request Descriptions

We anticipate that for most use cases the structure of regularly occurring requests like our shipment service discovery requests (compare to Figure 2) will remain fairly stable, but parameters and variable values will change. We therefore decided not to build a request from scratch within the BPEL process but to rather deploy a request template to the DSD-Middleware at design time which will be filled with variable values at runtime. This way the creation of the request description can be done in the editors designed for that within the DSD framework and is completely separated from the existing BPEL legacy order management. All the order management has to do and all that has to be changed in the BPEL process is that the process needs to send the name of the request template to use and the parameters (like address, package weight, package pickup time...) in BPEL friendly XML format to the webservice interface of the middleware. The format of those parameters (i.e. the XML schema) may be defined by the legacy BPEL process and the middleware therefore adapts to the existing process and not vice versa.

The BinderAgent component of the middleware is responsible for the management of deployed request templates. It will be called by the webservice interface, locate the template corresponding to a given request name and transform the given input XML parameters to ontological concepts and instances represented as Java objects (the data format used internally by the middleware). The information how to do that transformation can be defined declaratively in the request template's grounding by specifying XmlDsdMapping instances as shown in Figure 4. Each mapping identifies a variable from the request and a node from the given XML parameters that is used to fill that variable. The node is specified using an arbitrary XPath expression; this offers great flexibility. If the expression evaluates to a node list instead of a single node, multiple instances of the variable to fill will be created as necessary.

Where necessary a custom converter class and method name may be optionally specified which will be used by the middleware to unmarshall the contents of the node into DSD variables. The price variable for instance is filled with data taken from the "maximumPrice" child element of the given parameters. The unmarshalling is provided by invoking the "convertToPriceDescription" method of the "MaxPriceConverter" class.

```
...
mapping += anonymous XmlDsdMapping [
    variable = $price,
    dataNodePath = "maximumPrice",
    converterClassName = "MaxPriceConverter",
    converterMethodName = "convertToPriceDescription"
],
mapping += anonymous XmlDsdMapping [
    variable = $cargo,
    dataNodePath = "package"
    attributeMappings += anonymous XmlDsdAttributeMapping [
        attributePath = "weight/val",
        subNodePath = "weight"
    ],
    attributeMappings += anonymousXmlDsdAttributeMapping [
        attributePath = "dimension/length/val",
        subNodePath = "length"
    ],
    ...
],
...
```

Fig. 4. Excerpt from mapping definitions XML to DSD variables

Usually the deployment of such custom converter classes is not necessary. If no custom converter class is given, two cases need to be distinguished: If the variable to fill is of a simple type (corresponding to XML Schema's atomic types), standard marshalling will be used to fill it using the value from the specified node. If the variable has a complex type, an empty variable of that type will be initialized and XmlDsdAttributeMapping instances have to be provided that define how its attributes will be filled. These submappings work similar to the XmlDsdMappings but operate in the context of the variable and node specified by the parent mapping. As XmlDsdAttributeMappings can be nested arbitrarily deep this mechanism is flexible enough to deal with any content, including nested lists. As shown in Figure 4 the "cargo" variable will be filled with data from the "package" child element of the given parameters. If multiple "package" child elements are found, multiple "cargo" variables will be created. The fillings of the "cargo" variable's attributes are defined by the given attributeMappings. The "weight" attribute's "val" attribute for instance (compare to Figure 2) will be filled using the data from the child element "weight" of the node that had been identified by the "package" XPath expression. Since the type of the "val" attribute is a simple double type and no converter class is specified, standard unmarshalling will be used. As shown in the next mapping definition, variable attributes may be identified using concatenated paths. In this case the "val" attribute of the "length" attribute of the "dimension" attribute of the "cargo" variable is filled (Note that this attribute has been omitted in Figure 2 for the sake of clarity).

3.2 Request Execution by the DSD-Middleware

Once the BinderAgent has translated the input XML to DSD variables and filled the request template accordingly, that request is forwarded to the RequestAgent. The RequestAgent contacts the Repository [1] in order to obtain a list of available offer descriptions. Together with this list the request is then forwarded to the MatcherAgent. The MatcherAgent forms the heart of the middleware. Not only does it provide efficient semantic matching of the request against the offers, it also configures the offers optimal with regard to the request. More details about the matching process can be found in [3]. An important property of the Matcher-Agent is its ability to interact with a service provider during matchmaking. In the description of its offer a shipment service provider can, e.g., specify that the price of a shipment may be inquired by calling a getPrice operation with the size of the package to send as parameter. The MatcherAgent is then able to automatically call that operation and use the dynamically provided additional information in the matching process.

Upon completion of the matching process the MatcherAgent returns a list of properly configured service offers to the RequestAgent, ordered by how well the offers suit the request. In the most basic case of our shipping scenario the least expensive service would rank highest, in more advanced scenarios preferences concerning pickup times, speed of delivery and other properties can be included.

The RequestAgent picks the best offer and forwards it to the CallerAgent which invokes the OfferAgent at the middleware instance running on the service provider's server. Based on information provided in the offer description's grounding the OfferAgent has to bridge the gap between the semantic description of the offer and its actual implementation. Different implementations (like Java program, web service, ...) are mirrored by corresponding different types of groundings in the offer's service description. Depending on the type of the grounding found in that description, the OfferAgent thus delegates the invocation to the appropriate ServiceHandler. In order to perform the service invocation the ServiceHandler has to translate the given configured service offer description into a service invocation. In case of a web service the input parameters of that service have to be extracted from the configured offer description and transformed

---

[1] The implementation of the repository is pluggable and independent from the rest of the middleware. It is therefore not within the scope of this paper.

into an XML message the service can process. This is the complementary task of the translation performed by the BinderAgent. Besides providing essential information like the address of the service, the offer grounding therefore also has to define mappings which are this time used the other way round, namely to create XML data from DSD variables analogously to the proceeding explained in Section 3.1. In a similar fashion the reply of the web service is transformed back into DSD variables. These are transferred back through the middleware and returned to the calling BinderAgent. Finally, the BinderAgent transforms them into an XML message that is replied to COS-tec's BPEL order management process. Once again these transformations are performed using mapping definitions from the offer and request's grounding.

The system introduced in this paper has been implemented and tested. An elaborate scenario including selection, binding and invocation of a shipping service has been implemented in the context of the 2006 Semantic Web Services Challenge [4].

4   Evaluation

We offer an easy and lightweight way to enable dynamic binding for the component services used by BPEL processes. Our approach is beneficial, if several different providers competitively offer a certain necessary functionality used by the BPEL process (like shipment ordering, stock quote lookup, component purchasing, ...). In this case our approach enables the BPEL process to always use (i.e. choose and invoke) the best provider on a case by case basis. Thereby the different services do not have to adhere to a standardized protocol or data representation to enable to be bound and invoked automatically, but of course need to annotate or describe their service semantically using an agreed upon language - in this case DSD. To keep the approach lightweight, only limited support is currently offered for cases where one component service would have to be replaced by a whole workflow of other services. A discussion of this topic of automatic composition synthesis is beyond the scope of this paper.

BPEL uses the notion of partner links, roles and partners to identify conversations with varying actual services. It may be necessary to ensure that the same single partner service, once chosen, will be used in later calls to the same role. This is somewhat contrary to the idea of dynamic binding but if necessary can easily be ensured by giving the provider name as parameter in later calls of the DSD-Middleware. This will effectively limit the possible matches to the single provider registered with the given name. More flexible limitations of possible matches for dynamic bindings downstream the business process execution can be achieved similarly. This way one could ensure that certain providers are always (or never) used in combination.

During runtime the integrating of the DSD requests into BPEL processes includes up to four data transformations: The input from the BPEL process has to be transformed to DSD in order to be processed by the middleware. It has then to be transformed to a format understood by the chosen provider's implementation to invoke the service. Finally, output data has to be transformed the same way back. Although this might look like too much overhead, it is unavoidable to overcome heterogeneities regarding data representation and choreography between COS-tec's legacy process on the one hand and the various systems of many independent shipment service providers on the other hand. An xml message issued by COS-tec cannot be used directly to communicate with a dynamically discovered service provider since this would require a unified xml interface for all the various potential providers.

By supporting the necessary translations through declarative specifications within the semantic description of a service request or offer, the bulk of actual work concerning these translations can be performed by the DSD middleware and doesn't have to be implemented by the participants (COS-tec or the shipment service providers). Furthermore, by putting the translation rules into the description's groundings they are cleanly separated from other concerns and can be easily adapted, if a participant were to change its data format. If, for instance, one of the shipment service providers changes its data format, all it has to do is to publish an updated version of its offer description to the repository system used. COS-tec's order management system could still use that provider without any change, in fact COS-tec wouldn't even notice a change took place!

The approach presented in this paper could in principle be realized using any service description language that allows for a precise encoding of user preferences in the request and provides a matching algorithm that is able not only to find the most appropriate offer, but also to directly invoke it. While a detailed comparison of DSD with other such languages and discovery techniques is outside the scope of this paper, it can be found in [3]. There, we reach the conclusion that neither WSMO nor OWL-S, the two most widespread such languages currently meet these requirements. Extensions of these languages, however, would be a suitable basis for this approach. In the following section we will give a short overview of the related work that also tries to support dynamic binding for business processes.

5 Related Work

The work closest to the one presented in this paper is by Mandell and McIllraith [5]. They also propose to integrate dynamic service discovery and binding into BPEL processes. Discovery and matchmaking is performed by querying a knowledge base of DAML-S service profiles with requests expressed in the DAML Query Language (DQL). This machinery is then made availabe to BPEL processes through a "Semantic Discovery Service" (SDS). Although this idea is very similar to ours, the realization is not. The SDS is agnostic to the content of the service descriptions and invocation messages it receives. An invocation message of the SDS consists of two parts: The abstract service request description to be sent to the DAML-S knowledge base and the parameters to be sent to a discovered service. Both are simply forwarded. Thus the calling BPEL process has not only to deal with semantic descriptions directly, it also has to output parameters in a format that will be understood by the discovered services. This is very different from the configurable, adaptable mappings approach presented in this paper.

The METEOR-S project [6] aims at creating a framework to support dynamic selection of optimal partner web services. Developers create abstract processes that contain service templates (semantic requests). At runtime a configuration module binds these to concrete services using semantic discovery and an execution environment handles their invocation. Unlike the previously mentioned approach METEOR-S also deals with the problem of data mapping. Similar to our approach, developers may specify mappings between each element of an input data of a web service and the corresponding ontological concept. Compared to our work the way how the semantic technology is integrated by METEOR-S differs. While we provide a web service gateway to the DSD Middleware that enables to replace single (or multiple) statically bound service invocations by calls of the middleware, the METEOR-S framework takes whole abstract processes as input to transform it into a concrete process observing global constraints and a global optimization function. Thus, the targeted use case is somewhat different. But more importantly, the SWRL reasoner used by METEOR-S to perform this task is not as powerful as the DSD MatcherAgent as it lacks the ability to express user preferences and to invoke service operations during matchmaking to gather dynamic information (This difference applies to [5], too).

Just recently Lemcke and Drumm [7] introduced a work to show the benefits of integrating semantic Web service technologies into business processes. Just like this paper they use a logistics scenario and aim to support dynamic carrier selection. However, they use a set of predefined carriers to create a single business process for each of them at design time. At runtime they then use semantic technology to pick and instantiate the most appropriate process. Although the use case is the same, the focus of this work is less on discovery and binding and more on automated mapping of in- and output parameters to support the creation of the business processes at design time.

The work by Oberle et al. [8] makes a case for the necessity to trade of between the high maintenance costs of the WS-* approaches and the high modeling cost of semantic approaches. It thus suggests a compromise that explicitly does not aim at automating anything but only the most efficient things. We share this idea and the underlying motivation, but the resulting work aims at very different objectives. Based on a set of use cases Oberle et al. try to identify who could benefit to what extent from what kind of semantic modeling of web services. Thereby they aim at examining how to support the developers of web applications by exploiting which kind of semantic information. Thus, they focus on the usage of semantic technology during process design time, while we leverage semantic technology at process runtime.

6 Summary and Conclusion

In this paper we have shown how existing service-oriented applications can leverage the advantages offered by novel semantic web service technology without compromising trust in the application or encountering unreasonable effort during the transition.

The basic idea is to enable BPEL processes to bind to the semantics-based DSD middleware instead of statically binding to an external service provider. In places where the static binding is replaced by the DSD middleware binding, predefined templates will be used to issue semantic requests. The DSD middleware then uses its semantic technology to dynamically find and invoke the most suitable service provider from a potentially vast pool of candidates. This dynamic binding results in a robust system that always uses the best provider of functionality available without the need of manual intervention. Developers can choose at which steps of a BPEL process to replace the original static binding by the DSD-based one. This leaves the control about how much semantics to introduce in the discretion of the developer. This overcomes both the widespread lack of trust in semantic technology and the high entrance costs associated with a complete migration to semantic technology.

The approach presented in this paper offers an opportunity for a smooth transition from legacy web service applications to more powerful semantic web service technology. We believe such a seamless transition to be a necessary prerequisite for the adaptation of semantic service technology in real-life commercial settings.

References

1. Sprott, D., Wilkes, L., Veryard, R., Stephenson, J.: Web services roadmap. In: CBDI. Report Series - Guiding the Transition to Web Services and SOA (2003)
2. W3C World Wide Web Consortium: (www.w3c.org)
3. Klein, M., König-Ries, B., Müssig, M.: What is needed for semantic service descriptions - a proposal for suitable language constructs. International Journal on Web and Grid Services (IJWGS) 1(3/4), 328–364 (2005)
4. Küster, U., König-Ries, B., Klein, M.: Discovery and mediation using diane service descriptions. In: Second Workshop of the Semantic Web Service Challenge 2006, Budva, Montenegro, June 2006 (2006)
5. Mandell, D.J., McIlraith, S.A.: Adapting BPEL4WS for the semantic web: The bottom-up approach to web service interoperation. In: Fensel, D., Sycara, K.P., Mylopoulos, J. (eds.) ISWC 2003. LNCS, vol. 2870, Springer, Heidelberg (2003)
6. Verma, K., Gomadam, K., Sheth, A.P., Miller, J.A., Wu, Z.: The METEOR-S approach for configuring and executing dynamic web processes. Technical Report 6-24-05, LSDIS Lab, University of Georgia, Athens, Georgia, USA (2005)
7. Lemcke, J., Drumm, C.: Semantic business automation. In: Proceedings of the 3rd European Semantic Web Conference's Industry Forum, Budva, Montenegro (2006)
8. Oberle, D., Lamparter, S., Eberhart, A., Staab, S.: Semantic management of web services. In: ICWS05. Proceedings of the 2005 IEEE International Conference on Web Services, Orlando, Florida, IEEE Computer Society Press, Los Alamitos (2005)

Part II

First International Workshop on Modeling Service-Oriented Architectures: Business Perspective and Model Mapping

A Model-Driven Approach for QoS Prediction of BPEL Processes

Jiangxia Wu and Fangchun Yang

State Key Laboratory of Networking and Switching Technology,
Beijing University of Posts and Telecommunications, 100876 Beijing, China
wujiangxia@gmail.com, fcyang@bupt.edu.cn

Abstract. Business Process Execution Language (BPEL) is one of the most popular languages for Web service composition. To predict the QoS of composite service processes specified in BPEL gives the way to tell whether the process meet the non-function requirements, and to choose the process with better QoS from those with similar function. A model-driven approach for QoS prediction of BPEL processes is proposed in this paper, which has a two-layer architecture: One is the prediction model specifying necessary information for prediction and independent of specific languages, and the other is the semantic model of specific languages such as BPEL. A set of transformation rules is defined between the two layers so that processes specified in specific languages can be transformed to the prediction model. A prediction algorithm is defined based on the prediction model, and through the algorithm the average value of process QoS attribute can be computed. The approach can be used not only to BPEL processes but also to processes in other specifications such as BPML and BPSS, if the mapping rules between the semantic models of these languages and the prediction model are defined. The feasibility and good accuracy of the approach has been proved by the experiment.

Keywords: QoS prediction, Web service composition, BPEL, model-driven.

1 Introduction and Related Work

Business Process Execution Language (BPEL) is one of the most popular languages for Web service composition. To predict the QoS of BPEL processes gives the way to tell whether the process meet the non-function requirements, and to choose the process with better QoS from those with similar function. The research in QoS prediction of Web service composition is in its infancy. Zeng introduced the aggregation function approach for prediction [1]. The function is rather simple and has limited accuracy. Grassi proposed the Software Architecture based approach [2] which is based on the research of component system prediction and is concerned with the execution environment of Web services. Therefore, it is not feasible for Web service composition. Chadrasekaran introduced a simulation based approach [3] which relies on specific simulation tool. And the Workflow Based Approach (*WBA*) [4, 5] is proposed by Cardoso and Jaeger respectively and has better feasibility and accuracy than others methods. However, neither of the existing methods can be used

D. Georgakopoulos et al. (Eds.): ICSOC 2006 Ws, LNCS 4652, pp. 131–140, 2007.

for the prediction of BPEL processes, because they are not based on the semantic concepts of BPEL.

In this paper, we propose a model-driven approach for BPEL process prediction, which introduces a two-layer architecture: One is the prediction model specifying necessary information on composite services for prediction and independent of specific languages, and the other is the semantic model of specific languages such as BPEL. A set of transformation rules is defined between the two layers so that processes specified in specific languages can be transformed to the prediction model. And a prediction algorithm is defined based on the prediction model, by which the average value of QoS attributes of processes can be computed. The approach can be used for not only BPEL processes QoS prediction but also processes specified in any other languages such as BPML, WSCI etc., if the mapping rules between the semantic models of these languages and the prediction model are defined. The feasibility and good accuracy of the approach has been proved by the experiment.

The rest of the paper is organized as follows: Section 2 gives the formal definition of the prediction model. Section 3 proposes the transformation rules between semantic model of BPEL and the prediction model. Section 4 introduces the prediction algorithm and the analysis of the time complexity. The experiments and analysis are given in section 5. Finally, we conclude in section 6.

2 Prediction Model

2.1 Model-Driven Prediction

Model-Driven Architecture (*MDA*) is promoted by the Object Management Group (*OMG*) for software development [7]. The main idea of MDA is to achieve portability, interoperability, and reusability through an architectural separation and transformation of concerns between the design and implementation of software. The work described in this paper adopts the MDA strategy to predict the QoS of composite service processes specified in BPEL.

Model-driven QoS prediction is based on a two-layer architecture shown in figure. 1. One is the prediction model specifying necessary information on composite services for prediction and independent of specific languages, and the other is the semantic model of specific languages such as BPEL. A set of transformation rules is defined between the two layers so that processes specified in specific languages can be transformed to the prediction model. Based on the prediction model, a prediction

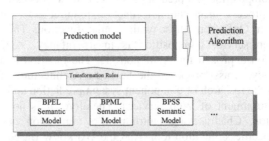

Fig. 1. The architecture of model-driven prediction

algorithm is defined to compute the average value of QoS attributes of processes specified in the prediction model. Thus, the approach can be used to predict the process in any languages such as BPML, BPSS etc., if the mapping rules between the semantic model of the language and the prediction model is defined.

2.2 Model Definition

The prediction model is the abstraction of information elements necessary for QoS prediction of a composite services process. It is independent of specific languages so it can be used for the prediction of process in any specification including BPEL. The model is made up of the following concept definitions.

Definition 1. Composite service process Γ. Γ is a 4-tuple with the format of (CP, T, C, Q). It is used to represent the composite service process to be predicted. Γ can be specified as a workflow [8]. And the tasks in workflows represent the service invocation operations, and the transitions between tasks represent the orders between invocation operations. The definition of the four elements of Γ is given below.

Definition 2. Composition pattern set (CP). CP represents the set of composition patterns which constitute the composite service process. Composition pattern is the abstraction of basic architecture of composite services [5, 6], which is composed of a set of tasks and defines the execution order of the tasks and the completion symbol of the pattern. There are seven types of composition patterns *Sequence*, *Loop*, *XOR_XOR*, *AND_AND*, *AND_DISC*, *OR_OR* and *OR_DISC*. The definition of each type is given in table 1. Composition patterns can be nested and sub-patterns can be treated as the tasks of the parent-pattern.

Table 1. Definition of composition pattern types

cp Type	Definition
Sequence	Containing n ($n>1$) tasks which are executed in sequence.
Loop	Containing 1 task which is executed repeatedly.
XOR_XOR	Containing n ($n>1$) tasks one of which is chosen and executed, completed when the task completes.
AND_AND	Containing n ($n>1$) tasks which are executed concurrently, completed when the n tasks complete.
AND_DISC	Containing n ($n>1$) tasks which are executed concurrently, completed when m out of n ($m<n$) tasks complete.
OR_OR	Containing n ($n>1$) tasks s ($n>s>1$) of which are executed concurrently, completed when the s tasks complete.
OR_DISC	Containing n ($n>1$) tasks s ($n>s>1$) of which are executed concurrently, completed when t out of s ($t<s$) the tasks complete.

Definition 3. Task set (T). T represents the set of tasks composing the composite service process.

Definition 4. Contain (C). C represents the relationship between composition patterns and the nodes it contains, and $C = \{(cp, node) \mid cp \in CP, node \in CP \cup T\}$. And

(cp, *node*)∈ C, iff cp∈ CP and cp contains *node*₀ Any node is contained by one and only one pattern, that is to say, if $\exists$ (p_1, *node*) ∈ C and $\exists$ ($p2$, *node*) ∈ C, then p_1 = p_2.

Definition 5. QoS description of tasks (Q). Q describes the QoS value of tasks, and Q = {(t, d, v) | t∈ T)}, in which t∈ T, and d represents the type of QoS such as *performance, cost, availability* and *reputation* [1], and v represents the average value of QoS.

3 Transformation

The semantic concepts of BPEL are the abstraction of the information described by the BPEL process specification, which are organized as the metamodel of BPEL. And the transformation rules between BPEL metamodel and the prediction model define the mapping from the concepts in BPEL to the concepts in the general model. And with the transformation rules BPEL processes specification can be converted into the general model which is the input of the prediction algorithm.

The metamodel of BPEL in UML [9] is shown in figure 2, which describes the main semantic elements of BPEL and the relationship among them. The semantic elements concerned with the prediction are *process* and *activity*. The detail mapping rules between the elements and the concepts in general model are described as follows.

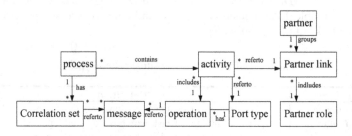

Fig. 2. BPEL metamodel

process element described as <process> in BPEL will be transformed to a composite service process Γ. And *activity* element is split into two types, one is basic activity, the other is structured activity.

3.1 Transformation of Basic Activity

The basic activity in BPEL represents the invocation operation of element services and is described as <invoke>, <receive> and <reply>. Basic activities will be transformed to tasks in composite service process. <invoke> represents a synchronized or asynchronous Web service invocation and will be mapped to a task t. And <receive> and <reply> together represent a synchronized invocation and will be mapped to a task t. The tasks corresponding to all basic activities in <process> make up with the tasks set T.

3.2 Transformation of Structured Activity

The structured activity in BPEL *specifies* the order of activities contained in it, and is described as <sequence>, <switch>, <while>, <pick>, and <flow>. The structured activities will be transformed to composition patterns (*cp*) of composite service process and the relationship between the structured activity and the activities it contains will be transformed to the elements in *C* of the composite service process. The structured activity can be nested and the nested activity can be mapped to nested *cp*.

<sequence> contains one or more activities that are performed sequentially, in the order in which they are listed. It is mapped to a *cp* with *sequence* type. <switch> contains one or more condition branches, one of which will be chosen to be executed according to the condition. It is mapped to a *cp* with *XOR-XOR* type. <while> represents repeated execution of a specified iterative activity until the given Boolean no longer holds true. It is mapped to a *cp* with *Loop* type. <pick> contains one or more event branches, one of which will be chosen to be executed according to the event. It is mapped to a *cp* with *XOR-XOR* type. And <flow> specifies one or more activities to be performed concurrently. It is mapped to a *cp* with *AND-AND* type. All the *cp*s corresponding to the structure activities in <process> make up the composition pattern set *CP*.

3.3 To Get the QoS Description *Q*

QoS description of tasks can not be extracted directly from the BPEL process specification. The QoS of tasks is the QoS of basic activities which is decided by the element service being invoked. There are two ways to get the QoS of services. One is to refer to the interface specification of services which can be located through the *porttype* and *operation* attributes of basic activities. A method of describing service QoS in WSDL specifications has been proposed in [10]. And the other is to get the QoS of services through test or monitoring. A method of getting service QoS through monitoring has been proposed in [11].

4 Prediction Algorithm

Based on the prediction model in section 2 we define the prediction algorithm to predict the average value of the QoS of composite service processes. The QoS attributes supported by the algorithm include *performance, cost* and *reputation*. The algorithm is independent of the specific definition of attributes and can be used for each attribute. In the algorithm, the QoS of processes are based on the QoS of composition patterns calculated through the QoS aggregation formula for composition patterns which take the QoS of the tasks in the pattern as input, and recursive procedures are used for the calculation of nested patterns. And the QoS of the most parent pattern is the prediction result of the process.

For each type of composition patterns and for each attribute of QoS, a QoS aggregation formula is defined. For example, the *performance* QoS aggregation formula for *sequence* composition pattern is defined as $\sum_i x_i$, and for *XOR-XOR* pattern is $\sum_i p_i x_i$, in which, x_i represents the *performance* value of tasks in the pattern and p_i represents the probability of the branch including the task being executed. The formulas for each pattern type and for the attributes of *performance, cost and reputation* are given in [6].

4.1 Algorithm Definition

The algorithm inputs include the composite service process Γ and the attribute d to be predicted. Through the algorithm the average value of the d attribute of the process Γ can be computed.

The algorithm is made up of three steps. First, the process is composed of nested composition patterns and we need to get the most parent composition pattern described as cp_0 and satisfying $\forall cp \in CP$, $(cp, cp_0) \notin C$. Second, in order to calculate the QoS of composite patterns, we need to get the attribute value of d of all nodes in cp_0. And then let *node* represent a node in cp_0. When *node* is a task, the QoS of *node* is the v in $(node, d, v) \in D$. And when *node* is a nested composition pattern, the QoS of *node* can be extracted through the recursive invocation of the algorithm. Thirdly, take the QoS value of nodes in cp_0 into the aggregation formula for the attribute of d and the pattern type of cp_0 to get the QoS of the composition pattern, which is the result of prediction.

4.2 Time Complexity

Theory 3.1. As the input is $\Gamma = (CP, T, C, Q)$, the time complexity of the algorithm is $O\left(|CP|\right) + O\left(|T|\right)$.

Let $|CP| = n$, $|T| = m$, and there is $|C| = m + (n - 1)$. To get the most parent composition pattern, the algorithm checks each element in C and debars those being contained by other patterns. The worst time complexity of the procedure is $(m + n - 1) \cdot t_1$, in which t_1 represents the constant time to deal with a single element in C. In addition, the time of the procedure of getting the QoS of all tasks is $m \cdot t_2$ and of getting the QoS of all composition patterns is $n \cdot t_3$, in which t_2 and t_3 respectively represent the constant time of getting the QoS of a service and of calculating an aggregation formula. As a result, the time performance of the algorithm is $(m + n - 1) \cdot t_1 + m \cdot t_2 + n \cdot t_3$, and the complexity is $O(n) + O(m)$, that is $O\left(|CP|\right) + O\left(|T|\right)$.

5 Experiment

To prove the feasibility and accuracy of the approach proposed in the paper, we give an example of BPEL process prediction. First, the performance of a BPEL process is predicted by the approach, and then the BPEL process is executed by Active BPEL to get the actual average process performance, and the actual value and prediction result are compared.

The example BPEL process specification is shown in figure 3, and the function of the process is to perform stock quote or exchange rate consultant according to the user request. There are four element services: *Receipt, StockQuote, ExchangeQuote* and *Response*, and the WSDL file URLs of the element services are shown in table 2.

And the definition of Web services *performance* is given in [1] as the interval between receiving the request and sending out the response, and the interval can be measured through the execution time of services.

```
<Process name="ConsultantService" ...>
<partnerLinks>...</partnerLinks>
<partners>...</partners>
<variables>...</variables>
<sequence>
    <invoke partnerLink="Receipt"
        portType="urn:ReceiptService" operation="ConsultantRequestReceipt"
        variable="ConsultantRequest" createInstance="yes".../>
    <switch>
        <case condition="urn:RequestServiceType==1">
            <invoke partnerLink="StockQuote"
                portType="urn:StockQuoteService" operation="StockQuoting".../>
        </case>
        <case condition=" urn:RequestServiceType==0">
            <invoke partnerLink="ExchangeQuote"
                portType="ExchangeQuoteService" operation="ExchangeQuoting".../>
        </case>
    </switch>
    <invoke partnerLink="Response"
        portType="urn:ResponseService" operation="ConsultantResponser"
        variable="ConsultantResponse" createInstance="yes".../>
</sequence>
</Process>
```

Fig. 3. The example BPEL process

Table 2. The WSDL file URLs of the element services in the example BPEL process

element service	WSDL URL
Receipt	http://www.telestar.bj.cn/spacejojo/wsdl/receipt.wsdl
StockQuote	http://services.xmethods.net/soap/urn:xmethods-delayed-quotes.wsdl
ExchangeQuote	http://www.xmethods.net/sd/2001/CurrencyExchangeService.wsdl
Response	http://www.telestar.bj.cn/spacejojo/wsdl/response.wsdl

The performance value of the example process can be computed as follow. The BPEL process is transformed to a corresponding prediction model according to the rules in section 4 to get the input of the algorithm, and the result prediction model is shown in table 3. And the performance of element services represented as the QoS description Q in the prediction model is gotten through service test. We record the performance data of element services in ten executions and take the average performance as the value in Q. And we suppose the branches in <switch> have the same probability to be executed. Through the prediction algorithm, we can get the prediction result of the process performance as16.05s.

Table 3. The result prediction model transformed from the example BPEL process

Element	Value
Γ	(CP, T, C, Q)
T	{t_receipt, t_stock, t_exchange, t_response}
CP	{cp_sequence, cp_switch}
C	{(cp_sequence, t_receipt), (cp_sequence, cp_switch), (cp_sequence, t_response), (cp_switch, t_stock), (cp_switch, t_exchange)}
Q	{(t_receipt, performance, 3.3), (t_stock, performance, 10.2), (t_exchange, performance, 9.3), (t_response, performance, 3.0)}

Table 4. The run-time performance of the example process and the included basic activities

instance	Process <sequence>	Receipt <invoke>	<switch> StockQuote <invoke>	<switch> ExchangeQuote <invoke>	Response <invoke>
1	16.97	3.67	–	9.32	2.54
2	15.46	3.00	–	9.05	3.13
3	18.67	3.77	–	9.06	3.34
4	17.5	3.68	10.16	–	3.33
5	18.02	3.78	10.55	–	3.42
6	19.63	3.06	10.53	–	3.47
7	19.09	3.64	10.00	–	3.47
8	15.72	2.99	–	9.30	3.04
9	16.53	3.41	–	9.78	2.99
10	16.3	3.67	–	8.95	2.91
11	16.84	3.08	10.05	–	2.89
12	16.11	3.63	–	9.79	3.35
13	18.06	3.08	10.36	–	2.96
14	16.05	3.40	–	9.31	3.31
15	17.73	3.35	10.44	–	3.36
16	15.42	3.20	10.04	–	3.47
17	16.53	3.57	–	9.68	3.11
18	16.81	2.97	10.01	–	3.33
19	15.39	2.93	–	9.26	2.89
20	16.81	3.54	10.43	–	2.91
Avg	16.98	3.36	10.24	9.35	3.18

And then the example process is executed by Active BPEL, which is an execution engine of BPEL based on Java [13]. The reason to choose Active BPEL is that it provides the log on the start and end time of the process as well as the basic activities in the process, so that the run-time performance of the process and the basic activities can be gotten. Active BPEL takes the process specification and the element service WSDL file URL as the input. According to the Active BPEL logs on 20 executions of the example process, the run-time performance of the process and the basic activities can be calculated and the result is shown in tabel 4. The actual average process performance can be gotten as 16.98s.

From the data in table 3 and table 4, we can see that there are errors between the estimation and the actual performance of element services, and this is one of the reasons leading to the error of process prediction. The process prediction error rate can be calculated through the formula of $\eta = \dfrac{|V_e - V_a|}{V_a}$ in which V_e and V_a respectively represent the prediction result and actual value. And the error rate of the performance prediction of the example process is 5.5%, which proves the approach has a good estimation in predicting the average QoS value of BPEL processes.

6 Conclusion

A model-driven approach for the QoS prediction of BPEL process is proposed in the paper. It has a two-layer architecture: One is the prediction model specifying necessary information on composite services for prediction and independent of specific languages, and the other is the semantic model of specific languages such as BPEL. A set of transformation rules is defined between the two layers so that processes specified in specific languages can be transformed to the prediction model. Based on the prediction model the prediction algorithm to predict the average value of the QoS attributes of composite service processes is defined. And we've proved the algorithm has a linear time complexity. Model-driven strategy makes it possible for the approach to be used for the prediction of processes specified in any languages, if the sets of mapping rules between the semantic models of the language and the prediction model are defined. The feasibility and good accuracy of the approach in BPEL process prediction has been proved by the experiment.

Acknowledgment. We thank the National Basic Research Priorities Programme (Grant No. 2003CB314806) for funding the project.

References

1. Zeng, L., Benatallah, B., Ngu, A.H.H., et al.: QoS-Aware Middleware for Web Services Composition. Software Engineering, IEEE Transactions on 30(5), 311–327 (2004)
2. Grassi, V.: Architecture-based Reliability Prediction for Service-oriented Computing. In: de Lemos, R., Gacek, C., Romanovsky, A. (eds.) Architecting Dependable Systems III. LNCS, vol. 3549, Springer, Heidelberg (2005)

3. Chadrasekaran, S., Miller, J.A., Silver, G.S., et al.: Composition, performance analysis and simulation of web services. Electronic Markets: The International Journal of Electronic Commerce and Business Media (2003)
4. Cardoso, J.: Quality of Service and Semantic Composition of Workflows. PhD thesis, Department of Computer Science, University of Georgia, Athens, GA (USA) (2002)
5. Jaeger, M.C., Rojec-Goldmann, G., Muhl, G.: QoS aggregation for service composition using workflow patterns. In: EDOC 2004. Proceedings of the 8th International Enterprise Distributed Object Computing Conference, Monterey, California, IEEE Computer Society Press, Los Alamitos (2004)
6. Jaeger, M.C., Rojec-Goldmann, G., Muhl, G.: QoS aggregation in Web service compositions. In: EEE 2005. Proceedings of the IEEE Int. Conf. on e-Technology, e-Commerce and e-Service, pp. 181–185. IEEE Computer Society Press, Los Alamitos (2005)
7. Miller, J., Mukerji, J.: MDA Guide Version 1.0.1, OMG (2003)
8. van der Aalst, W.M.P., van Hee, K.M., Houben, G.J.: Modeling workflow management systems with high-level Petri nets. In: Proceedings of the second Workshop on Computer-Supported Cooperative Work, Petri nets and related formalisms, pp. 31–50 (1994)
9. Mongiello, M., Castelluccia, D.: Modelling and Verification of BPEL Business Processes. In: MBD/MOMPES 2006. Proceedings of the Fourth Workshop on Model-Based Development of Computer-Based Systems and Third International Workshop on Model-Based Methodologies for Pervasive and Embedded Software (2006)
10. Gouscos, D., Kalikakis, M., Georgiadis, P.: An Approach to Modeling Web Service QoS and Provision Price. In: Proceedings of the Fourth International Conference on Web Information Systems Engineering, pp. 121–130 (2003)
11. Liu, Y., Ngu, A.H.H., Zeng, L.: QoS Computation and Policing in Dynamic Web Service Selection. In: Proceedings of the Thirteenth International World Wide Web Conference, New York (2004)
12. van der Aalst, W.M.P.: Web Service Composition Languages: Old Wine in New Bottles. In: Proceedings of the 29th EUROMICRO Conference New Waves in System Architecture EUROMICRO (2003)
13. Stoilova, K., Stoilov, T.: Comparison of workflow software products. In: CompSysTech. Proceedings of the International Conference on Computer Systems and Technologies (2006)

Modelling of Service Compositions: Relations to Business Process and Workflow Modelling

Michael C. Jaeger

Technische Universität Berlin, FG Formal Models, Logic and Programming
Sek. FR 6-10, Franklinstrasse 28/29, D-10587 Berlin, Germany
mcj@cs.tu-berlin.de

Abstract. The service oriented architecture (SOA) represents a trend in the IT industry for the development of a flexible and unifying software infrastructure. In an SOA, software components provide their functionality as a service by using uniform interface description and invocation protocols. The provision of software components in an uniform manner allow their efficient composition to form new complex services. Currently, the compositions of services is a popular field of research with many ongoing efforts.

However, the sheer number of existing proposals and efforts to describe service compositions in this field have led to term Web Services Acronym Hell (WSAH) [1] and an obvious confusion. This paper intends to serve as an orientation for explaining what the differences between business processes and workflow control flow languages are and why service compositions are used in this field. It will also introduce past and existing proposals for Web service composition languages for understanding why so many different languages for modelling workflows, business processes and compositions exist.

1 Introduction

Services in an SOA use standardised interface descriptions and uniform invocation protocols. The Web services proposal by the W3C has defined such elements of an SOA by using Internet protocols for the invocation and XML-based description formats for the description and messages in an SOA [2]. A service composition results from combining existing services to realise a new, more complex functionality. The SOA reflects the task-orientation of modern businesses that form a business process. Using services in this setup leads to services that fulfil individual tasks of a process. Arranging them together to a composition provides the implementation of a process. One candidate for describing and defining compositions of Web services is the Business Process Execution Language for Web Services ("BPEL4WS"). In the remainder of this paper, a language like BPEL4WS is named composition language. However, in this field some problems of understanding arise:

– The BPEL4WS proposal carries "Business Process Execution" in its name. Is a service composition equivalent with the realisation of a business process? What is the relation between business processes and compositions?

D. Georgakopoulos et al. (Eds.): ICSOC 2006 Ws, LNCS 4652, pp. 141–153, 2007.
© Springer-Verlag Berlin Heidelberg 2007

- Considering the definition of the Workflow Management Coalition (WfMC) provided in their comprehensive workflow reference model saying that "a workflow is the computerised facilitation or automation of a business process, in whole or part" [3]: Does a service composition represent a workflow when realising a business process? Based on this definition it seems odd why there is a "business process execution language" used for service compositions, but not an analogous "workflow execution language" which would be the more consistent name with respect to the definitions of the WfMC.
- Why there are so many different composition languages? What are their origins and in which direction will they evolve in the future?

This work intends to give a clarification and to answer the posed questions in the following way: In Sections 2 and 3, a rough overview about business processes, workflows and their modelling languages is given. In Sections 4 and 5, differences between both are discussed and the main considerations why service compositions match these two fields are introduced. And then, based on the given clarifications, composition languages are discussed which are found most in today's literature in Section 5.1. After these main three parts, the paper ends with the conclusions in Section 6.

2   Business Processes

In the mid-90s, the work of Hammer and Champy, who introduced business process reengineering as a main strategy to improve existing businesses and organisations [4], brought the IT industry to put more efforts in the development of software systems that facilitate the creation and management of business processes. The basic idea of this strategy is to design a process in the most modern and optimised way leading in a process definition without legacy artefacts. Every business process should have a dedicated customer and thus offer a clear benefit. In addition, a process should also have a defined process owner, who is in charge and responsible in order to provide customers with a defined point of contact.

At that time, different organisational units where divided by their functional responsibilities, and a process typically crossed different units. As a result, processes performed inefficiently and in case of problems, a responsible party was hard to identify. To overcome these lacks of efficiency, the business process reengineering was proposed as an optimisation effort of existing activities. As a side-effect of standardised processes, monitoring and benchmarking tasks produce results that are more suitable for comparison. And based on the defined processes, mistaken activities or misunderstandings between involved actors are reduced and thus the productivity is improved.

Apart from the evident advantages, analysis from the performed business process reengineering efforts have also revealed a couple of disadvantages. Most noticeable are that too radical changes will lead to social problems in an organisation [5, p. 239]. Moreover, a strong focus on the process optimisation also runs the risk of poor improvements on what the individual activities produce.

2.1   Modelling Business Processes

One motivation of modelling business processes is to achieve a clear and common understanding between the management and the involved actors and users of the process. For modelling processes, different graphical and textual languages exist, which can be used to create diagrams or a description of a business process that is ready for interpretation by software systems. Graphical representations can be flow diagrams, block diagrams, or basic graphs. Considering a graph, a node represents usually an activity, an event, or an entity where directed edges represent the (causal) relations between the elements.

One early introduced graphical language for the modelling of processes is the event-driven process chain (EPC) [6]. As its name suggests, the basic element of an EPC is the event, which is a defined condition and thus can be the result of a process, a function, or an external event. Contrary to events, a function is an active element which changes a state and thus is the object between different events. Events and functions, can be combined with combination operators, like ANDs or XORs. EPCs are suitable for the modelling of control flows that define the order of occurring events and executed functions. To model the data flow of a process (or also the flow of goods) extensions are proposed that appear in literature as so-called extended EPCs [5, p. 221].

The Business Process Management Initiative (BPMI) has introduced the Business Process Modeling Language (BPML) as a textual language for describing business processes [7]. The BPMI represents a non-profit organisation with the goal to support and coordinate the activities in the field of business processes among its members. The BPML is intended to serve as a comprehensive description of a business process, which also covers aspects of implementing business processes. It consists of different elements to describe the control flow as well as the data flow of a process. The standard textual representation used for BPML documents is XML. The BPMI has also released a graphical notation called Business Process Modelling Notation (BPMN) to provide a set of symbols and layout conventions for drawing business process models [8]. In the recent past, the BPMI has merged their efforts with the business process modelling activities of the Object Management Group (OMG), which represents a non-profit organisation for pursuing interests in the area of object-oriented software technologies.. As a result from this merger, the work focusses on new releases of the BPMN adopted by the OMG.

The Business Process Specification Schema (BPSS) has a slightly different focus than the BPML. The BPSS is part of the ebXML suite which supports establishing agreements to facilitate electronic businesses on an inter-organisational level. The motivation background for this effort is to provide a specification for helping developing countries to participate in electronic commerce without being dependent on technologies offered by particular vendors. The ebXML is driven by the United Nations Centre for Trade Facilitation and Electronic Business (UN/CEFACT) and a Technical Committee at Organisation for the Advancement of Structured Information Standards (OASIS). The first release that can be traced back was submitted in 2001. At that time, compositions of services in an SOA were not mentioned at all.

The Business Process Execution Language (BPEL), also named BPEL for Web Services (BPEL4WS) represents another proposal for specifying business processes. This proposal covers the modelling of processes and the description about the involvement of concrete Web services. At the moment, a committee at the OASIS coordinates the development of BPEL. Before, BPEL was carried out by a joint venture of the software industry. Originally, it resulted from a merger of the Web Services Flow Language by IBM (WSFL, [9]), which shows influences from IBM's MQ Series workflow software [10], and XLANG [11], which was intended to serve as the process modelling language in Microsoft's BizTalk software.

Besides the mentioned EPC, BPMN, BPEL, WSFL, and XLANG, other approaches to model business processes exist. The given selection represent the commonly mentioned proposals in papers discussing the area of service compositions. In addition, the WSFL, XLANG and BPEL4WS proposals directly cover the realisation of processes with services by forming service compositions, which also indicate that the border between business processes and service compositions becomes blurred. Another popular proposal for modelling business processes is the Unified Modelling Language (UML) from the OMG, for example by using activity diagrams [12, cf. section 2.13.2.1]. Originally intended for "software-intensive" systems as the foreword of the UML specification explains, this modelling language is already implemented by different software products for the development of service compositions.[1]

3   Workflow Management

The management of workflows has got a different origin from the management of business processes. Workflow management systems (WFMS) were first applied for specific application cases. One of the systems mentioned as the first steps is the so called OfficeTalk which came as a part of the Xerox Star computer system [15]. The Xerox Palo Alto Research Centre (PARC) has developed this system in the 70s to support the work with documents in a typical office environment. This did not represent typical WFMS of today. However, OfficeTalk reflects the way humans would work on documents without computers – a non-computer-supported workflow. Clearly, workflow has in this sense a strong relation to support collaboration and document management. By covering this application scenario, the workflow management systems brought a couple of benefits. The most important advantage is the automated execution of tasks, which do not require an interactive handling, in order to accelerate the workflow. By the automated processing of data, the application of a WFMS anticipated that documents are kept in the software systems by bundling different systems together. Cumbersome re-entry of data which is time-costly should be avoided. And, when workflow management systems coordinate the work, also data can be derived that indicates the performance of the performed processes. Clearly,

---

[1] Examples are the Oracle BPEL Process Manager [13], or the WebSphere Integration Developer by IBM [14].

this represents an analogy to the main benefits identified for the business process reengineering.

From this early beginning, WFMS developed further to support other application domains than the work around documents in an office. Also, WFMS became more compatible to coordinate tasks performed by external systems. As an example, Mahling et al. explain the evolution of the Poise system [16]: in its first version, it represented an office information system supporting the handling of documents, such as entering information or realising static workflows. In the mid-80s, a subsequent development called Polymer offered a more sophisticated concept of modelling workflows that resulted in more flexible workflows and in a better coverage of different application scenarios. Based on that, Polyflow was introduced in 1995 as a full-featured WFMS in the sense of the reference model by WfMC [3].

3.1   Modelling Control Flows in Workflows

Since the development of WFMS begun, vendors have provided proprietary modelling languages. Van der Aalst et al. have introduced a set of patterns that describe structural characteristics and functional capabilities of WFMS and involved languages. Their analysis covers about 15 different WFMS [17].

Besides the reference model, the WfMC has introduced the XML Process Definition Language (XPDL, [18]). XPDL was intended to serve as a platform independent description language that allows to share workflow descriptions between tools and execution environments of different vendors. As a consequence, the authors have chosen the XML as its textual notation because of its wide support among different platforms. Besides the efforts from the industry side, research work covers also the modelling and specification aspect. Most approaches consider the application of EPCs, process calculi or (high-level) Petri nets as a foundation. Petri nets, also called Place-/Transition-Nets (P/T-Nets), are named by its "inventor" Carl Petri and serve as a formal language for modelling and specifying discrete events of dynamic systems. They show a high degree of versatility and are also applied to the specification of telecommunication protocols, or used as description of logistic chains. Petri nets were introduced by Petri in the year 1962; the ISO covers Petri nets today as a proposed standard [19].

Janssens et al. have introduced an analysis of existing workflow modelling efforts that use Petri nets [20]. Their analysis covers 12 contributions. The main reasons for using Petri nets for modelling workflows are that they offer a graphical notation and a formally defined semantic of its elements which allow the application of formally proven analysis techniques [20,21]. Among the contributions in this field, van der Aalst et al. have defined a Petri net variant which they call *Workflow Nets* for modelling workflows [22]. Based on this work and the patterns analysis, van der Aalst et al. have developed "Yet Another Workflow Language" (YAWL, [23]). This language extends the concepts of Workflow nets to support the workflow patterns while keeping a formal foundation that allows the anticipated verification of workflow models.

4   The Workflow Versus Business Processes Discussion

The previous two sections have introduced two fields that seem to have many issues in common. The resulting question is what makes these two different? The two terms business process and workflow modelling are used synonymously sometimes, suggesting that using either the one or the other refers to historic reasons. The two main communities who represent the workflow corner and the business process community, i.e. the WfMC and the BPMI, have discussed this questions in more detail. In a retro-perspective of the workflow reference model published by the WfMC [24], the authors acknowledge the growing momentum of business process management efforts, which have developed in parallel to the workflow-related efforts. The WfMC explains that a difference results from the evolution of the technologies in the workflow area. However, WFMS meet today the requirements of business process management as well. Consequently, their proposal sees the original reference model as the foundation for a new reference model that covers also business process management.

Members from the BPMI promote a different view. Smith and Fingar have initiated a discussion by publishing that a workflow represents just a process expressed using a process calculus [25] and thus is purely concerned with process description. According to their view, this clear focus makes workflows and WFMS less suitable for the new requirements of today's businesses. They explain that workflows are rather static (i.e., application dependent) and do not support changes of the process. Their statement has received a response from the workflow community which has motivated the two authors to publish a clarification [26]. What remains is that according to the viewpoint of the BPMI, a workflow represents just one aspect among the different fields subsumed by the business process management: in addition to workflows, business process management systems cover the integration of different computer systems as well as the non-computerised parts of business processes.

When it comes to the application of the terminology and the referring languages such as for looking at composition languages, a clarification must be achieved to distinguish what is different and what is claimed to be different. Apparently, the difference between both results from their different origins. The underlying problems such as the expressiveness of the modelling languages, how verifications can be applied, or which graphical modelling language is the most efficient, appear for both directions quite similar.

5   Realising Business Processes and Workflows with Service Compositions

The similarities between a process or workflow model and the composition of services in an SOA are evident. Modelling business processes usually involves a description about required activities and a specification about their execution order; this also represents what is basically required for describing a service composition. Also, business processes should have a defined input and output while the implementation of each task becomes secondary, what poses a similarity to the interface-orientation of services [27,28]. Moreover, an SOA provides different architectural characteristics which are promoted as the requirements on the IT-infrastructure in today's businesses [26]:

- **Technology Independence.** [29,30,31] The basic motivation to promote the SOA in companies is to establish a middleware that ties together functionality offered by different systems regardless of their hard- and software. This resembles the *access transparency* defined by the ISO RM-ODP [32, p. 17]. The heterogeneity of IT systems in companies is the standard in large businesses, because different departments of an enterprise have usually started the application of computer systems in most cases independently from each other.
- **Location Transparency.** [27,30,32] By definition, services offer their interface over a network. Web services uses Internet protocols for descriptions and messaging. Service consumers can use services across the local network or the boundaries of the local organisation. Although an organisation might not want to invoke any service that is just available anywhere in the world, the use of Internet protocols offers a greater level of flexibility.
- **Loose Coupling.** [29,30] The term loose coupling in an SOA is similar to the understanding of dynamic typing in the field of programming languages. Usually, in an SOA, loose coupling means that a service consumer knows what kind of service is required at design time. However, the binding ("coupling") to a real available service takes place at the run-time. Loose coupling enables service consumers to revise existing bindings during the run-time when necessary.

5.1 Modelling Service Compositions

Among the proposals for modelling service compositions, most languages provide direct support for Web services as this represents the major SOA implementation used today. The current situation shows different composition languages that share the same goal what resembles the situation with workflow or business process modelling. Also, some business process modelling languages are considered to create service compositions. To provide a better orientation among these, the following three groups are proposed:

- **Abstract level languages, L1.** These languages are primarily intended to describe a composition with activities in the way that services might realise these activities. However, concrete services are not mandatory to make the description complete. When not mentioning available particular services, such a description handles the activities or involved services as black boxes.
- **Concrete level languages, L3.** On the concrete level, the description covers the invocation of concrete services from a technical view. Usually, a service does not provide an atomic, stateless operation, but also provides different operations and requires to manage a session or a state. A description

must cover states when interoperating with services as well as considering particular operations. These languages do not focus entirely on service composition, because they are also concerned with the interoperation of different parties rather than realising a process.

- **Languages covering both levels, L2.** Some languages are right in the middle of both, not showing a clear process modelling focus and also not a clear interoperation focus. An example for such a language represents BPEL which allows the description of a business process among with an executable description involving available Web services. Compared with L3-languages, L2 would represent typical service composition languages.

The reader should note that this categorisation does not provide a formal basis nor an argumentation like if concept x is found in a language z, then it belongs to level y. This categorisation has the purpose to give an orientation. It resembles the idea of the model-driven architecture (MDA, [38]) which is a proposal for the model-centric development of software systems. This proposal distinguishes

Table 1. Composition Languages Overview

L	Acronym	Full Name, *Reference* Supporting Parties, Remarks
1	XPDL	XML Process Definition Language [33] WfMC, contributing authors were from Global 360, FileNet, Staffware/TIBCO, Prozone and Fujitsu Software
1	BPML	Business Process Modelling Language [7] BPMI, mentions only one contributing author from Intalio
1	BPSS	Business Process Specification Schema [7] *(Part of the ebXML Suite)* UN/CEFACT, an United Nations Body for Electronic Trade and an OASIS TC, including members from Cyclone Commerce, Fujitsu, SAP AG and Sun Microsystems
2	WSFL	Web Services Flow Language [9] IBM, moved into the BPEL4WS proposal
2	XLANG	subtitled "Web Services for Business Process Design" [11] Microsoft, moved into the BPEL4WS proposal
2	BPEL4WS	Business Process Execution Language for Web Services [34] IBM, Microsoft and BEA, moved into the WS-BPEL proposal
2	WS-BPEL	Web Services Business Process Execution Language [35] An OASIS TC involving about 18 industry parties, among them BEA Systems, IBM, Microsoft, Oracle, Sun Microsystems, SAP AG
3	WSCI	Web Service Choreography Interface [36] W3C Note submitted by BEA, Intalio, SAP AG und Sun Microsystems
3	WS-C	Web Service Choreography [37] W3C Working Group, continuing the WSCI proposal

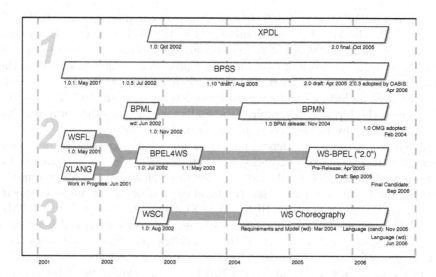

Fig. 1. Release Dates of Process Description and Service Composition Languages

(software) models at different stages of the development process. The two main categories of models are platform-independent models (PIM) and platform-specific models (PSM). PIMs do not contain modelling artefacts resulting from specific technologies, platforms or standards; they represent an *abstraction* from technical details. Based on these, PSMs are derived from PIMs to provide the technical information necessary for the implementation of the software.

Table 5.1 lists a selection of composition languages with their acronyms and their proposed categorisation. In addition, Figure 1 shows a chronological overview about their introduction dates. The two BPEL proposals, WSFL, and XLANG were mentioned already in Section 2.1. These candidates can be clearly called Web service composition languages and fit into the second group.

Regarding the languages at the first level, Table 5.1 mentions XPDL, BPML, and BPSS. These languages provide elements to support the invocation of Web services; however, their involvement is not mandatory. The BPSS is completely independent from particular SOA technologies. To provide the ties to concrete SOA implementations like Web services, separate specifications called a Collaboration Protocol Profile (CPP) and a Collaboration Protocol Agreement (CPA) are proposed. A BPSS document can refer to a CPP or CPA to provide a description of the involved services, for example, by referencing to a WSDL description. However, since the BPSS has a clear focus on enabling electronic trade, it is thus not the preferred candidate for implementing business processes with service compositions.

The Web Service Choreography Interface (WSCI) represents the foundation for the third group. The WSCI proposal directly focusses on specifying the required message flow between Web service requesters and providers resulting from their offered operations [36]. Consequently, the authors of BPML mention explicitly that WSCI and WSDL specifications are complementary to BPML [7, section 1.2]. The WSCI has been submitted to the W3C as a technical note in 2002. In beginning of 2003, a W3C working group named Web Services Choreography has begun its work to take the WSCI proposal as input to elaborate this aspect further [37]. By choreography, the working group refers to the *characteristic of describing linkages and usage patterns between Web services*. The working group uses the term choreography in a similar manner as other proposals use collaboration, conversation, coordination or orchestration.

When comparing the different languages and specifications, not only thier focus but also their expressiveness is a useful criteria. Such a comparison has already been conducted by Wohed, van der Aalst et al. They have presented a comprehensive analysis about the structural capabilities of languages to specify Web service compositions for BPEL4WS, XLANG, and WSFL [39,1], BPML, and WSCI [40], and XPDL [10]. Their result is an analysis about which language directly supports which pattern of their workflow patterns. Apart from these languages, other proposals exist which were in previous sections. Considering graphical notations, EPCs and the BPMN are suitable for the description of service compositions as well. However, none of these efforts shows a noticeable impact in this area. For this purpose the UML plays a more important role, as research work has already indicated [41,42].

6   Conclusions

This paper has proposed a classification of composition languages and languages for modelling business processes. The classification helps to identify different players in the Web Services Acronym Hell (WSAH) [1]. The classification is roughly based on separating composition languages for abstract process design from languages for defining how to involve concrete Web services. Moreover, it was discussed that composition languages have much in common with the modelling of workflows. By using their workflow patterns, Wohed, van der Aalst et al. give a detailed explanation about the capabilities of composition languages with their problems and – more important – they also explain how previously introduced workflow modelling languages have coped with that.

The overview has identified different parallel efforts working on composition languages, which is still an ongoing process. Apparently, the OASIS-driven WS-BPEL has the biggest momentum in the service composition area. It gathers together main industry players, such as IBM, Microsoft, Oracle, SAP, and Sun Microsystems. Besides, the WS Choreography working group shows also ongoing activity for the definition of service compositions on a technical level.

References

1. van der Aalst, W.M.P., Dumas, M., ter Hofstede, A.H.M.: Web Service Composition Languages: Old Wine in New Bottles? In: EUROMICRO'03. Proceedings of the 29th EUROMICRO Conference New Waves in System Architecture, Belek, Turkey, September 2003, pp. 298–304. IEEE Computer Society Press, Los Alamitos (2003)

2. Booth, D., Haas, H., McCabe, F., Newcomer, E., Champion, M., Ferris, C., Orchard, D.: Web Services Architecture (February 2004), http://www.w3c.org/TR/ws-arch/

3. Hollingsworth, D.: The Workflow Reference Model. Technical Report TC00-1003, Workflow Management Coalition, Lighthouse Point, Florida, USA (1995)

4. Hammer, M., Champy, J.: A Manifesto for Business Revolution. Harper Business (1993)

5. Frank, H., Gronau, N., Krallman, H.: Systemanalyse im Unternehmen, 3 edn. Oldenbourg Verlag, München, Germany (October 2000)

6. Keller, G., Nüttgens, M., Scheer, A.W.: Semantische Prozeßmodellierung auf der Grundlage Ereignisgesteuerter Prozeßketten (EPK). Veröffentlichungen des Instituts für Wirtschaftsinformatik (IWi) 89, Universität des Saarlandes, Saarbrücken, Germany (1992)

7. Assaf, A., et al.: Business Process Modeling Language (BPML). Technical Report Version 1.0, BPMI.org (2002)

8. White, S.A.: Business Process Modeling Notation (BPMN). Technical Report Working Draft (1.0), BPMI.org (August 2003)

9. Leymann, F.: Web Services Flow Language (WSFL 1.0). Technical report, IBM Software Group (2001), http://www-4.ibm.com/software/solutions/webser-vices/pdf/WSFL.pdf

10. van der Aalst, W.M.P.: Don't go with the flow: Web services composition standards exposed. In: Jan/Feb 2003 Issue of IEEE Intelligent Systems, January 2003, pp. 72–76. IEEE Computer Society Press, Los Alamitos (2003)

11. Thatte, S.: XLANG - Web Services for Business Process Design (2001), http://www.gotdotnet.com/team/xml_wsspecs/xlang-c/default.htm

12. Object Management Group (OMG): Unified Modeling Language: Superstructure. OMG formal document/05-07-04 (August 2005)

13. Shaffer, D., Dayton, B.: Orchestrating Web Services: The Case for a BPEL Server. Technical report, Oracle Corporation, Redwood Shores, California, USA (June 2004)

14. Lynch, E., Venkatapathy, C.: Sustaining your Advantage with Business Process Integration based on Service Oriented Architecture. White Paper (October 2005)

15. Johnson, J., Roberts, T.L., Verplank, W., Smith, D.C., Irby, C., Beard, M., Mackey, K.: The Xerox Star: A Retrospective. Computer 22(9), 11–26 (1989)

16. Mahling, D.E., Craven, N., Croft, W.B.: From Office Automation to Intelligent Workflow Systems. IEEE Intelligent Systems 10(3), 41–47 (1995)

17. van der Aalst, W.M.P., ter Hofstede, A.H.M., Kiepuszewski, B., Barros, A.P.: Workflow Patterns. Distributed and Parallel Databases 14(1), 5–51 (2003)

18. Marin, M., Brunt, J., Zurek, W., Stephenson, T., Bojanic, S., Gouri, G.: Workflow Process Definition Interface – XML Process Definition Langauge, Version 1.0. Technical Report WFMC-TC-1025, Workflow Management Coalition, Lighthouse Point, Florida (October 2002)

19. ISO/IEC: ISO/IEC 15909-1: High-level Petri nets – Part 1: Concepts, Definitions and Graphical Notation. Published Standard (December 2004)

20. Janssens, G.K., Verelst, J., Weyn, B.: Techniques for modelling workflows and their support of reuse. In: van der Aalst, W.M.P., Desel, J., Oberweis, A. (eds.) Business Process Management. LNCS, vol. 1806, pp. 1–15. Springer, Heidelberg (2000)

21. van der Aalst, W.M.P.: Workflow Verification: Finding Control-Flow Errors Using Petri-Net-Based Techniques. In: van der Aalst, W.M.P., Desel, J., Oberweis, A. (eds.) Business Process Management. LNCS, vol. 1806, pp. 161–183. Springer, Heidelberg (2000)
22. van der Aalst, W.M.P., van Hee, K.M., Houben, G.J.: Modelling Workflow Management Systems with high-level Petri Nets. In: De Michelis, G., Ellis, C., Memmi, G. (eds.) Proceedings of the second Workshop on Computer-Supported Cooperative Work, Petri nets and related formalisms, pp. 31–50 (1994)
23. van der Aalst, W.M.P., Aldred, L., Dumas, M., ter Hofstede, A.H.M.: Design and implementation of the YAWL system. Technical Report FIT-TR-2003-07, Centre for IT Innovation, QUT (2004), http://www.tm.tue.nl/it/research/patterns
24. Hollingsworth, D.: The Workflow Reference Model 10 Years On (extracted from Workflow Handbook 2004). In: Workflow Management Coalition, Lighthouse Point, Florida (February 2004)
25. Smith, H., Fingar, P.: Workflow is just a Pi Process, January 2004. Business Process Trends, Columns and Articles (2004)
26. Smith, H., Fingar, P.: Business Process Fusion Is Inevitable. Business Process Trends, Columns and Articles (March 2004)
27. Bolcer, G.A., Kaiser, G.: SWAP: Leveraging the Web to Manage Workflow. In: IEEE Internet Computing, January-February 1999, pp. 85–88. IEEE Computer Society Press, Los Alamitos (1999)
28. Dijkman, R.M., Dumas, M.: Service-Oriented Design: A Multi-Viewpoint Approach. International Journal of Cooperative Information Systems (IJCIS) 13(4), 337–368 (2004)
29. Huhns, M.N., Singh, M.P.: Service-oriented computing: Key concepts and principles. In: IEEE Internet Computing, January and February 2005, pp. 75–81 (2005)
30. Papazoglou, M.P.: Service-Oriented Computing: Concepts, Characteristics and Directions. In: WISE'03. Proceedings of the Fourth International Conference on Web Information Systems Engineering, Roma, Italy, December 2003, pp. 3–12. IEEE Computer Society Press, Los Alamitos (2003)
31. Yang, J.: Web Service Componentization. Communications of the ACM 46(10) (2003)
32. ISO/IEC: ITU.TS Recommendation X.902 — ISO/IEC 10746-1: Open Distributed Processing Reference Model - Part 1: Overview (August 1996)
33. Shapiro, R., Marin, M., Brunt, J., Zurek, W., Stephenson, T., Bojanic, S., Gouri, G.: Process Definition Interface – XML Process Definition Language, Version 2.0. Technical Report WFMC-TC-1025, Workflow Management Coalition, Lighthouse Point, Florida (October 2005)
34. Tony, A., et al.: Business Process Execution Language for Web Services Version 1.1. Technical report, BEA Systems, IBM Corp., Microsoft Corp., (2003), http://www-106.ibm.com/developerworks/webser-vices/library/ws-bpel/
35. TC, O.W.B.: WS-BPEL Specification Editors Draft (December 2005), http://www.oasis-open.org/committees/download.php/127 91/ wsbpel-specification-draft-May-20-2005.html
36. Assaf, A., et al.: Web Service Choreography Interface (WSCI) 1.0. Technical report, W3C (2002), http://www.w3.org/TR/wsci
37. Burdett, D., Nickolas, K. (eds.): WS Choreography Model Overview, W3C Working Draft 24 March 2004. Technical report, W3C (2004), http://www.w3.org/TR/ws-chor-model/
38. Object Management Group (OMG): Model Driven Architecture. ormsc/2001-07-01 (August 2001)

39. Wohed, P., van der Aalst, W.M.P., Dumas, M., ter Hofstede, A.H.: Pattern Based Analysis of BPEL4WS. Technical Report FIT-TR-2002-04, QUT, Queensland University of Technology, Queensland, Australia (2002)

40. van der Aalst, W.M.P., Dumas, M., ter Hofstede, A.H.M., Wohed, P.: Pattern Based Analysis of BPML (and WSCI). FIT Technical Report FIT-TR-2002-05, Queensland University of Technology, Brisbane, Australia (2002)

41. Skogan, D., Grønmo, R., Solheim, I.: Web Service Composition in UML. In: EDOC'04. Proceedings of the 8th IEEE Intl Enterprise Distributed Object Computing Conf., Monterey, California, September 2004, pp. 47–57. IEEE Computer Society Press, Los Alamitos (2004)

42. Grønmo, R., Jaeger, M.C.: Model-Driven Methodology for Building QoS-Optimised Web Service Compositions. In: Kutvonen, L., Alonistioti, N. (eds.) DAIS 2005. LNCS, vol. 3543, pp. 68–82. Springer, Heidelberg (2005)

Extending the UN/CEFACT Modeling Methodology and Core Components for Intra-organizational Service Orchestration

Philipp Offermann[1], Christian Schröpfer[1],
and Maximilian Ahrens[2]

[1] Faculty of Electrical Engineering and Computer Sciences,
Technische Universität Berlin, Germany
{Philipp.Offermann, Christian.Schroepfer}@sysedv.tu-berlin.de
[2] Deutsche Telekom Laboratories, Berlin, Germany
maximilian.ahrens@telekom.de

Abstract. When creating a company's IT structure based on a service-oriented architecture (SOA), it is necessary to first analyze the business domains and process areas of the company, then to model the business processes to be supported by the SOA and finally to convert the models into a service orchestration description. Currently, few methodologies exist to support this. At our department, we have proven that the UN/CEFACT Modeling Methodology (UMM) can be used for intra-organizational process integration. In this article we analyze if the UMM is sufficient for SOA, which artifacts are missing and how the UMM could be extended. The UMM was created to model the collaboration between different legal entities to perform collaborative business processes. There exist methods to convert these models into executable service choreography descriptions expressed in the Business Process Specification Schema (BPSS) or the Business Process Execution Language (BPEL). However, the business process models can also be used as a basis for an intra-organizational service orchestration. By extending the UMM it is possible to enable the automated generation of service orchestrations using Core Components and the Business Process Modeling Notation (BPMN).

Keywords: UN/CEFACT Modeling Methodology (UMM), Core Components (CC), Business Process Execution Language (BPEL), Business Process Modeling Notation (BPMN), Service Orchestration, Service-Oriented Architecture (SOA).

1 Introduction

Service-oriented architecture (SOA) is a new design paradigm for software systems and IT governance. While the technical concepts behind the SOA are well established, comprehensive methodologies are still rare. At our department we have proven, using action research, that the UN/CEFACT Modeling Methodology (UMM) can be used for intra-organizational process integration.[1] In this article we analyze if the UMM methodology is sufficient for SOA and how it could be extended.

D. Georgakopoulos et al. (Eds.): ICSOC 2006 Ws, LNCS 4652, pp. 154–165, 2007.

1.1 Service-Oriented Architecture

Service-oriented architectures are a current trend in the IT industry. Many big companies like IBM, Microsoft, BEA and SAP are supporting and developing standards for or are converting their products to an SOA.[2-5] Additionally, organizations like the World Wide Web Consortium (W3C), OASIS and the Object Management Group (OMG) are developing and publishing standards related to SOAs.[6-8]

The Gartner Group defines an SOA as follows: "SOA is a software architecture that builds a topology of interfaces, interface implementations and interface calls. SOA is a relationship of services and service consumers, both software modules large enough to represent a complete business function. So, SOA is about reuse, encapsulation, interfaces, and ultimately, agility."[9]

The most common implementation environment for an SOA is Web services. A Web service is a program that offers its functionality through a defined interface over open protocols.[6] The difference to classical modularization of program logic is that the functionality encapsulated by Web services is derived from the business functions composing the business processes and not from the IT systems.[10-12]

Therefore, the concept of an SOA is not restricted to the technical side, but also reaches out to business process management (BPM).[13] By designing services in a way that they represent business functionality, it is possible to align the structure of business processes with the organization of the IT infrastructure supporting these processes.

1.2 Service Orchestration

To be able to align the IT structure with the business processes, it is necessary to describe the sequence in which Web services are called and to make sure that this sequence is structurally equivalent to the sequence of business functions described in the business process model.

Different description languages, called web service orchestration languages, have evolved to describe the sequence of Web services and make this sequence executable. Service orchestration languages are used to support intra-organizational processes through a central coordination, while service choreography languages support inter-organizational processes without a central coordination.[14] Out of the service orchestration languages, the Business Process Execution Language (BPEL) has most support from industry and research.[15]

For representing the structure of business processes, different modeling notations exist, e.g. Event-Process Chain (EPC), ICAM Definition Language (IDEF) and UML Activity Diagrams. There are ways for converting these process models into executable process description languages, e.g. UML to BPEL.[16]

Additionally, special business process modeling notations that are based on the orchestration languages have evolved to better support the conversion from the business process model into the executable service orchestration. One of these is the Business Process Modeling Notation (BPMN).[8]

1.3 The Missing Methodology

What has been missing until now is a methodology giving a guideline how to analyze businesses and model its processes for orchestrating services. For achieving a perfect alignment of the business processes with the IT structure, in a first step the business processes have to be identified, analyzed and explicitly written down, preferable in the form of diagrams. This process usually starts with a business domain analysis to identify different fields of business processes before modeling the business processes in detail. Then, several refinement layers of the business process activities have to be modeled to describe the business process on a granularity level suitable for a support through Web services.

Finally, the business processes described in a modeling notation have to be converted into an executable description. This also includes binding the services to the business activities. For finding the right Web services, the requirements have to be included as precisely as possible in the business process models. In a first step, the inputs and outputs of the business activities should be specified. For a more detailed description, pre and post conditions as well as non-functional requirements can be included too.

The UMM has been subject to thorough research at our department. It provides a methodology that can be used for intra-organizational process integration. [1] This is why we are interested in analyzing if the UMM is sufficient for SOA, which artifacts are missing and how it could be extended. We will first introduce the UMM, then show its limitations and propose extensions so that required artifacts for intra-organizational service orchestration are created.

2   UN/CEFACT Modeling Methodology

The UN/CEFACT Modeling Methodology (UMM) provides a methodology and models to describe inter-organizational business processes. The idea behind this is to have a unified methodology for identifying and modeling the information exchange between participants when executing a business to business (B2B) process that spans different companies.[17]

2.1   The Methodology

The UMM is based on three views, the Business Domain View, the Business Requirements View, and Business Transaction View. These views present the different perspectives that are used at different stages of the modeling process. The models are based on UML 1.4.2.[18]

Business Domain View. The first view in the process of modeling the business collaboration is the Business Domain View. It takes a very high level perspective. For this view, in a first step, business areas and process areas are identified, using diagrams based on the UML Package Diagram. Then for every process area business processes and stakeholders are identified, using diagrams based on the UML Use Case Diagram.

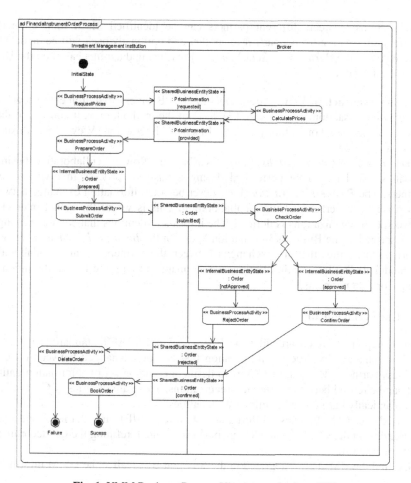

Fig. 1. UMM Business Process View example, from [17]

Business Requirements View. After finishing the Business Domain View, following the methodology, the Business Requirements View has to be completed. It differentiates three views: Business Process View, Business Entity View, and Partnership Requirements View.

The *Business Process View* contains business processes. These processes are modeled as Business Process Activity Models based on the UML Activity Diagram notation. In the process models, entity states are used as defined in the Business Entity View. The *Business Entity View* describes all entities that are used in the Business Process Activity Models, using a diagram based on the UML Class Diagram, and the lifecycles of the entities, using diagrams based on the UML Statechart Diagram. An entity state can either be an Internal Business Entity State for an entity state that is internal to a business process of a single partner, or a Shared Business Entity State for an entity state that is shared between different partners participating in a process. An example Business Process View is displayed in figure 1. Based on the exchange of Shared Business Entity States, requirements for collaborations between different partners can be identified. Each transaction that transfers information from a partner to another and optionally back will be modeled in more detail in the *Partnership Requirements View*, using diagrams based on the UML Use Case Diagram.

Business Transaction View. After modeling the "Business Requirements View", the "Business Transaction View" is the last stage of the methodology. It consists of three views: Business Choreography View, Business Interaction View, and Business Information View.

The *Business Choreography View* describes the flow of collaborative business activities that have to be performed during a business process involving several partners. The *Business Interaction View* describes the information exchange between two partners to perform a single collaboration. This is where the actual interaction between two organizations is defined. The information entities that can be exchanged are described in the Business Information View. In the *Business Information View* all Information Entities that are exchanged between the partners during a collaboration are modeled. The Information Entities can be mapped to a more formal definition by using Core Components.

2.2 Core Components

Core Components (CC) are, like the UMM, a UN/CEFACT standard.[19] CC are used to semantically describe information that can be exchanged between different business partners. The aim of CCs is to define a common set of information entities that can be reused between different organizations. There are libraries of CC available to semantically harmonize the information entities.[20]

Based on CC, Business Information Entities (BIE) are defined, specifying restrictions on the CC. BIE put CC in a business context, refining the CC according to their specific use.

CC and the UMM are integrated in the way that BIE realize the UMM information entities.

2.3 Service Choreography

Based on the business collaborations modeled in the Business Choreography View and concrete transactions modeled in the Business Interaction View, it is possible to generate a service choreography for the parties involved. The Business Process Specification Schema (BPSS) has been specially developed for this purpose.[21]

What has not yet been envisioned by the UMM is the generation of a service orchestration for a single company. The advantage of this would be to use a single methodology for describing the orchestration of services within a company together with the choreography necessary for the collaboration between companies. This limitation is due to the aim of the UMM.

2.4 Limitations of the UMM

The UMM is aimed at modeling the information exchange between different parties involved in a business process. Until modeling the business processes and information flow in the Business Process View and the Business Entity View, the methodology is general and can be used either for analyzing the business processes of a single company or the collaboration between different partners. But starting with the Partnership Requirements View, the methodology specializes on the collaboration of the different parties involved. That results in very detailed diagrams about the collaboration, down to the level of a concrete request and an optional response.

For a service orchestration, it is necessary to also specify the business processes internal to the partners involved in more detail. Unfortunately, as the internal business processes are not interesting for the collaboration, it is not foreseen in the methodology to model them in any greater detail. While the UMM is sufficient for modeling collaborative business processes, it comes to its limitations when trying to orchestrate services. A different methodology is necessary for modeling internal business process as a basis of a service orchestration.

3   Modeling Processes for Service Orchestration with the UMM

It would be of great advantage to use a single methodology to model the processes inside a company as well as to model the collaboration between companies. From such models, in addition to the service choreography, a service orchestration could be derived. Additionally, when all the processes are modeled uniformly, it is easier to in- or outsource parts of the process.

3.1   Using the Methodology on a Finer Granularity Level

One idea to enable service orchestration using the UMM is to use the methodology on a finer granularity level. If, for example, the different partners involved in a business process are not different companies, but different departments inside the same company, the transactions analyzed in the Business Transaction View are transactions inside the company. Still, this would result in a service choreography, only this time inside the company and not between companies.

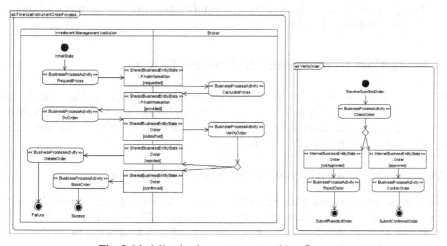

Fig. 2. Modeling business processes with refinements

To model the information exchange necessary for every single business function, and therefore for every single service supporting the business process, every service would have to be interpreted as a different partner involved in the process. While this would be possible for single services, it clearly reaches its limitation when every service has to be modeled as a partner. On the one hand, the models in the Business Domain View and especially in the Business Requirements View would be too complex. On the other hand, modeling every single service as a partner would lead to an explosion of the number of models in the Business Transaction View.

Therefore, for generating a service orchestration out of a UMM model, using the methodology on a finer granularity level does not seem to be a feasible solution.

3.2 Using the Process Model for Service Orchestration

Another approach to generate a service orchestration is to use the process model from the Business Process View. The Business Process Activity Model is based on UML Activity Diagrams. These diagrams are well suited for business process modeling, and a transformation into a service orchestration described in the BPEL exists.[16]

As a Business Process Activity, the activity used in Business Process Activity Models, may contain another Business Process Activity Model, a refinement of activities is possible in the UMM. This can be used to refine process models down to a level where they can be used for service orchestration.

A service orchestration can only be generated for a control flow within a partition (concerning only one partner). Otherwise, it would not be an orchestration but a choreography. Additionally, modeling the activities on a level necessary for a service orchestration is of no use for identifying the need for a collaboration. It would be a better solution to model a process internal to a partner on the highest level as only one activity. This is sufficient for identifying the need for a collaboration. At the same time when refining the activity, it contains a whole process part being performed by one partner. Hence the refinement can be used to generate a service orchestration.

Figure 2 illustrates this. On the left side, a business process with only one activity per partner per collaboration is shown, sufficient to identify necessary collaboration. On the right side, one activity is refined. This refinement can later be used to generate a service orchestration description.

4   Using Core Components for Business Entities

What has been considered for the service orchestration until now is the control flow of internal business processes. Apart from the control flow, Business Process Activity Models describe the business entity flow and business entity states too. This information flow can be used for orchestrating services.

4.1   Modeling the Business Entities for Service Orchestration

Information about the business entity flow is used to identify what kinds of objects are exchanged during a collaborative business process. The concrete structure of the information exchanged between partners is defined at a later stage in the Business Transaction View.

When modeling the entity flow in a business process being used as a basis for a service orchestration, the relevant entities are information entities. In contrast to general business processes where physical products could be exchanged, Web services only exchange information. Therefore only the information flow has to be modeled in the regarded business processes.

For a service orchestration, the information about the data flow can be used to describe the services that are necessary to support the business process. It is therefore helpful to extensively use the Internal Business Entity State, the entity stereotype used internally in a business process, for the modeling of a service orchestration.

Unfortunately, in the UMM there is no official link between the entities modeled in the Business Entity View that are used in the Business Process View and the entities modeled in the Business Information View that are used in the Business Interaction View. But only in the Business Information View the entities are specified in detail. Therefore, a link between a Business Entities from the Business Entity View and an Information Entity from the Business Information View should be established to enable a more detailed description of the information exchange in the Business Process Activity Model. This is possible as the Business Entity View and the Business Information View are based on UML Class Diagrams. It could be envisioned to unify the Business Entity and the Information Entity into one single stereotype when modeling business processes for a service orchestration.

4.2   Using Core Components for a Common Semantic

The flow of information entities is relevant for a service orchestration. For modeling this flow, entities being used as input and/or output of business activities should be modeled using a common semantic. In the UMM, this can be realized by using Core Components. As explained above, a Business Information Entity can realize a UMM Information Entity. By this a common semantic is used to describe the information exchange in the Business Transaction View. Unfortunately, the Business Transaction View defines a choreography of information exchanges only, but doesn't help when creating a service orchestration.

By linking Information Entities with Business Entities as proposed above, the semantics of the CC can be used in the Business Process View. The information flow used for creating the service orchestration is semantically based on CC. This is useful when trying to bind the business activities to concrete services, as input and output parameters are described semantically.

5   Using the BPMN for Business Process Activity Models

Modeling business processes for service orchestrations, another UMM extension can be proposed by replacing the UMM Business Process Activity Model with the Business Process Modeling Notation.

5.1   The Business Process Modeling Notation

The Business Process Modeling Notation (BPMN) is an Object Management Group (OMG) standard.[8] While UML Activity Diagrams were developed to describe object oriented software systems, the BPMN was developed to model business processes.[22] At the same time, a defined mapping between the BPMN and the BPEL exists.[8, 23]

BPMN and UML Activity Diagrams are very similar. The only pattern that can not be modeled in UML Activity Diagrams is the Interleaved Parallel Routing pattern.[24] As the UML and the BPMN are OMG standards, it is possible that the two notations will be merged at some point.[24] Still, modeling business processes with the BPMN has the advantage that due to its extended syntax complex situations can be model much more explicitly. This results in diagrams that are much more readable.

The BPMN can be used to model private (internal) business processes, abstract (public) processes and collaboration (global) processes. Of interest in this article are collaboration processes and private business processes.

Collaboration processes use at least two swim lanes. In figure 3 a collaboration process is shown. For modeling an information exchange between different parties, a Message Flow with a special arrow is used for message exchanges between the parties. This clearly depicts which flows are needed in a collaboration.

In contrast to the collaboration process, a *private business process* uses one swim lane only, enabling the modeling for internal business processes.

5.2   Using BPMN Instead of Business Process Activity Models

The idea is to replace the UMM Business Process Activity Model with a BPMN model. There are four advantages:

1. Many constructs are much clearer in the BPMN than the equivalent UML Activity Diagram notation when modeling down to a granularity level of services, as special denotations exists e.g. for rollback and messages.[24]
2. The BPMN was developed to be transformed into a service orchestration and has a defined mapping to the BPEL.
3. While the OMG designed UML Activity Diagrams for modeling object oriented software systems, the BPMN is the OMG's standard for business process modeling. Hence one should assume that for modeling business process it is better to use the notation that was designed for this task.
4. The collaborations between partners can be identified more easily using BPMN because of its special message flow notation and the possibility to informally group elements. An example for this is drawn in figure 3.

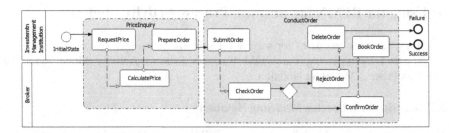

Fig. 3. Using groups for indicating collaboration in the BPMN

Replacing the Business Activity Model by a BPMN model is straight forward as the Business Activity Model is based on UML Activity Diagrams, which BPMN models are very similar to. An example of the business process shown in figure 1 modeled in the BPMN can be seen in figure 3. What is not shown in the example are the BPMN Data Objects that would relate to the Business Entities of the Business Entity View. By relating Business Entities to Information Entities, the BPMN Data Objects can also be based on Core Components, making it possible to semantically annotate the data flow in the same way as in Business Process Activity Models.

6 Summary and Outlook

It is possible to extend the UN/CEFACT Modeling Methodology to better support the modeling and generation of service orchestration. Only few extensions are necessary.

6.1 Propositions

The following extensions of the UMM are proposed:

1. Use the UMM Business Process View model on a granularity level as high as possible for depicting a collaborative business process. Then use refinements to model internal business processes down to a detail level necessary for supporting business activities by services.
2. Establish a link between UMM Business Entities and UMM Information Entities. For a service orchestration only the information exchanged between business activities is of interest. Thus, by establishing the link, the Business Entities can be based on Core Components. This is also useful for a consistent semantic description of the services necessary to support the business activities.
3. Replace the UMM Business Process Activity Model by a Business Process Modeling Notation model. This helps specifying the internal business process, makes it easier to transform the model into an executable service orchestration and even facilitates the identification for necessary collaborations.

6.2 Advantages

By following these extensions of the UMM, the methodology can not only be used to generate service choreographies, but also service orchestrations internal to a business partner. One methodology can be used to model both aspects of a service-priented architecture, the business and its processes as well as the service orchestration and the service choreography. The end-to-end process starting with the business domain analysis and ending with the orchestration and choreography description is supported by one single methodology. This helps businesses, because knowledge of only one technique has to exist and one set of models can be used for business and technical aspects.

6.3 Outlook

There are many points that are still open and subject to further research within this area. The future work of the authors will focus on three of them. The most important point is evaluating the concept by conducting an empirical study on the applicability of the proposed extensions. For this, secondly, a tool has to be created incorporating all necessary modeling notations to support the methodology. Finally, a semantic description of Web services to be used in conjunction with the proposed modeling technique based on Core Components should be developed.

References

1. Dietrich, J.: Nutzung von Modellierungssprachen und -methodologien standardisierter B2B-Architekturen für die Integration unternehmensinterner Geschäftsprozesse (unpublished Dissertation). TU Berlin, Fachgebiet Systemeanalyse und EDV (2006)
2. International Business Machines Corporation: developerWorks : SOA and Web services (2006), http://www-128.ibm.com/developerworks/webservices
3. Microsoft Corporation: .NET Architecture Center: Service Oriented Architecture (2006), http://msdn.microsoft.com/architecture/soa/
4. BEA Systems: Dev2Dev Online: Service-oriented Architecture (2006), http://dev2dev.bea.com/soa/
5. SAP AG: SAP - Enterprise Service-Oriented Architecture: Blueprint for Service-Based Business Solutions (2006), http://www.sap.com/platform/esa/index.epx
6. World Wide Web Consortium: Web Services Architecture (2004), http://www.w3.org/TR/ws-arch/
7. OASIS Open: OASIS Commitees by Category: SOA (2006), http://www.oasis-open.org/committees/tc_cat.php?cat=soa
8. Object Management Group: Business Process Modeling Notation Specification (2006), http://www.omg.org/cgi-bin/doc?dtc/2006-02-01
9. McCoy, D., Natis, Y.: Service-Oriented Architecture: Mainstream Straight Ahead. Gartner Research (2003)
10. Szyperski, C.: Component Oriented Programming. Springer, Heidelberg (1998)
11. Schmelzer, R.: Solving the Service Granularity Challenge (2005), http:// www.zapthink.com/report.html?id=ZAPFLASH-200639
12. Foody, D.: Getting web service granularity right (2005), http://www.soa-zone.com/index.php?/ archives/ 11-Getting-web-service-granularity-right.html
13. Leymann, F., Roller, D., Schmidt, M.T.: Web services and business process management. IBM Systems Journal 41, 198–211 (2002)
14. Newcomer, E., Lomow, G.: Understanding SOA with Web Services. Addison-Wesley, Reading (2005)
15. Andrews, T., Curbera, F., Dholakia, H., Goland, Y., Klein, J., Leymann, F., Liu, K., Roller, D., Smith, D., Trickovic, I., Weerawarana, S.: Business Process Execution Language for Web Services Version 1.1 (2003), ftp://www6.software.ibm.com/software/developer/library/ws-bpel.pdf
16. Skogan, D., Gronmo, R., Solheim, I.: Web service composition in UML. Enterprise Distributed Object Computing Conference, 2004. In: EDOC 2004. Proceedings. Eighth IEEE International, pp. 47–57 (2004)
17. UN/CEFACT: UN/CEFACT's Modeling Methodology (UMM) (2006), http://www.untmg.org/index.php?option=com_docman&task=view_category&Itemid=137&subcat=1&catid=63&limitstart=0&limit=5
18. Object Management Group: Unified Modeling Language Specification Version 1.4.2 (2004), http://www.omg.org/cgi-bin/doc?formal/04-07-02

19. UN/CEFACT: ISO\DTS 15000-5: 2006 Core Components Technical Specification 2nd edn. UN/CEFACT Version 2.2 (2006), http://www.untmg.org/index.php?option=com_docman&task=docclick&Itemid=137&bid=43&limitstart=0&limit=5

20. United Nations Economic Commission for Europe: Core Component Library (UN/CCL) (2006), http://www.unece.org/cefact/codesfortrade/codes_index.htm#ccl

21. UN/CEFACT: UN/CEFACT – ebXML Business Process Specification Schema (2003), http://www.untmg.org/index.php?option=com_docman&task=view_category&Itemid=137&subcat=3&catid=63&limitstart=0&limit=5

22. White, S.A.: Introduction to BPMN. IBM Corporation (2004), http://www.bpmn.org/Documents/Introduction%20to%20BPMN.pdf

23. White, S.A.: Using BPMN to Model a BPEL Process. IBM Corp., United States (2005), http://www.bpmn.org/Documents/Mapping%20BPMN%20to%20BPEL%20Example.pdf

24. White, S.A.: Process Modeling Notations and Workflow Patterns. IBM Corp., United States (2004),
http://www.bpmn.org/Documents/Notations%20and%20Workflow%20 Patterns.pdf

A Pattern-Based Approach to Business Process Modeling and Implementation in Web Services

Steen Brahe[1] and Behzad Bordbar[2]

[1] Danske Bank and IT University of Copenhagen, Denmark
stbr@danskebank.dk
[2] School of Computer Science, University of Birmingham, UK
b.bordbar@cs.bham.ac.uk

Abstract. There are often three groups of experts involved in the design and implementation of business processes in a service oriented enterprise; *business analysts*, *solution architects* and *system developers*. They collaborate with each other to transform a high-level design created by a business analyst to a final executable workflow, based on a service composition language such as the Business Process Execution Language (BPEL). In this paper, we present a new approach to support and semi-automate this transformation process, thus producing applications of higher quality in shorter time. The idea is to capture existing knowledge in the enterprise, which is required for transforming models from one abstraction level to another, as reusable, parameterized patterns. These patterns are used for tool based model transformations of the business processes. To support our approach, we shall make use of Domain Specific Modeling Languages (DSMLs) designed for each enterprise to capture models of a business process at different levels of abstraction, each suitable for the use of one of the groups of experts. The presented approach bridges the gap between business and IT by providing customizable language-, tool- and transformation support for the different groups of experts within the enterprise and is illustrated by an example.

1   Introduction

Information technology is undergoing a rapid change of role from being a mere provider of support for businesses, to an active role in driving the revenue and profit [1]. There is an ever-increasing pressure on modern enterprises to adapt to the changes in their environment by evolving to respond to any opportunity or threat [2]. To address such challenges, Service Oriented Architecture (SOA) has received considerable attention as it provides the foundation for implementing business processes via composition of (existing) services.

Using SOA and service composition requires a collaborative effort of different groups of experts; *business analysts* model the process at a high conceptual level, *solution architects* map such conceptual designs to architectural models, and *system developers* implement architectural models in a service composition language such as Business Process Execution Language (BPEL) [3]. However, there is a gap between business and IT, due to different terminology, levels of granularity, varied models, approaches, tools and method that each employ [2].

D. Georgakopoulos et al. (Eds.): ICSOC 2006 Ws, LNCS 4652, pp. 166–177, 2007.

In this paper we present a new approach to close the gaps between different model representations of a business process by using tool-based transformations from one model to another. The main idea of the approach is to capture knowledge required for the transformations as reusable, parameterized patterns, which can be used to conduct the transformations via software tools. To achieve this, we combine Model Driven Development (MDD) techniques [4] and Domain Specific Modeling Languages (DSMLs) [5,6] fitted specifically for the enterprise. DSMLs are used to capture models of the business process at different abstraction levels for the three groups of experts. This enables creation of precise, machine-readable models, which are also easier to communicate. MDD techniques are used for automatic transformations of models captured in domain specific languages. Hence, the presented approach aims to assist the experts belonging to each of the three groups to create precise models of the business process at their abstraction level and to support automatic propagation of changes in the model created by the analyst to the model created by the architect and further to the model created by the developer

The paper is organized as follows. Section 2 provides a brief introduction on DSML, MDD and service composition. Section 3 presents the outline of our approach. Section 4 illustrates the approach with the help of an example of a mortgage approval process in an imaginary bank. Section 5 evaluates the approach. Section 6 introduces a prototype implementation and section 7 contains the conclusion.

2 Preliminaries

This section describes concepts and notions used in the rest of the paper. It introduces the use of Domain Specific Modeling Languages, Model Driven Development, and service composition as an implementation to support business processes.

2.1 Domain Specific Modeling Language

A general purpose process modeling language such as the Business Process Modeling Notation (BPMN) [7] or UML activity diagrams [8] are not designed to support enterprises in creating models using their own vocabulary and terminology. In contrast, a DSML created specific for an enterprise allows the experts to create models using locally known domain concepts and to provide domain specific information to model precisely. In this paper we shall make use of domain specific modeling languages, which are based on UML activity diagrams and extended for a particular domain by a UML profile [8]. A profile is constructed by using the extensibility elements: stereotypes, tagged values, and constraints [8], which are machine readable modeling construct used by UML tools. For example, in an activity diagram we may wish to specify, if a task is carried out by a software system or a human agent. To do so, a profile containing the stereotypes <<*Automatic*>> and <<*HumanActivity*>> can be applied to the activity diagram. Such stereotypes clarify if a task is carried out by software or by a human being. A stereotype is applied to a task to indicate the task type. Using these stereotypes or specialized task types extends activity diagrams into a new (here, rather simplistic) language.

Through out the paper we use the term task for the single actions or activities that make up a business process. We use the term task type to classify various tasks. For example, *HumanActivity* is a task type, which embodies tasks such as posting a letter or assessing a risk related to a mortgage by a human actor. A domain specific process modeling language consists of a number of task types that can be used for modeling.

2.2 Model Driven Development

In the Model Driven Development (MDD) paradigm, models are treated as primary software artefacts, from which the implementation is created with the help of software tools [4]. Adopting MDD in a software development process is expected to speed up development time and improves the quality of the delivered system.

The Model Driven Architecture initiative (MDA) [9] implements the MDD approach around a set of technologies and standards like MOF, UML and XMI. Central to the MDA is the idea of model transformations. Defining a transformation from one kind of model, the source model, to another kind of model, the target model, one is able to reuse that transformation for all source models of the same type. MDA provides mechanisms to define DSMLs and a conceptual framework for defining transformations between different DSMLs. Models are created by using constructs from meta-models. Meta-models are models, which formally defines the syntax of which models can be created. A meta-model defined for a specific domain can be seen as a Domain Specific Modeling Language. Using MDA technologies, a meta-model is defined either by using MOF, a meta modeling language, also called a meta-meta-model [9] or by using the UML profiling mechanism [8]. A transformation is a set of rules that specify mapping between the source and the target language. Several methods exist for defining model transformations ranging from complex frameworks utilizing languages as ATL and QVT to simple Java based frameworks as SiTra. For simplicity, we describe transformation rules in English.

2.3 Service Composition

Enterprises that adopt a Service Oriented Architecture often require combining services to support their business processes. As a result, service composition languages, such BPEL, are designed to allow combining and coordinate service invocations. BPEL is an XML based-language for describing business processes and business interaction protocols.

Research into the application of MDD techniques to the web service domain has recently received considerable attention. A popular area of research is model transformations from platform independent languages to Web service languages, among others, Class Diagrams to WSDL [10] and Activity diagrams to BPEL [11].

3   A Pattern Based Approach to Model Transformations

This section illustrates the outline of our method for bridging the gaps between Business and IT using DSMLs and MDD techniques as depicted in Fig. 1.

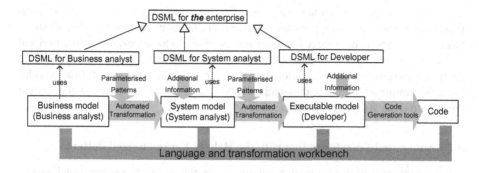

Fig. 1. A pattern based approach for modeling collaboration

The analyst creates a business model of the process. The architect transforms this model to an *architectural model* by applying a predefined and automatic transformation to the business model. The transformation uses *parameterized patterns* to create the architectural model. These patterns represent knowledge previously kept by the architect of how to map business models to architectural models in the enterprise. The patterns are parameterized, hence, the architect is asked to include values of *Additional Parameters* required by the transformation. Additional Parameters are information that are required in the architectural model, and which is not represented in the business model. Following the creation of the architectural model by the architect, a developer transforms it to an *executable model* in a similar fashion. The architect and the developer do not change generated models; instead the information they must provide to the final implementation is given as values of additional parameters during transformation. The transformation workbench incorporates this information into the generated models automatically. We shall now describe the approach and the use of parameterized patterns in further details.

3.1 Parametrized Patterns

Derived from Alexander's work on architectural patterns, and now commonplace in software engineering [12], patterns have been embraced by the workflow and business process community [13,14]. A pattern describes a recurring problem that occurs in a given context, and based on a set of guiding principles, suggests a solution. In our approach, a *pattern* is a common architectural, or implementation solution to reoccurring tasks of same type. For instance, a business analyst may for simplicity model a single task in a process, but describe that it should be executed a number of times. The architectural pattern for the task is an iteration over a service invocation. Each time such a task is modeled by the analyst, the architect creates the same kind of solution. We use patterns to capture and describe such common solutions to tasks of the same type.

The patterns described in this paper are domain, or enterprise, specific, i.e. they are specific to each individual enterprise. They make use of attributes and parameters related to the models. Hence, we shall use the phrase *parameterized patterns* [15] to distinguish such patterns from high level patterns described in [12]. In our approach, a parameterized pattern includes three pieces of information; a *pattern template*, *additional parameters* and *transformation rules*. Pattern templates capture the overall structure of a task type in the source language represented at a lower level of abstraction and is defined in the target language. Additional parameters specify information required for fitting and customizing the pattern template for a specific task. Transformation rules use values of the additional parameters and attribute values of the task to change and fit the pattern template into the target model.

3.2   Automated Transformation with the Help of Parameterized Patterns

Fig. 2 depicts an outline of our approach for conducting model transformation between different DSMLs using the information captured as design patterns. This results in refinement of a model to a lower level of abstraction as depicted in Fig. 1.

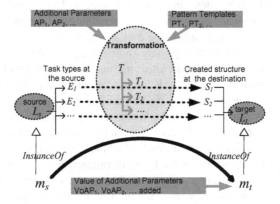

Fig. 2. Model transformation between DSMLs with the help of patterns

Let us consider a source DSML L_s and a target DSML language L_t. For example, in transformation from the Business model to the System model, see Fig. 1, L_s and L_t are DSMLs for business analysts and system analysts, respectively. Suppose that L_s consists of a number of domain specific task types $E_1, E_2, \ldots$ The aim is to transform a source model m_s defined in the language L_s to a target model m_t defined in the language L_t. To achieve this, a transformation T, which contains transformation rules for mapping tasks from L_s to tasks of L_t, is used. The transformation T consists of a number of sub transformations T_j, responsible for the transformation of one task type E_j in the source model to a structure S_j in the target language L_t. The global transformation T orchestrates and coordinates which sub transformations should be executed at the different tasks contained in the source model m_s, collects all generated structures by the sub transformations and connects the generated structures together to the target model m_t.

A sub transformation T_j captures and represents a parameterized pattern, and hence it represents domain specific knowledge of how to represent a task type at a lower level of abstraction in the target language L_t. This makes the sub transformations the most essential part of the transformation. The sub transformation T_j is defined by the following elements:

1. **Pattern template** PT_j. A model template defined in the target language L_t. The model template represents the structure of the source task E_j transformed to L_t.
2. **Additional Parameters** AP_j. When transforming a source task E_j to a lower abstraction level (L_t), additional information may be required to enrich and customize the pattern template so the structure S_j defined in the L_t can be generated.
3. **Transformation rules.** Rules that specify how the pattern template PT_j is customized into the structure S_j. The rules make use of Values of Additional Parameter ($VoAP_j$) and values of attributes at the source task E_j.

4   Example: Process Modeling in Estate Bank

In this section we shall illustrate the above approach with the help of an example of an imaginary enterprise called Estate Bank. In contrast to a real business process, which can be quite complex, we use a simplified process as the purpose of the example is to illustrate our approach. Fig. 3 models a mortgage approval process inside Estate Bank. When a customer requests for a mortgage at the bank, a risk analysis (AssessRisk) task is executed. Based on the risk, either the loans for the mortgage is created (CreateLoans) or the request is rejected (Reject).

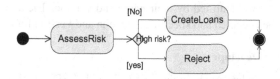

Fig. 3. A mortgage approval process in Estate Bank

A business analyst defines the above model of the mortgage approval process. The team of system architects and, subsequently, the team of developers must create an executable system from such a model. Due to space limitation we shall only define a subset of the modeling languages and transformations. Firstly, we describe subsets of the different languages used by the three groups of experts. Then, we shall define the essential sub-transformations for a selected number of task types from the different languages. Finally, we illustrate the transformation of the CreateLoans task in the mortgage process from the business level to the architect level and further to the development level by using the different sub transformations.

4.1   A DSML for Business Analysts

Consider a domain specific language L_B containing three task types named *HumanActivity* (E_1^B), *Automatic* (E_2^B) and *Bundle* (E_3^B). A task of type *HumanActivity*, as the name suggest, is a task which is handled by a human actor. For example, the AssessRisk task used in Fig. 3 can be carried out by an employee at the bank, and hence the task is a *HumanActivity*. An *Automatic* task is a task, which is executed by a computer program. For example, the Reject task in the mortgage process is an *Automatic* task type as a computer program in Estate Bank automatically is able to send a rejection letter or an email. A *Bundle* task is one which is executed a number of times. For example, in the mortgage process, creating a number of different loans with different interest rate based on the customer request can be considered a bundle . These task types are high-level enough to be used by the business analyst for creating business process models. For a full-blown realistic example in a real enterprise, several additional types are required. However, the three task types are sufficient to explain our approach.

4.2   A DSML for Solution Architects

The solution architect refines models created by the business analyst. As a result, the DSML, called L_A, used by the solution architect requires more information than the DSML used by the business analyst. Here, we shall exemplify refinement of the task type Bundle from the previous sections. Two of the task types used by the solution architects are *Loop* (E_1^A) and *Service* (E_2^A), which are used in refining the task type *Bundle* from the analyst language. A task of type *Loop* indicates that an iteration should be executed over a sequence of other tasks. The architect may use a *Loop* to indicate that a certain service must be called a number of times, e.g. creation of several loans but with different interest rates. A task of type *Service* indicates calling a specific service available for the use of Estate Bank, for instance creation of a loan with a specific interest rate. Such services are identified by their name and version. The architect determines which service to be executed and specifies the name and version for the service task.

4.3   A DSML for Developers

The developer uses a language similar to BPEL and WSDL. Considering these languages express the system in lower level of abstraction, the DSML, called L_D, for the developer requires more information than the one for the solution architect. The language is not specific to Estate Bank as it is similar to the BPEL language. We present three exemplary task types: *Assign* (E_1^D), *Invoke* (E_2^D) and *Loop* (E_3^D). A task of type *Assign* maps data between variables and is used to initialize input data to service invocations. A task of type *Invoke*, similar to BPEL's *invoke*, is described by a WSDL document. A task of type *Loop* iterates over a sequence and can be compared with a "for" or "while" loop in traditional programming languages. Models created in the DSML for the developers can be compiled directly to BPEL code without any additional parameters required. The models must be defined completely, i.e. the models must be rich enough to be "executable".

Table 2 depicts the task type *Bundle*, of the DSML for the business analyst and its refinement by the architects and developers. Whenever a business analyst models a task as a *Bundle* type (E_3^B), for example the task CreateLoans in the mortgage process Fig. 3, she/he must specify values of the required attributes of the task as listed in Table 1. Firstly, the description attribute clarifies the purpose of the *Bundle*. Secondly, the iterations attribute, if the number is known at modeling time, specifies the number of times the *Bundle* should execute.

Table 1. Task types and their attributes

DSML	Task type	Attributes	Description
Business L_B	Bundle E_5^B	description	A description of what is bundled
		iterations	The number of iterations if it is known
Architect L_A	Loop E_1^A	iterations	The number of iterations
		knownAtBuildTime	Number of iterations is known at build time?
	Service E_2^A	name	The name of the service to invoke
		version	The version of the service to invoke
Developer L_D	Assign E_1^D	data mappings	Mapping of data between variables
	Invoke E_1^D	wsdl	Document describing the service to call

As illustrated in Table 2, the architectural pattern PT_3^{BA} for modeling the equivalent to a Bundle at the architectural level is a loop task type, and inside the loop, a service task type is present. The pattern expresses the common solution to reoccurring model elements of type *Bundle*. The loop task type requires values for two attributes :

-knownAtBuildTime: Boolean. True, if the iteration numbers is known at build time
-number:= the number of times the iteration should run.

Both these attributes can be extracted from the attributes of the *Bundle* task, so no additional information is required here. The *service* task type also requires data for two attributes:

Service name:= The name of the service which the bundle invokes multiple times.
Service version:= The version of the service to be invoked.

Table 2. Sub transformation for *Bundle* task type from business to architectural level

Pattern template PT_3^{BA}	Add. params AP_3^{BA}	Rules
	-Service name -Service version	Set name and version at *Service* attributes

These attributes cannot be extracted from the *Bundle* task type at the business level, as they are information about the architecture of services in Estate Bank, so they must be provided as additional parameters AP_3^{BA} during the transformation. The business analyst has only provided a description of the purpose of the task of type *Bundle*. The architect uses his/her knowledge of Estate Banks services to describe which service and what version to call and specify the attribute values of the *Service* task. A sub transformation T_3^{BA} can be defined for transformation of the *Bundle* task type at the business level to the architectural level. Table 2 shows the pattern template, a textual description of the transformation rules and the required additional transformation parameters.

The *Bundle* sub transformation generates a model structure S_3^A defined in the architect language. This structure contains two tasks, one of type *Loop*, and one of type *Service*. The structure can be transformed to the development level by use of two different sub transformations, one sub transformation T_1^{AD} for the *Loop* task type and one (T_2^{AD}) for the *Service* task type.

Table 3 illustrates that a *Loop* task at the architectural level is transformed to an *Assign* task and a *Loop* task at the development level. The *Service* task at the architectural level is transformed to a sequence of an *Assign* task followed by an *Invoke* task at the development level. The two assign nodes at the development level both need additional parameters for determining how to map data for variables to the loop node and the invoke task respectively. This information can be provided at modeling time, however since the focus of the paper is on the control flow part of the models, we will not deal with this aspect here.

The *Loop* node requires a conditional statement (logic) to determine when is should terminate. This is similar to the conditional statements, for example in "if" and "while" clauses, in conventional programming languages. The *Invoke* node need to know the WSDL document defining the service to invoke. The logic and the document have to be provided for the transformations as values of additional parameters, $VoAP_j$.

Table 3. Sub transformation of *Service* and *Loop* task type from architect to developer level

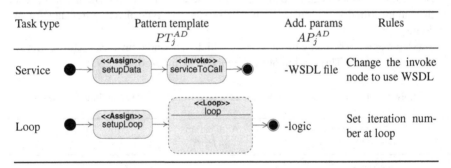

Task type	Pattern template PT_j^{AD}	Add. params AP_j^{AD}	Rules
Service		-WSDL file	Change the invoke node to use WSDL
Loop		-logic	Set iteration number at loop

The described parameterized patterns allow the CreateLoans task, if modeled as a *Bundle* type, to be transformed into code with only limited work done by the architect and the developer. They only have to provide specific information during the transformations. The architect has to provide the service name and version of the service that in the IT systems fulfils the requirements specified by the business analyst. The developer has to provide a WSDL document based on the service name and version and logic for when the loop should terminate. Based on these additional transformation parameters, the described sub transformations in Table 2 and Table 3 handle the rest of the work of transforming the business model to an implementation. This is illustrated in Fig. 4.

Similarly, the other tasks, AssessRisk and Reject, of the mortgage process can be transformed by other subtransformations to an implementation. Fig. 5 illustrates the complete mortgage process transformed to the developers DSML where also the AssessRisk and the Reject task has been transformed. The different Assign tasks, map1, map2, map3 and map4, are used for mapping data for service invocations; for the AssessRisk service which is handled by a human actor, for initializing the while loop for creating the different loans requested by the customer, for the CreateLoan service which create one loan and for the Reject service which sends a rejection to the customer.

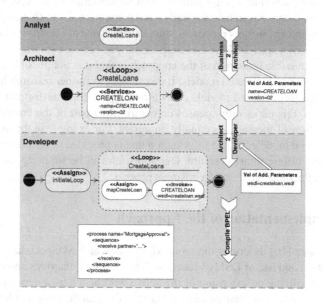

Fig. 4. Transformation of the CreateLoans task from analyst to architect to developer to code

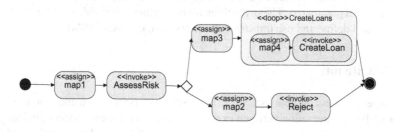

Fig. 5. Mortgage Approval process transformed to developer DSML

5   Discussion

As the example illustrates, the analyst and the architect are able to create precise, machine-readable models in well known domain specific concepts by using languages fitted specially for their needs. By using the suggested approach, i.e. having defined sub transformations for the specific domain concepts, tools can now collect the required information for the concrete tasks in a source models, automatically transform the source model to the target domain and finally generate the implementation code. The model can be transformed to an implementation, where only required additional transformation parameters have to be provided by the architect and the developer. The developer and the architect are not required to remember or know all details about the patterns and which additional parameters are required. For example, the tool can provide assistance in form of wizards.

Following the gathering of information, the transformation of the task to the lower abstraction level is carried out automatically. As a consequence, the challenge of modeling and implementing business processes, then becomes one of identifying and defining domain specific concepts, DSMLs and transformations between different DSMLs. An outcome and a possible limitation of the approach is that it is not possible to introduce manual corrections to generated models. It is a subject to further research how manual changes applied to generated models can survive repeatable transformations. Due to space limitation, this paper only focuses on control flow part of the business process. Modeling the flow of messages is equally important. For example in the mortgage example it should be modeled which information that is provided to the process and what information the different tasks require. Our approach can be similarly used to model and transform the message flow of a business process.

6   Tool Implementation of the Approach

Our earlier paper [16] describes the tools ADModeler and ADSpecializer, which enable the creation and use of DSMLs based on UML activity diagrams and profiles. We are currently finalizing an extension of the above workbench by a new module called ADTransformer, a transformation engine feasible for transforming models based on different profiles for UML activity diagrams. ADTransformer implements the concepts of sub transformations, parameterized patters, patterns templates, transformation rules and additional parameters. Using the three tools together one is able to define and utilize DSMLs, and define and use transformations between different DSMLs.

7   Conclusion

This paper presents an approach for bridging the gap between business and IT by facilitating better interaction between experts involved in business process modeling and implementation. The main idea is to capture domain knowledge related to different groups of experts as domain specific modeling languages and reusable, parameterized transformation patterns. Using an example, the paper demonstrates that domain specific modeling combined with customizable model transformations can simplify the process of modeling and implementing business processes. Using our tool-based approach will result in shorter time to market from business process idea to implementation, higher quality of the resulting code based on automated transformations, an assurance for what is conceptually modeled is actually also implemented, and better interaction between different groups of experts.

References

1. Wagner, H.-T., Beimborn, D., Franke, J., Weitzel, T.: IT Business Alignment and IT Usage in Operational Processes: A Retail Banking Case. In: HICSS'06. Proceedings of the 39th Annual Hawaii International Conference on System Sciences, vol. 8, pp. 172–194 (2006)
2. Arsanjani, A.: Empowering the business analyst for on demand computing. IBM Systems Journal 44, 67–80 (2005)
3. BEA, IBM, Microsoft, SAP, A., Systems, S.: Business Process Execution Language for Web Services (BPEL4WS). Version 1.1 (2003),
   http://www-128.ibm.com/developerworks/library/specification/ws-bpel/
4. Stahl, T., Völter, M., Bettin, J., Haase, A., Helsen, S.: Model-Driven Software Development: Technology, Engineering, Management. Wiley, Chichester (2006)
5. Chen, K., Sztipanovits, J., Neema, S.: Toward a semantic anchoring infrastructure for domain-specific modeling languages. In: EMSOFT '05. Proceedings of the 5th ACM international conference on Embedded software, pp. 35–43. ACM Press, New York (2005)
6. van Deursen, A., Klint, P., Visser, J.: Domain-Specific Languages: An Annotated Bibliography. ACM SIGPLAN Notices 35, 26–36 (2000)
7. White, S.: Business Process Modeling Notation, Version 1.0, final adopted version (2006), Avaible at http://www.bpmn.org/Documents/OMG-02-01.pdf
8. UML2.0: UML 2.0 Superstructure Specification, Final Adopted Specification (2004), available at http://www.omg.org/docs/formal/05-07-04.pdf
9. Kleppe, A., Warmer, J., Bast, W.: MDA Explained: The Model Driven Architecture–Practice and Promise. The Addison-Wesley Object Technology Series. Addison-Wesley, Reading (2003)
10. Bezivin, J., Hammoudi, S., Lopes, D., Jouault, F.: An Experiment in Mapping Web Services to Implementation Platforms. Technical report, LINA, University of Nantes (2004)
11. Bordbar, B., Staikopoulos, A.: On Behavioural Model Transformation in Web Services. In: Conceptual Modelling for Advanced Application Domain (eCOMO), Shanghai, China, pp. 667–678 (2004)
12. Gamma, E., Helm, R., Johnson, R., Vlissides, J.: Design Patterns: Elements of Reusable Object-Oriented Software. Addison-Wesley, Reading (1994)
13. Eriksson, H., Penker, M.: Business Modeling with UML. Business Patterns at Work. John Wiley & Sons, Chichester (2000)
14. van der Aalst, W., Hofstede, A., Kiepuszewski, B., Barros, A.: Workflow Patterns. Distributed and Parallel Databases 14, 5–51 (2003)
15. MacDonald, S., Szafron, D., Schaeffer, J., Anvik, J., Bromling, S., Tan, K.: Generative design patterns. In: IEEE International Conference on Automated Software Engineering, pp. 23–34. IEEE Computer Society Press, Los Alamitos (2002)
16. Brahe, S., Østerbye, K.: Business Process Modeling: Defining Domain Specific Modeling Languages by use of UML Profiles. In: Rensink, A., Warmer, J. (eds.) ECMDA-FA 2006. LNCS, vol. 4066, pp. 241–255. Springer, Heidelberg (2006)

Integrating Semantic Business Policy into Web Service Composition

Xu Meng and Chen Junliang

State Key Laboratory of Networking and Switching Technology,
Beijing University of Posts and Telecommunications,
Beijing, China
xumengmoon@gmail.com, chjl@bupt.edu.cn

Abstract. Web services composition is becoming increasingly important as the 3rd part service providers are now getting ready to provide more complex service-based applications. Accordingly it is critical to integrate the business policy with web service composition dynamically to adapt to changing business environments. Business policy needs to be represented explicitly, to be understood by semantics, and to be applied automatically. To support the business control in the interactive web service composition, this paper proposed a SWRL-based business policy model which does the rule reasoning based on semantics. And a business policy driven services recommend method was present to apply this model to the web service composition, which bridges the gap between business requirements and academic research. As a result, 3rd part service providers can focus on the business goals to be achieved, instead of having to create detailed control and data follows for the work at hand.

1 Introduction

Web services embody the paradigm of Service-Oriented Computing: applications from different providers are offered as web services that can be used, composed, and coordinated in a loosely coupled manner. One of the key challenges for contemporary enterprises is to generate complex services using by available web services on the Internet. The Web Service Composition (WSC) is really a business process which determines how the composition should be structured and scheduled. We believe business processes can be dynamically built by composing web services if they are constructed based on and governed by business rules.

Currently, one of the feasible WSC methods is workflow based schema, just like BPEL, which predefines the workflow of services. However, the predefined method lacks of flexible mechanisms to satisfy the user's personal requirements. The interactive method presented in [1][2] is a reasonable composition solution, which invites users to join the procedure to select the successive service. As semi-automated composition method, it has been argued in several literatures, in which the core algorithm is how to get the candidate services. According to the execution result of the last service (preS), the user could select the successive service from candidate services. When users select the successive services (sucS), they want to find the needed service quickly, rather than search in a great deal and unrelated services.

D. Georgakopoulos et al. (Eds.): ICSOC 2006 Ws, LNCS 4652, pp. 178–189, 2007.

Our work is motivated by the requirements of integration of business process with interactive WSC method. In the exist work of interactive WSC method, they consider the business process rarely, however, business process is critical in the service recommend process. Otherwise, the 3rd SP couldn't control the service logic, so the interactive MSC has less feasibility to be applied in reality. We have developed a semi-automatic WSC platform which utilizes service relation [3][4] to recommend services for users. In this paper, we proposed a solution to integrate business process to interactive WSC, which is achieved though using of business policy and rule inference.

There has been increasing work in designing business policy based WSC system [5]-[8]. However, there are some challenges in developing such a system. Firstly, business policies need be written in a language that both people and machine can easily understand, so business rules should be combined with Semantic Web [9]. Secondly, when conflicts arise in the context of using policies, it needs an efficient and appropriate manner to detect and resolve conflicts. Thirdly, business policy must be integrated to the interactive WSC method to control the business logic dynamically.

We analyze the business policy special for WSC and propose SWRL [10]-based Business Policy Model which includes of knowledge and rules. Based on SBPM, we present a Business Policy driven Services Recommend Method (BPSRM) to provide the candidate services which satisfy the business requirement. Our prototype and case analysis verify that BPSRM could integrate the business policy to WSC dynamically and seamlessly, which allows create personal services semi-automatically and bridges the gap between business requirements and academic research.

The remainder of this paper is organized as follows. Section 2 discusses related works. Section 3 reviews the business rules, introduce the SBPM. In section 4, we present the BPSRM. Section 5 briefly describes the prototype and shows the effect by case analysis. Section 6 provides some concluding remarks and outlines the future work.

2 Related Works

There are many ongoing research efforts in the business policy related technology. Some rule description language was used to express business rules: Defeasible Logic was used to describe the business rule in [6], which has strong expressive power and is executable. While the tool for maintaining rules and reasoning is absent, and it never argued the application to web service composition. RuleML based on SCLP was used to describe business rules in [7], and it has the characteristic that could be extended easily. However, it never refers to web service composition, and it could only reasoning with the condition, rather than control the service logic. Description Logic was applied in [8] to enhance current business integration approaches, and the semantic technology was applied in reasoning of non-function properties when service selecting. The business policy that used in the above works only refers to the service constraints, which is only a part of business rules. In this paper, we use the ontology and rule technology to modeling the business policy, which could express all business policies including service condition constraint and action enabler in focus and could be reasoned base on semantics. We argue the action of the business policy in the service logic control, rather than just in the constraint of selection in the services which have alike function.

In the research of integration business with WSC area, they dealt with business policy in different way. In the workflow method, a hybrid web service composition method [11] explicitly separates business rules from the process specification and adds the business rules to BPEL using the aspect-oriented programming method. PLM-flow [12] could create workflow automatically through the business rule which were defined by template including backward-chain and forward-chain. However in the above method, they never use the reason based on semantics. Based on semantic reason technology, we could use the object orientated method, the rule expression has semantics rather than just denotations. We use SWRL to modeling the business policy supporting semantics, and proposed the business policy expression more general than the above. So in the interactive WSC method, business policy could guide and govern the composition procedure.

3   Business Policy Model

In the following subsections, we present a SWRL – based business policy model (SBPM) which includes of knowledge and business rules. Business rules are defined as SWRL rules that are executed by a rule inferring engine.

3.1   Business Policy

Business rule encompasses a collection of terms (definitions), facts (connection between terms) and rules (computation, constraints and conditional logic) [4], which reflect the business policy. According to [4], the business policy is shown in Table 1.

Table 1. Business policy classification

Type	Rule	definition	Example
Supporting Business Rules	**Inference**	Tests conditions and upon finding them true, establishes the truth of a new face	R1: If customers are younger than 18, they are younger
	Computation	Checks a condition and when result is true, provides an algorithm to calculate the value of a term	R2:Today – birth date = age
Supporting Business Behavior	**Constraint**	Expresses an unconditional circumstance that must be true or false	R3: If customers are under 18, they cannot buy products for adults.
	Action Enabler	Checks conditions and upon finding them true initiates some action	R4: If no fight is found, book a train ticket.

Table 1 shows the two basic types of business rules. Supporting business tasks enable business tasks and processes implemented with web services. Supporting business rules such as computation and inference rules are not directly involved with the web service composition. They provide interpretation tools for operational business rules.

3.2 SBPM

Business policy needs to be represented explicitly, to be understood by semantics, and to be applied automatically. Contemporary literature on the combining of ontology and rule primarily addresses that the rule could be constructed on the ontology to extend the expressive power of ontology [13]. SWRL [9] combines the RuleML and OWL [14] to overcome many limitations in Description Logic and is considerably more powerful than either OWL DL or Horn rules alone.

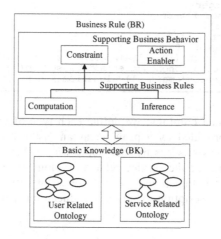

Fig. 1. SWRL-based Business Policy Model

According to the business rule defined by Business Rules Group and the classification in Table 1, a SWRL-based business policy model (SBPM) was shown in Fig.1. SBPM includes two parts: one is Supporting Business Rules - Basic Knowledge (BK) which defines the concept and relationships that should be used in rules; another is Supporting Business Behavior - Business Rules (BR) which is defined by SWRL. BR is supported by BK, and it extends the expressive capability of BR in essence. They construct the business policy in common and SBPM could be a repository of the reasoning system.

3.3 Business Knowledge

We have realized an interactive WSC system which mainly faces to information providing service, and we use the GIS related services and information services as examples in the following text.

Because there are two roles in business activity, which are the user and the available service, we model BK as two parts: one part is user related ontology which saves the information about user; another is service related ontology which saves the service and relationships among them. The user related ontology includes of knowledge that used to describe the user, which is shown in BK_1.

BK₁ A snippet of user related ontology

```
DatatypeProperty(gender)
DatatypeProperty(age)
DatatypeProperty(name)
Class(Person)
  intersectionOf(
  restriction (name allValuseFrom(xsd:string))
  restriction (gener allValuseFrom(xsd:string))
  restriction (age allValuseFrom(xsd:integer)))
  restriction (birthDate allValuseFrom(xsd:integer))
Class(Younger) (
  subClassOf(Person))
Class(User)
  intersectionOf(
    subClassOf( Person)
    restriction (ID allValuseFrom(xsd:string))
    restriction(phoneNumber allValuseFrom(xsd:string))
    restriction(email allValuseFrom(xsd:String)))
```

In the service related ontology, we define each type of web service as a class and a web service provided by a provider as an instance in the service related ontology, and organizes services by their topic what is achieved according to the service content. Therefore the service related ontology saves the relationships of service causing by their topics and the occurrence of service description file (in OWL-S). For further description, we have introduced this part in [3]. The example is shown in BK₂.

BK₂ A snippet of service related ontology

```
ObjectProperty(hasService)
Class(Spot
  intersectionOf(
    restriction (hasService queryAddress)
    restriction (hasService queryPhoneNo)
    restriction (hasService showAroundMap)
    restriction (hasService sendMessage)
    restriction (hasService locate)))
Class(Entertainment
  intersectionOf(
    subClassOf(Spot)
    restriction (hasService queryAverage)))
Class(Cinema
  intersectionOf(
    subClassOf(Entertainment)
    restriction (hasService queryFilmInfo)
    restriction (hasService buyFilmTicket)
    restriction (hasService queryNearCinema)))
Class(sendMessage)
Class(sendMMS
  intersectionOf(
    subClassOf(sendMessage)))
Class(sendSMS
  intersectionOf(
    subClassOf(sendMessage)))
```

3.4 Business Rule

Business rules are usually expressed in the form *if conditions then action* which accords with the syntax of SWRL. The business rule templates use the SWRL expression which is

antecedent => consequent, where *antecedent* and *consequent* = $a_1 \wedge \ldots \wedge a_n$ where a_i can be of the form C(x), P(x,y), or swrlb:buildin where C is an OWL description, P is an OWL property, and swrlb:buildin is a SWRL built-ins [11] which support the operation including Comparing, Boolean values, Strings, Date, Time, and et al.

For services invocation and constraints, we defiant five properties to express the relation between user and services:

i) *success*(User, Service). A user has invoked this service successfully, which means that the service has no exception when invoked.

ii) *failed*(User, Service). A user has invoked this service but it returned abnormally, maybe exist some exceptions.

iii) *enable*(User, Service). It defines the constraints that the service could be invoked by the user in the current state.

iv) *disable*(User, Service). It defines the constraints that the service couldn't be invoked by the user in the current state.

v) *do*(User, Service). Service should be executed in one step.

The detail templates of different rule types are shown in Table 2. According to the examples of Table 1, the rules are expressed in the following.

Table 2. Business Rules Templates

	a_i in antecedent	a_i in consequent
Inference	C(x)|P(x, y)|swrlb:buildin	C(x)|P(x, y)|swrlb:buildin
Computation	Empty	C(x)|swrlb:buildin
Constraints	C(x)|P(x, y)|swrlb:buildin	enable(x,y)|disable(x,y)|do(x,y)
Action enabler	success(x, y)|failed(x,y)	enable(x,y)|disable(x,y)|do(x,y)

BR A snippet of BR

```
R1:User(?x)∧Age(?x,?y)∧swrlb:smallerThan(?y,18) ⇒ Younger(?x)

R2:User(?x)∧Today(?y)∧birthDate(?x,?a)∧age(?x,?b) ⇒
swrlb:substract(?b,?y,?a)

R3:User(?x)∧Adult(?x) ⇒ BuyAdultCommodity(?a)∧disable(?x,?a)

R4:User(?x)∧BuyAirTicket(?y)∧failed(?x,?y) ⇒ BuyTrainTicket(?a)
∧do(?x, ?a)
```

4 A Business Policy Driven Web Service Composition

In this section, we give details on how to realize the dynamical WSC and execution governed by SBPM.

4.1 WSC Process

Business policy driven WSC involved five major steps (see Fig.2): business policy repository building, facts creation, rule inference, recommend candidate service and user invocation.

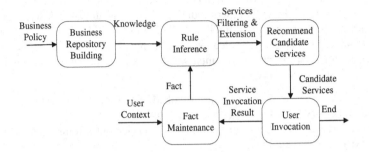

Fig. 2. Business Driven Interactive WSC Process

Firstly, the 3rd part SP input the business policy to build the business policy repository. Secondly, the WSC process begins with a user's request and the user context is the fact of reasoning. Thirdly, the inference engine could do the reasoning with business policy repository and return the results about the business constraints. Fourthly, according to the results, system gets the candidate services and provides them to users. Lastly, the user invokes the service and the execution result is maintained to update the fact. In the following text, we will discuss the inference face and conflict handling in detail.

4.2 Facts and Inference

Context-sensitive technology has been introduced to web service composition [15] in which the user context was defined as user profile and user location. In our paper, we think that the user profile and the services list that invoked by the user in the current session are critical for the successive service. Therefore, we extend the context with the services list that invoked by the user. The user context constructs the reasoning fact, which is defined as follows.

User Context is a 4-tuple <userID, preSList, PreS, F> where userID is the identifier of a user; preSList is a set of services S invoked by the user, S is a 2-tuple <Sname, State> where Sname is the name of service, and State is the result of service Sname, which will be "success" or "fail"; PreS is the service S that was invoked in the last choice; Fact is the assertion that come from preSList and preS.

SWRLJessTab [16] is a Protégé (since v3.2beta) [17] plugin intend to bridge between Protege OWL, RACER and Jess, for reasoning with SWRL. The reasoning results are consisted of *do*, *enable*, *disable* services list.

4.3 Conflict Handling

SWRL has been proposed as a standard in W3C, and it has been extensively studied, has clear semantics, and is supported by automated reasoning techniques. But it falls short as an appropriate basis for our purposes in business policy on inability to deal with rule conflict that most rule languages have. For the rule's conflicts checking, the primary method is to check the conflict manually, and define the priority of rules to deal with the conflict. Whereas SWRL doesn't support priority any, so the priority of rules is infeasible in our model.

Rather than define the priority of rules, we proposed a simple method that define the priority of properties. The priority of properties of service is:

$P(disable) > P(do) > P(enable)$ where P stands for priority.

If the reasoning result has conflict such as *disable*(user, buyTicket) and *enable*(user, buyTicket), we hold the predication *disable*(user, buyTicket) that has the higher priority.

4.4 Service Recommend Algorithm

IO-matching is a relative mature approach, in which the successive service (sucService)'s input is could feed to the previous service (preS) as an input. The core idea of the DSAC is that it uses the IO-matching method as a basic step, then extends and revises it by the result of service relation reasoning. BPSCM add the business policy reasoning to DSAC to make the service logic be governed by business policy. The concrete approach is listed as follows:

i) By using the business inference and conflict handling, we could get three lists – *doList*, *enableList*, and *disableList*.
ii) After DSAC method, we could get the candidate service, which are saved in *doList*.
iii) Remove the services in *disabledList*, add the service in *enableList*, and trigger the services in *doList* automatically.

5 The Prototype and Case Analysis

Integrated Intelligent Service Platform (IISP) [4] realized an interactive web service composition method – DSAC [3]. IISP used a call center agent to assistant the user to complete the service composition procedure. The system recommends candidate services to users by a call center agent, and after the user makes a choice, the agent invokes the selected service and gives back the results. So the user just dial the customer service center, an agent will service you. The basic services of our system are: GIS related services, telecom services and integrated information services.

5.1 Implementation of the Prototype

The working interface of agent is shown in Fig. 3, we could see the candidate services that accord with the business policy are list in the right fuscous frame, and the agent could help the user choose a service according to the user's request or make clues to the user. The user's request could be record by agents, and the inputs and outputs are processed by agents. For space reason, the service execution flow is not detailed here

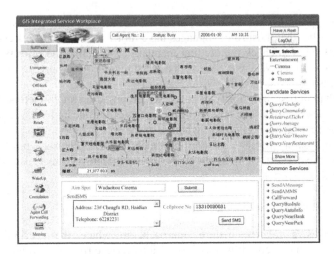

Fig. 3. Interface of IISP to agents

5.2 Case Analysis

In this scenario, we analyze a case to verify that the BPSCM could govern and guide the process of composite service.

Case: suppose that in the business policy repository, the basic knowledge is consisted of BK_1 and BK_2, and the rules include the examples in Table 1. We would like to add the business rules shown as follows to express our business policy.

R5: if the user query the address of some spot, then system send a map around the spot to the user by MMS.

R6: if the user is a younger, he (she) couldn't by the ticket of cinema.

R7: if the user hasn't subscribed the mobile service, he (she) couldn't use the mobile related service.

R8 : If the user hasn't subscribed the mobile service, the system recommend the user to register for the mobile service.

Therefore, we could add the rules to business rule file (BRS) like this:

```
R5:User(?x)∧queryAddress(?y)∧sucess(?x,?y) ⇒
showAround(?a)∧sendAMMS(?b)∧do(?x,?a)∧do(?x,?b)
R6:User(?x)∧Younger(?x)⇒byFilmTicket(?a)
∧disable(?x, ?a)
R7:User(?x)∧haveMsgAuthorization(?x,?y)∧swrlb:equal(?y,
"no")⇒sendMessage(?a)∧disable(?x,?a)
R8:User(?x)∧haveMsgAuthorization ?x,?y)∧swrlb:equal(?y,
"no")⇒applyMsgAuthorization(?a)∧enable(?x,?a)
```

A scenario is the following: When a user named moon calls the call center, the agent accepts the user's request and serves him. The agent tells the user what services he could invoke. Firstly, the user asks that "I want to query the address of XiTian

Cinema", then agent invokes the service *queryAddress,* and input the parameter "XiTian Cinema". Once the service *queryAddress* is invokded, we analysis the process in detail.

I) Fact is shown as follows:

```
Individual(Today)
  Value(year "2006")
  Individual(User )
  Value(ID "moon")
  Value(birthday "1989")
  Value(phoneNo "13800000000")
  haveMessage("no")
  success("moon", "queryAddress")
```

II) After reasoning with the business rule, the new assertions are the following:

```
Individual(User, typeOf Person, User, Younger)//From R1
  value(age "17")                     //From R2
  disable("moon", "buyFilmTicket")    //From R1,R6
  do("moon", "showAround")            //From R5
  do("moon", "sendAMMS")              //From R5
  disable("moon", "sendMessage")      //From R7
  enable("moon", "applayMsgAuthorization") //From R8
```

In the BK2 there are

sendAMMS $\subseteq$ sendMessage and sendASMS $\subseteq$ sendMessage,

therefore we remove the assertion *disable*("moon", "sendMessage") and add two assertions *disable*("moon", "sendAMMS") and *disable*("moon", "sendASMS").

For service *sendAMMS,* there's some conflict because it appears in both *disableList* and *doList*. The rank of *disableList* is higher than *doList*, thus we remove the *do*("moon","sendAMMS").

III) The comparison of DSAC and BPSCM including automate invocation and candidate services are shown in Table 3.

Table 3. Comparison of DSAC and BPSCM

	DSAC	BPSCM
Automate Invocation	null	*showAroundMap*
Candidate Services	*queryNearestRestaurant* *queryNearestCinema* *queryTransferInfo* *buyfilemTicket* *sendASMS*	*queryNearestRestaurant* *queryNearestCinema* *queryTransferInfo* *applyMsgAuthorization*

From the above case, we could draw a conclusion that: Firstly, SBPM has enough expressive power to represent both business rule and knowledge that needed by the business policies. Secondly, the reasoning power of SBPM could be integrated with the web service composition process seamlessly and the service logic could adapt the variety of policy flexibly by BPSRM. Thirdly, SBPM is a general model to get the constraints and restrictions coming from business policy, so it could be applied in other web service compositions method preferably.

6 Conclusion

It is clear that current business policy driven web service composition are not capable of dealing with the complex and entirely business policy and never refer to how to use the business policy to guide the interactive services composition.

In this paper, we have presented a SWRL-based business policy model SBPM which has strong expressive power to represent the business policy, and its reasoning result could be integrated with the web service composition process dynamically. The inferring result which is consisted of constraints and extension of services is combined with the web service composition flexibly. A prototype was implemented to verify our idea, and the case analysis illustrated that BPSRM could get a set of effect candidate services which satisfy business policy for user. As a result, end user can focus their business goals to be achieved, and the interactive WSC could be governed by business goals. Our future work includes researching the performance of SBPM inferring and semi-automatically constructing the ontology and extracting business rules from documents.

Acknowledgments. The National Natural Science Foundation of China under grant No. 60432010 and National Basic Research Priorities Program (973) under grant No. 2007CB307100 support this work. We gratefully acknowledge invaluable feedbacks from related research communities.

References

1. Sirin, E., Parsia, B., Hendler, J.: Filtering and Selecting Semantic Web Services with Interactive Composition Techniques. Intelligent Systems 19(4), 42–49 (2004)
2. Arpinar, I.B., Zhang, R., Boanerges, A., et al.: Ontology-driven Web service Composition Platform. In: Proceedings of the IEEE International Conference on E-Commerce Technology, pp. 146–152 (2004)
3. Xu, M., Meng, X.W., Chen, J.L., Mei, X.: The Research of Load Balancing for Integrated Service Platform. Journal of Beijing University of Posts and Telecommunications, 94–97 (20065A) (in Chinese)
4. Xu, M., Chen, J., Peng, Y., Mei, X.: A Semantic Association-Based service creation method. In: the Proceedings of Web Intelligence Conference, IEEE/WIE/ACM, HongKong, pp. 666–669 (2006)
5. von Halle, B.: Business Rules Applied: Building Better Systems using the Business Rules Approach. Wiley, Chichester (2001)
6. Antoniou, G., Arief, M.: Executable Declarative Business Rules and Their Use in Electronic Commerce. In: Nyberg, K., Heys, H.M. (eds.) SAC 2002. LNCS, vol. 2595, pp. 6–10. Springer, Heidelberg (2003)

7. Grosof, B.N.: Representing E-Commerce Rules via Situated Courteous Logic Programs in RuleML. In: WITS '01. Proceedings of the 11th Workshop on Information Technologies and Systems (2001)
8. Trastour, D., Preist, C., Coleman, D.: Using Semantic Web Technology to Enhance Current Business-to-Business Integration Approaches. In: Proceedings of the Seventh IEEE International Enterprise Distributed Object Computing Conference, pp. 222–230. IEEE Computer Society Press, Los Alamitos (2003)
9. Spreeuwenbergn, S., Gerrits, R.: Business Rules in the Semantic Web, are there any or are they different? In: Proceedings of 2nd European Semantic Web Conference (2005)
10. Horrocks, I., Patel, P.F.: A Proposal for an OWL Rules Language. In: Proceedings of WWW2004, New York, pp. 723–731 (2004)
11. Anis, C., Mira, M.: Hybrid Web Service Composition: Business Processes Meet Business Rules. In: ICSOC'04. 2ed International Conference on Service Oriented Computing, pp. 30–38. ACM Press, New York (2004)
12. Zeng, L., Flaxer, D., Chang, H., Jeng, J.-J.: PLMflow–Dynamic Business Process Composition and Execution by Rule Inference. In: Buchmann, A.P., Casati, F., Fiege, L., Hsu, M.-C., Shan, M.-C. (eds.) TES 2002. LNCS, vol. 2444, pp. 144–150. Springer, Heidelberg (2002)
13. Antoniou, G., Damasio, C.V., Grosof, B., et al.: Technical report: Combining Rules and Ontologies-A survey, http://rewerse.net/deliverables/m12/i3-d3.pdf
14. Antoniou, G., van Harmelen, F.: Web Ontology Language: OWL. In: Staab, S., Studer, R. (eds.) Handbook on Ontologies in Information Systems, pp. 67–92. Springer, Heidelberg (2003)
15. Maamar, Z., Mostefaoui, S.K., Mahmoud, Q.H.: Context for Personalized Web Services. In: Proceedings of the 38th Hawaii International Conference on System Sciences, pp. 89–98 (2005)
16. Martin, O., Holger, K., Samson, T., et al.: Supporting Rule System Interoperability on the Semantic Web with SWRL. In: Gil, Y., Motta, E., Benjamins, V.R., Musen, M.A. (eds.) ISWC 2005. LNCS, vol. 3729, pp. 974–986. Springer, Heidelberg (2005)
17. Protégé: http://protege.stanford.edu/

Model Driven Service Domain Analysis

Stephan Aier[1] and Marten Schönherr[2]

[1] Institute of Information Management, University of St.Gallen
Mueller-Friedberg-Strasse 8, 9000 St. Gallen, Switzerland
stephan.aier@unisg.ch
[2] Faculty of Computer Science and Electrical Engineering,
Technical University Berlin,
Franklinstr.28/29, 10587 Berlin, Germany
mschoenherr@sysedv.tu-berlin.de

Abstract. Currently scientists and practitioners are discussing Service Oriented Architectures (SOA) as an approach to reconcile business requirements and IT. The alignment of business and technology in organizations is a key challenge in the discipline of Enterprise Architecture (EA). Therefore the contribution starts with a discussion of SOA as an EA integration concept to synchronize business requirements and IT architecture in an efficient way. Differentiating methodological and technological aspects of EA the paper shows the need for methods in the field of domain analysis supporting the design of a SOA. The main contribution of the paper is an algorithm based modeling tool and methodology to support service domain clustering. Service clusters are being used for service definition and management. Due to enormous complexity it is necessary to support architects by finding and defining appropriate clusters. For modeling interdependencies in EA the paper's focus is on business processes, information systems and interfaces. Our approach adopts network-centric algorithms used in the field of social network analysis to define and/or identify service domain clusters in complex scenarios. Edge remover algorithm is used to compute the relevant model aspects. The results of our approach will be demonstrated in a case study.

Keywords: SOA, Enterprise Architecture, Process Oriented Integration, Service Domain Clustering.

1 Challenges of Managing Complex Enterprise Architectures

During the last decades IT has been grown a determining success factor. As a result especially in large organizations existing IT infrastructures can be described as extremely complex and heterogeneous. Therefore interoperability is one of the main issues developing and operating these infrastructures. As a matter of fact the conventional way of using individually coded point-to-point interfaces to connect systems is getting beyond control due to increasing overall system complexity. On the one hand one has to consider the costs for IT operation and maintenance of up to thousands of individual interfaces and on the other hand adaptations caused by the introduction of new systems (or system upgrades) and/or procedural-organizational stipulations are

D. Georgakopoulos et al. (Eds.): ICSOC 2006 Ws, LNCS 4652, pp. 190–200, 2007.
© Springer-Verlag Berlin Heidelberg 2007

almost non-manageable due to complexity of element interdependencies. The recently discussed prominent approach to this issue is a Service Oriented Architecture (SOA). The paradigm of SOA is a distributed integration infrastructure [1]. One of the key benefits is a major challenge as well—SOA's integration level. SOA not only aims at systems integration at a primarily technical level, but on process integration driven by business requirements and implemented by utilizing information technology.

Such an integration approach inevitably affects organizational as well as techno-logical questions. In an empirical study we found out, that in companies using integra-tion technologies as SOA, a third of their applications are integrated utilizing those integration platforms and a further third are planned to be integrated this way in the near future [2]. To sum it up it can be said that integration technologies as SOA are major elements of enterprise architectures (EA).

The definition of EA is a central part of this paper. The term of (enterprise) archi-tecture is used in multiple meanings and suffers from a lack of consistent definition appropriate to specific research domains as Business Informatics, Computer Science or Management Science. Therefore in the following we will describe our understand-ing of enterprise architecture and the role of integration concepts in the context given.

In a few words an architecture can be defined as an abstract and holistic concept of structures and patterns considering planning aspects [3]. Architectures are generally results of planning efforts and offer by definition a master plan supporting holistic implementation for future actions. These universal characteristics can be used for planning and designing of enterprise structures and strategies too. Furthermore an enterprise architecture considers organizational, technical and psychosocial aspects for planning and building Information Systems (IS) in a socio-technical manner. This contribution particularly focuses on organizational and technical dimensions of EA. Therefore we use the terms *organizational architecture* and *IT architecture* (Fig. 1).

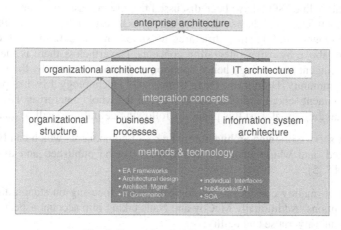

Fig. 1. Enterprise Architecture, see [1]

Organizational architecture contains all non-technical elements of the EA and is best compared with the so called instrumental understanding of organizations which covers all general explicit regulations to define the operational and organizational structure. Accordingly we differentiate the organizational architecture in organizational structure and business processes. On a par with the organizational architecture is the IT architecture which contains all technical elements of the EA. In particular IT architecture covers the IS which are described with their own architecture: the IS architecture. Both architectures organizational and IT architecture will be considered being equivalents but observed separately to accommodate the fact that both architectures are extremely relevant for the organization's efficiency and unfortunately do have complex interdependencies to each other.

Scientific literature very often refers to the terms Organizational and IT Architecture but uses multiple term understandings. Depending on the authors scientific background the organizational architecture contains technical concepts too [4] and the IT architecture organizational aspects respectively. By definition SOA delivers not just concepts for connecting IS but reconcile IS and business processes. Both integration aspects are already considered in the technical definition of SOA which describe a business process driven IS integration. Therefore SOA could serve as a mediator between different elements of an EA.

After all, designing and deploying integration concepts require both—methodology and technology. This contribution will focus on aspects of methodology (for aspects of technology see [1]). Therefore the following section will deal with the need for and the difficulties of managing services in a SOA. Thereafter we will show how clustering algorithms can be employed to derive services domain clusters from enterprise architectures. Eventually we will discuss methodologies for applying the algorithms proposed in practice.

2 The Need for Managing Service Oriented Architectures

Issues in the field of SOA have been discussed heavily the last few years. Both scientists and practitioners emphasize the potential of SOA especially by reconciling business requirements and IT infrastructures as stated in the definition of enterprise architecture above by using integration concepts. Nevertheless there is the need for finding a stringent terminology hence common understanding used by the majority of the SOA community. Definitions range from a solely technology driven approach to a new management school approach on how to run the whole enterprise. To find a stable understanding for at least this paper the following definitions shall be analyzed:

> "[A service oriented architecture is] a set of components which can be invoked, and whose interface descriptions can be published and discovered." [5]

Gold et al. mainly consider technological aspects focusing on standardized interface descriptions. Additionally McCoy and Natis taking into account aspects of stakeholder, granularity, reuse and agility:

> "SOA is a software architecture that builds a topology of interfaces, interface implementations and interface calls. SOA is a relationship of services and service consumers, both software modules large enough to represent a complete business function. So, SOA is about reuse, encapsulation, interfaces, and ultimately, agility." [6]

In the context of existing software systems and the introduction of SOA as a new overall enterprise architecture integration paradigm, issues as management and optimization need to be addressed too:

> "SOA is the concept of service-enabling new and existing software; linking internal and external service-enabled software systems; and implementing an enterprise wide infrastructure to enable, manage, and optimize services use and interaction" [7] (see also [8, 9])

Aside from primary SOA terminology many authors have a common understanding of secondary characteristics. Summed up these are the distributed manner of SOA, the aspect of combining (orchestration of) rich software components (services), loose coupling of applications using services and the standardization of interface descriptions [8, 10, 11]. To summarize the relevant issues Lubinsky and Tyomkin highlight the business process driven integration and therefore derive the following three main aspects of a SOA [8]:

- Service descriptions
- Business Processes
- Service [Lifecycle] Management

Due to reasons of complexity especially in large organizations the solely technical view on SOA is not sufficient to successfully implement it. Methodological aspects need to be considered too. The differentiation between technical and methodological issues has been discussed quite early [12-14]. This paper contributes to the methodological aspects of SOA. Concerning service management as a term which summarizes methods to design and run SOA the following issues are relevant in the design time hence the phase when service characteristics as granularity and reuse are considered. Aside from basic service characteristics as mentioned, a service management defines a service lifecycle mainly to avoid service redundancy. Due to reasons of complexity according to business process requirements mapped to technically executable services, a methodology needs to be introduced to support early phases in the service lifecycle, the design time of a SOA. In the context of a SOA methodology terms as service management, domain engineering, governance, maturity and roadmaps can be found [15, 16]. The most generic approaches can be found in the field of domain engineering [17, 18]. The Domain Engineering introduced by the Carnegie Mellon SEI differentiates the following three activities [17]:

- Domain Analysis
- Domain Design
- Domain Implementation

In the context of service definition the domain analysis needs to be considered. Output of a domain analysis is a domain model representing relevant features used for the specific context. To derive a domain model SEI proposes to use the context analysis defining the extent of a domain, the domain modeling providing a description of the relevant issues and the architecture modeling creating the architectural artifacts [17].

Adopting the general methodology of SEI to the requirements of a SOA especially in the context of an architectural migration from existing IT architectures to SOA a domain model needs to be created. A service domain can be described as a specific modeling view that consists of modularly defined functionality which is necessary to support business processes and the underlying basic data. Within dedicated IT projects, these requirements have to be implemented. The main characteristics of domains are [19]:

- Domains encapsulate their functionality and data.
- Functionality is implemented redundancy-free, information is consistent.
- Functionality and data can be used everywhere, they can be combined to support ever new business processes.
- New projects can build upon existing assets, investments are secured.

The following chapters describe methodologies, tools and algorithms to define service domains based on the generic SEI approach of a domain analysis, clustering existing enterprise architectures hence business processes, information systems and interfaces.

3   Deriving Service Domain Clusters

For clustering enterprise architectures first of all a model of the respective architecture is needed. Minimally the model should include the following elements:

- Business processes, that means the consecutive activities (tasks) and their relationships,
- IT systems,
- the usage of IT systems along a process,
- and the interrelationships and interfaces among IT systems along a process.

Such an enterprise model can be considered a graph often called network, too. In the following sections we will give a short introduction to graph theory and algorithms for graph partitioning. Thereafter we will introduce our implementation of a software system implementing those algorithms for enterprise architectures.

3.1   Graph Theory and Clustering Approaches

A graph consists of vertices V and edges E. All elements of our model (activities and IT systems) can be considered vertices and their relations can be considered edges. If a connection between two IT systems is used several times along a process the model will have several edges between two vertices. These edges may also be combined into a single edge with the weight w. In this case the graph will be called weighted graph.

A network with n vertices is represented by an $n \times n$ adjacency matrix A with elements

$$A_{ij} = \begin{cases} 1 & \text{if the vertices } i \text{ and } j \text{ are connected} \\ 0 & \text{otherwise} \end{cases} \qquad (1)$$

In a weighted graph A_{ij} represents the weight of an edge between the vertices i and j [20].

The partitioning of such graphs into several modules is called clustering while a cluster consists of elements that are all similar to each other in some way [21]. In our case of an enterprise architecture similarity means that vertices have a common subset of neighbors and are dependent from each other in some way. Typically this is a business activity which depends on the availability of an IT system.

Clustering approaches have a certain tradition in the analysis of social networks [22, 23]. Girvan/Newman proposed a clustering algorithm to identify communities in social networks [24]. Such a network consists of individuals (vertices) who know each other and thus have a relationship (edge). A community is defined by a number of people who know each other.

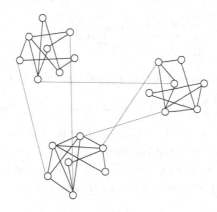

Fig. 2. A network with three communities, see [24]

Based on the analysis of shortcomings of existing clustering algorithms Girvan/Newman developed a "betweenness" algorithm. The basic idea of their algorithm is to remove the edges that are most in between in a network. The remaining vertices connected to each other form the communities. Therefore they generalized Freeman's betweenness [25] to edges and defined the edge betweenness of an edge as the number of shortest paths between pairs of vertices that run along it. The shortest paths between communities run along only a few edges. That it is why these edges will have a rather high edge betweenness. By removing these edges one can separate the communities. The algorithm valid for a weighted network is the following [20]:

1. Calculate the betweenness for all edges in the network.
2. Divide the betweenness by the weight of the respective edge.
3. Remove the edge with the highest resulting betweenness.
4. Recalculate betweennesses for all edges affected by the removal.
5. Repeat from step 3 until no edges remain.

In various papers they proved the performance of their algorithm in determining communities in social networks [20, 24, 26].

On an abstract level the problem of identifying modules in enterprise architectures is identical with the problem described for social networks. By applying the algorithm on the enterprise architecture model we identify appropriate modules as candidates for service domains in a SOA. Since one has to repeat the steps three to five for the weighted network several times it is also possible to identify a service domain hierarchy and eventually services. In every run through the algorithm, already identified modules will be further separated.

One of the important questions is when to stop the algorithm practically. Because it obviously does not make any sense to run through the algorithm as stated until no edges remain. This results in n modules which equals the number of vertices. So the question is when is a "good" modularity reached? Girvan/Newman propose the modularity Q as an indicator for the quality of clustering results [26].

Therefore they calculate the fraction of edges that fall within a module.

$$\frac{\sum_{ij} A_{ij}\delta(c_i,c_j)}{\sum_{ij} A_{ij}} = \frac{1}{2m}\sum_{ij} A_{ij}\delta(c_i,c_j) \qquad (2)$$

Where c_i is the module the vertex i belongs to. The function $\delta(u,v)$ is 1 if u = v and 0 otherwise, and $m = \frac{1}{2}\sum_{ij} A_{ij}$ is the number of edges in the graph. If the degrees k of vertices (the degree k_i of a vertex i is defined by the number of vertices connected with i) in a network are preserved but otherwise connect vertices together at random, then the probability of an edge existing between vertices i and j is $k_i k_j / 2m$, where k_i is the degree of vertex i. Thus the modularity Q, is given by

$$Q = \frac{1}{2m}\sum_{ij}\left[A_{ij} - \frac{k_i k_j}{2m}\right]\delta(c_i,c_j) \quad [26] \qquad (3)$$

Values for Q range between 0 and 1. A value of 0 indicates a poor clustering result while 1 is a perfect cluster but a rather theoretical value. Usually values between 0.3 and 0.7 indicate good values for realistic examples.

3.2 EA Builder Software System

For modeling, analyzing and clustering we developed a software system called EA Builder [27]. The software system supports modeling of business processes, organizational structures and IT systems (Fig. 3).

Contrary to a broad range of existing enterprise class modeling solutions the meta-model of EA Builder also supports the modeling of IT systems integration on process level—regardless whether the integration solution is implemented through a middleware, SOA or classic point-to-point (P2P) interfaces.

The performance of the clustering algorithm for enterprise architecture models has been verified on a number of specially prepared test cases discussed in [28]. In the following figures we will demonstrate the functioning of the EA Builder software system with the fictitious medium-sized company WMYPC (We Make Your PC). The company sells customized computer systems starting from small multimedia

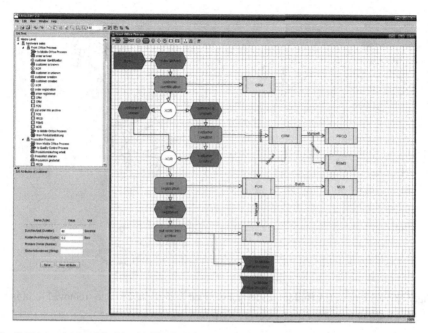

Fig. 3. EA model modeled in the EA Builder system; the screenshot shows an extended event driven process chain incorporating various IT systems which again are integrated with other IT systems along the process

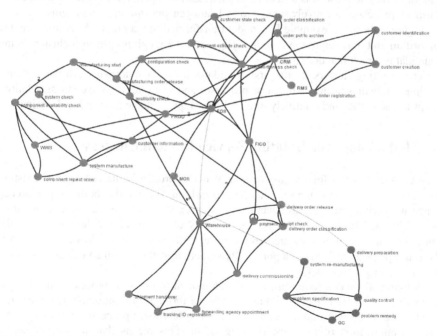

Fig. 4. Screenshot of EA Builder model transformed in a graph, 3 edges removed resulting in 2 clusters

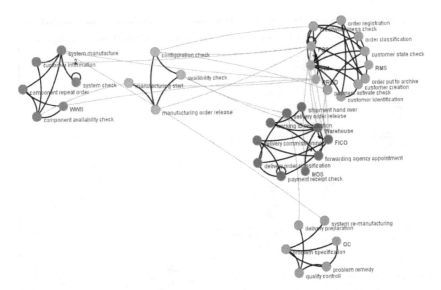

Fig. 5. Screenshot of EA Builder model transformed in a graph, 20 edges removed resulting in 5 clusters, grouped view

computers to enterprise class server systems. The processes are supported by six individually implemented information systems and one off the shelf software product. The aim of the test scenario was to realize an adequately complex business environment with business processes selectively supported by heterogeneous information systems.

Figure 4 shows an example EA model transformed into a graph. After applying the algorithm and thus removing 20 edges (figure 5) the graph is split in 5 clusters being candidates for service domains.

The resulting clusters are the first candidates for service domains. All the elements within a domain (cluster)—business processes and IT systems—have strong relationships to each other and relatively weak relationships to elements of other domains.

4 Methodology for Building Service Domain Clusters

The classic scenario for the application of our approach is the redesign of existing complex IT landscapes in a service oriented fashion. We call this bottom-up approach since we derive a service architecture from an existing complex enterprise architecture. This will be the scenario for the majority of organizations thinking about the introduction of a service oriented architecture. Compared to a top-down approach this bottom-up approach leads to a potentially smooth transition from an existing architecture to the target architecture.

A frequently stated requirement is the alignment of business processes and IT systems [29, 30]. This is exactly what we achieve through our approach. Once the EA model is transformed into a graph, we do not differentiate processes and IT systems for the application of the clustering algorithm. This means that we do not derive optimized process clusters or IT clusters—although this would be possible too. The clusters derived reflect the actual interplay of business processes and IT systems. Thus the resulting service domain clusters consisting of business processes and IT systems are potentially well designed concerning Business-IT alignment.

However, the resulting clusters reflect the as-is structure of the modeled company "only". The as-is structure does not necessarily correspond with an existing organization chart or IT map, since it will show the actual structure—not the supposed one. Depending on the overall integration strategy it now has to be decided how to proceed with this information. One possible scenario would be to define an internal integration approach per service domain and then an additional approach for the integration of the different domains. This results in a stable architecture with local flexibility through encapsulated service domains. Such encapsulated domains may be desirable for a variety of reasons—technology, business requirements, and also politics. Eventually encapsulation leads to a better manageable complexity of enterprise architecture.

5 Conclusion

The paradigm of Service Oriented Architectures (SOA) potentially leads to more flexible enterprise architectures and an improved Business-IT alignment. Besides technological means, methodologies for the implementation of SOA in existing and complex enterprise architectures are required in order to realize the benefits promised. Building service domain models in a bottom-up approach may be a step in the right direction. In this paper we introduced a software system—the EA Builder—which derives service domain candidates based on the clustering of enterprise architecture models. A key feature of our approach is the simple but as it seems effective way of achieving a true business process oriented design by clustering business processes and IT systems in a common network.

The artificial models, we tested our approach with so far, showed some very good results. The next steps of improvement will need real world examples of grown complex enterprise architectures to show the potential of this clustering approach.

References

1. Aier, S., Schönherr, M.: Evaluating Integration Architectures – A scenariao-based Evaluation of Integration Technologies. In: Draheim, D., Weber, G. (eds.) TEAA 2005. LNCS, vol. 3888, pp. 3–16. Springer, Heidelberg (2006)
2. Aier, S., Schönherr, M.: Sustainable Enterprise Architecture with EAI – An Empirical Study. In: Milutinovic, V. (ed.) Proceedings of the International Conference on Advances in Internet, Processing, Systems, and Interdisciplinary Research, IPSI-2005, MIT Cambridge/IPSI, Cambridge, Boston MA (2005)
3. Bass, L., Clements, P., Kazman, R.: Software Architecture in Practice, 2nd edn. Pearson Education Inc., Boston (2003)
4. Nadler, D.A., Gerstein, M.S., Shaw, R.B.: Organizational Architecture – Designs for Changing Organizations. Jossey-Bass, San Francisco (1992)
5. Gold, N., Knight, C., Mohan, A., et al.: Understanding Service-Oriented Software. IEEE Software, pp. 71–77. IEEE Computer Society Press, Los Alamitos (2004)
6. McCoy, D., Natis, Y.: Service-Oriented Architecture: Mainstream Straight Ahead Gartner Research (2003)

7. New Rowley Group: Building a more flexible and efficient IT infrastructure – Moving from a conceptual SOA to a service-based infrastructure (2003) http://www.newrowley.com/reseach.html
8. Lubblinsky, B., Tyomkin, D.: Dissecting Service-Oriented Architectures. Business Integration Journal, 52–58 (2003)
9. Roth, P.: Moving to A Service Based Architecture. Business Integration Journal, 48–50 (2003)
10. Sleeper, B., Robins, B.: The Laws of Evolution: A Pragmatic Analysis of the Emerging Web Services Market. The Stencil Group, San Francisco (2002)
11. Weinreich, R., Sametinger, J.: Component Models and Component Services: Concepts and Principles. In: Council, W.T., Heinemann, G.T. (eds.) Component-Based Software Engineering: Putting Pieces Together, pp. 22–64. Addison Wesley, Boston (2001)
12. Hagel, J., Brown, J.S.: Your Next IT Strategy. Harvard Business Review 79, 105–113 (2001)
13. Gisolfi, D.: Web Services Architecture: Part 1- An Introduction to Dynamic e-business (2001), http://www-106.ibm.com/developerworks/webservices/library/ws-arcl/
14. Kirtland, M.: A Platform for Web Services. Microsoft Developer Network (2001), http://msdn.microsoft.com/library/default.asp?/en-us/dnwebsrv/html/websvcs_platform.asp
15. IBM Corporation (2005), http://www-128.ibm.com/developerworks/webservices/library/ws-soa-simm/
16. Sonic (2006), www.sonicsoftware.com/soamm
17. SEI (2004), http://www.sei.cmu.edu/domain-engineering/
18. Open Group (2006), http://www.opengroup.org/architecture/togaf8-doc/arch/p4/maturity/mat.htm
19. Bath, U., Herr, M.: Implementation of a service oriented architecture at Deutsche Post MAIL. In: Aier, S., Schönherr, M. (eds.) Enterprise Application Integration – Serviceorientierung und nachhaltige Architekturen, Gito, Berlin pp. 279–297 (2004)
20. Newman, M.E.J.: Analysis of Weighted Networks. In: Phys. Rev. E, 70 (2004)
21. O'Madadhain, J., Fisher, D., Smyth, P., et al.: Analysis and Visualization of Network Data using JUNG. Journal of Statistical Software (2005)
22. Wasserman, S., Faust, K.: Social Network Analysis: Methods and Applications. Cambridge Univ. Press, Cambridge (1999)
23. Scott, J.: Social Network Analysis: A Handbook, 2nd edn. Sage, London (2005)
24. Girvan, M., Newman, M.E.J.: Community Structure in Social and Biological Networks. Proceedings of the National Academy of Science 99, 7821–7826 (2002)
25. Freeman, L.C.: A Set of Measures of Centrality based upon Betweenness. Sociometry 40, 35–41 (1977)
26. Newman, M.E.J., Girvan, M.: Finding and Evaluating Community Structure in Networks. Phys. Rev. E 69 (2004)
27. Aier, S.: Public Information on EA Builder on the Internet (2006), http://www.ea-builder.com
28. Aier, S.: How Clustering Enterprise Architectures helps to Design Service Oriented Architectures. In: SCC'06. Proceedings of the IEEE International Conference on Services Computing, Chicago, pp. 269–272. IEEE Computer Society Press, Los Alamitos (2006)
29. Duffy, J.: IT/Business Alignment: Delivering Results (2001), http://www.cio.com/analyst/123101_idc.html
30. Luftman, J.: Measure Your Business-IT Alignment (2003), http://www.optimizemag.com/article/showArticle.jhtml?articleId=17701026

Author Index

Lecture Notes in Computer Science

Sublibrary 2: Programming and Software Engineering

For information about Vols. 1–4085
please contact your bookseller or Springer

Vol. 4440: B. Liblit, Cooperative Bug Isolation. XV, 101 pages. 2007.

Vol. 4408: R. Choren, A. Garcia, H. Giese, H.-f. Leung, C. Lucena, A. Romanovsky (Eds.), Software Engineering for Multi-Agent Systems V. XII, 233 pages. 2007.

Vol. 4406: W. De Meuter (Ed.), Advances in Smalltalk. VII, 157 pages. 2007.

Vol. 4405: L. Padgham, F. Zambonelli (Eds.), Agent-Oriented Software Engineering VII. XII, 225 pages. 2007.

Vol. 4401: N. Guelfi, D. Buchs (Eds.), Rapid Integration of Software Engineering Techniques. IX, 177 pages. 2007.

Vol. 4385: K. Coninx, K. Luyten, K.A. Schneider (Eds.), Task Models and Diagrams for Users Interface Design. XI, 355 pages. 2007.

Vol. 4383: E. Bin, A. Ziv, S. Ur (Eds.), Hardware and Software, Verification and Testing. XII, 235 pages. 2007.

Vol. 4379: M. Südholt, C. Consel (Eds.), Object-Oriented Technology. VIII, 157 pages. 2007.

Vol. 4364: T. Kühne (Ed.), Models in Software Engineering. XI, 332 pages. 2007.

Vol. 4355: J. Julliand, O. Kouchnarenko (Eds.), B 2007: Formal Specification and Development in B. XIII, 293 pages. 2006.

Vol. 4354: M. Hanus (Ed.), Practical Aspects of Declarative Languages. X, 335 pages. 2006.

Vol. 4350: M. Clavel, F. Durán, S. Eker, P. Lincoln, N. Martí-Oliet, J. Meseguer, C. Talcott, All About Maude - A High-Performance Logical Framework. XXII, 797 pages. 2007.

Vol. 4348: S. Tucker Taft, R.A. Duff, R.L. Brukardt, E. Plödereder, P. Leroy, Ada 2005 Reference Manual. XXII, 765 pages. 2006.

Vol. 4346: L. Brim, B. Haverkort, M. Leucker, J. van de Pol (Eds.), Formal Methods: Applications and Technology. X, 363 pages. 2007.

Vol. 4344: V. Gruhn, F. Oquendo (Eds.), Software Architecture. X, 245 pages. 2006.

Vol. 4340: R. Prodan, T. Fahringer, Grid Computing. XXIII, 317 pages. 2007.

Vol. 4336: V.R. Basili, D. Rombach, K. Schneider, B. Kitchenham, D. Pfahl, R.W. Selby (Eds.), Empirical Software Engineering Issues. XVII, 193 pages. 2007.

Vol. 4326: S. Göbel, R. Malkewitz, I. Iurgel (Eds.), Technologies for Interactive Digital Storytelling and Entertainment. X, 384 pages. 2006.

Vol. 4323: G. Doherty, A. Blandford (Eds.), Interactive Systems. XI, 269 pages. 2007.

Vol. 4322: F. Kordon, J. Sztipanovits (Eds.), Reliable Systems on Unreliable Networked Platforms. XIV, 317 pages. 2007.

Vol. 4309: P. Inverardi, M. Jazayeri (Eds.), Software Engineering Education in the Modern Age. VIII, 207 pages. 2006.

Vol. 4294: A. Dan, W. Lamersdorf (Eds.), Service-Oriented Computing – ICSOC 2006. XIX, 653 pages. 2006.

Vol. 4290: M. van Steen, M. Henning (Eds.), Middleware 2006. XIII, 425 pages. 2006.

Vol. 4279: N. Kobayashi (Ed.), Programming Languages and Systems. XI, 423 pages. 2006.

Vol. 4262: K. Havelund, M. Núñez, G. Roşu, B. Wolff (Eds.), Formal Approaches to Software Testing and Runtime Verification. VIII, 255 pages. 2006.

Vol. 4260: Z. Liu, J. He (Eds.), Formal Methods and Software Engineering. XII, 778 pages. 2006.

Vol. 4257: I. Richardson, P. Runeson, R. Messnarz (Eds.), Software Process Improvement. XI, 219 pages. 2006.

Vol. 4242: A. Rashid, M. Aksit (Eds.), Transactions on Aspect-Oriented Software Development II. IX, 289 pages. 2006.

Vol. 4229: E. Najm, J.-F. Pradat-Peyre, V.V. Donzeau-Gouge (Eds.), Formal Techniques for Networked and Distributed Systems - FORTE 2006. X, 486 pages. 2006.

Vol. 4227: W. Nejdl, K. Tochtermann (Eds.), Innovative Approaches for Learning and Knowledge Sharing. XVII, 721 pages. 2006.

Vol. 4218: S. Graf, W. Zhang (Eds.), Automated Technology for Verification and Analysis. XIV, 540 pages. 2006.

Vol. 4214: C. Hofmeister, I. Crnković, R. Reussner (Eds.), Quality of Software Architectures. X, 215 pages. 2006.

Vol. 4204: F. Benhamou (Ed.), Principles and Practice of Constraint Programming - CP 2006. XVIII, 774 pages. 2006.

Vol. 4199: O. Nierstrasz, J. Whittle, D. Harel, G. Reggio (Eds.), Model Driven Engineering Languages and Systems. XVI, 798 pages. 2006.

Vol. 4192: B. Mohr, J.L. Träff, J. Worringen, J. Dongarra (Eds.), Recent Advances in Parallel Virtual Machine and Message Passing Interface. XVI, 414 pages. 2006.

Vol. 4184: M. Bravetti, M. Núñez, G. Zavattaro (Eds.), Web Services and Formal Methods. X, 289 pages. 2006.

Vol. 4166: J. Górski (Ed.), Computer Safety, Reliability, and Security. XIV, 440 pages. 2006.

Vol. 4158: L.T. Yang, H. Jin, J. Ma, T. Ungerer (Eds.), Autonomic and Trusted Computing. XIV, 613 pages. 2006.

Vol. 4157: M. Butler, C.B. Jones, A. Romanovsky, E. Troubitsyna (Eds.), Rigorous Development of Complex Fault-Tolerant Systems. X, 403 pages. 2006.

Vol. 4143: R. Lämmel, J. Saraiva, J. Visser (Eds.), Generative and Transformational Techniques in Software Engineering. X, 471 pages. 2006.

Vol. 4134: K. Yi (Ed.), Static Analysis. XIII, 443 pages. 2006.

Vol. 4119: C. Dony, J.L. Knudsen, A. Romanovsky, A.R. Tripathi (Eds.), Advanced Topics in Exception Handling Techniques. X, 302 pages. 2006.

Vol. 4111: F.S. de Boer, M.M. Bonsangue, S. Graf, W.-P. de Roever (Eds.), Formal Methods for Components and Objects. VIII, 447 pages. 2006.

Vol. 4089: W. Löwe, M. Südholt (Eds.), Software Composition. X, 339 pages. 2006.